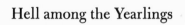

Hell among the Yearlings

All ready for action, Edmund Randolph riding the trap line for coyotes, Birney, Montana, 1925.

The Lakeside Classics

HELL AMONG
THE
YEARLINGS

By Edmund Randolph

The Lakeside Press

R. R. DONNELLEY & SONS COMPANY

CHICAGO

Christmas, 1978

PUBLISHERS' PREFACE

THE 1978 volume of *The Lakeside Classics* marks the beginning of the fourth twenty-five year series in this cherished tradition which was instituted in 1903 by Thomas E. Donnelley, then president of our Company.

Now, as in the beginning, our purpose is to provide interesting subject matter in a book that is easy to read, pleasant to hold, presented in a simple but tasteful format, and produced by modern methods.

To recognize this milestone we have made a few changes, most of which will be unnoticed by the general reader. One difference that will be noted immediately, however, is in the color of the cover cloth. The change to brown follows the established pattern of a new color every twenty-five years. The first series was green, the second, red, and the third, just completed, was blue.

Regardless of color changes, the cloth has been of the same quality and texture since 1903, and produced by the same Interlaken Mill, now owned by The Holliston Mills. Originally starch coated, the cotton cloth is now pyroxylin coated for greater durability.

The paper continues to be made especially for the series by the S. D. Warren Company who have provided the paper since the first volume. Originally made of rags, it was changed to wood pulp with the introduction of alpha pulp in 1953. Alpha is top quality and free of all impurities to give it a long life. The color or shade of the paper is specially formulated for *The Lakeside Classics*, and Warren has named it "Special Classic" text paper.

Surely the most significant change concerns the method of printing. This is the first volume to be printed in large part on a narrow-web offset press. The books previously were printed on sheets exclusively, and that system is again utilized for the first sixteen pages of this volume. The use of rolls required a slight alteration in paper formulation, but the quality, texture, and color remain the same.

The narrow-web presses deliver folded signatures which are then sewn with thread for easy opening, gilded at the top and trimmed fore-edge and foot. This is the first volume in the series to be trimmed in this manner.

As has been the practice since the 1973 volume, composition has been handled electronically with a computer-directed cathode ray tube that generates full lines of characters at the speed of light. We also have continued the same easy-to-read typeface, Bulmer, which we have used throughout the previous twenty-five year series. The case stamping and top gilding remain 23-carat gold for permanence. This year we have updated the company logo which is stamped on the front cover.

As in the past, production has involved coordinated teamwork between various departments and

Divisions. Typesetting and composition were done in our Electronic Graphics Division, design in the Creative Services Division, both in Chicago; the map was created by our Cartographic Services Center in Lancaster, Pennsylvania; and printing, binding, and mailing were done in our Crawfordsville (Indiana) Manufacturing Division.

Just as we have changed the color of the binding and certain production procedures as mentioned above, we also have changed our practice of selecting authors, at least for this edition. For the first time we have chosen a book written by a still-living author.

Edmund Randolph, the author, is of Virginian descent through his mother, but is not related to the noted Virginia Randolph family. His paternal ancestors, the Randolphs, came to the middle Atlantic states in the latter part of the seventeenth century. They were planters, patriots, and landowners. One of them, Nathaniel, donated some of his lands to establish the campus of Princeton University.

Edmund Dutilh Randolph, the author's grandfather, was a Philadelphia businessman who, sometime in the 1870s, went to New York, where for twenty-five years, he was President of the Continental National Bank. He also was a railroad director, Treasurer of the New York Life Insurance Company, and a devoted Senior Warden of Trinity Church at Broadway and Wall Street.

His son, Edmund (1864–1922), founded and

headed the brokerage firm of E. and C. Randolph, and was prominent in the world of yachting. His "New York 50" Class sloop, Spartan, won many racing trophies, among them the King's Cup, off Newport, Rhode Island, in 1913.

The present Edmund, the author of *Hell among the Yearlings*, was born December 3, 1903, in his father's house on East 48th Street, one of three children. The family lived in comparatively plush style during those days of the gold standard dollar, and before there was any federal income tax.

He entered Princeton University's Class of 1926 and during his freshman vacation he made his first trip to Montana with a classmate, both being promised (through still another classmate) summer jobs working in the forestry department of the Anaconda Copper Company. They successfully completed a two-week crash course provided by the company at Missoula and were hired as apprentice lumberjacks at a forestry camp near Ovando, a district in the midst of the extensive Anaconda timberlands, and fifty miles from the nearest town. There, Randolph received his first impression of a life in sharp contrast to everything he had known before, and to his surprise, he liked it.

The next year, his health took a turn downhill. It was discovered that he had a "spot" on his lung. He also had a painful operation on his leg for a bone infection, whereupon his guardian and the trustees, on medical advice, recommended another trip to the high, dry west, to speed recuperation. He was sent to the Eaton Ranch, near Sheridan, Wyoming. From there he proceeded to the town of Birney and the Tongue River country of southeastern Montana, which is the setting for this narrative.

After the period of this book, there was a return to the eastern domestic life: family duties, a Wall Street job (which faded out toward the end of the Great Depression), the purchase of a Long Island home in 1935 and travel abroad with his wife and son. Randolph also became interested in studying and practicing writing, publishing articles in newspapers and magazines, and doing work for the script department of Warner Brothers Pictures, Inc. This eastern life did not mesh too well with his former Montana pattern, but he still managed an occasional trip to the Tongue River country, and kept himself somewhat informed on cattle ranching. As the Depression dragged on, he had a premonition that some day he might want to return there.

When Hitler launched World War II, Randolph noted the rise in cattle prices and, feeling that our country would be dragged into hostilities sooner or later, began to put out feelers for a possible return to the range. He got in touch with his first Tongue River benefactor and original partner, Albert Gallatin Brown, Sr. The Brown Cattle Company was prospering and its ranges were all filled to the limit. Brown could not handle any more cattle, and grass was at a premium everywhere.

However, Brown drove Randolph some ninety miles to the Antler Ranch, a large scale steer operation headquartered on the Little Bighorn River near Wyola, Montana, and introduced him to the owner, Matthew H. Tschirgi. Brown and Tschirgi were old friends, having punched cows together as youngsters, in the days of the open range.

Matt Tschirgi, who owned and/or controlled several hundred thousand acres of range in the Crow Indian Reservation, soon solved Randolph's grass problem. Randolph, still living on Long Island, bought a small string of heifers and signed a contract with Tschirgi to run them on a 50-50 sharing basis which lasted many years.

In 1956 the Randolphs sold their Long Island home and moved to Denver, where Ned (as most people know him) has been a frequent contributor to the *Denver Post* and the *Rocky Mountain News*.

He still owns his log house and 610 acres of his original claim under the old Homestead Act, on which he holds a government patent (not just a title). He intends to hold this property to the bitter end, which may come with the ruthlessly advancing technology of strip mining for coal, which threatens the whole Tongue River valley. The monstrous drag lines may some day gobble up his little cabin, but they can never eradicate his memories of it.

IT IS CUSTOMARY in this part of the Publishers' Preface to comment about various aspects of our Company's business. We are not at all embarrassed if some remarks may have a familiar ring to readers of previous Prefaces. 1978 was another record-breaking year in sales and profits. All major categories, magazines, catalogs, books, and directories, contributed their share. Results have been expressed in current dollars, but even discounting for inflation, there has been real growth. In the last ten years our sales have more than doubled and our net income also has more than doubled. During this period we have invested more than $350,000,000, almost twice as much as the total net worth of the Company in 1968. Our total assets, too, have doubled in this ten-year period; and the assets invested per employee are now well over $40,000, about twice what they were ten years ago. The amount of investment required for each employee underscores the need for policies that encourage capital formation. We hope our friends in Washington fully recognize this as they deal with the problems of inflation and unemployment.

At present, funds for our capital expansion are generated from retained earnings, thanks to a conservative dividend policy which pays out roughly one-third of after-tax earnings. Even so, our Board of Directors increased the rate of dividends for the seventh consecutive year. There has been a yearly dividend continuously since 1911.

This year, we neared the completion of a major expansion program that to some extent involved all manufacturing divisions. The Old Saybrook Division has been re-equipped and the new gravure Division in Gallatin, Tennessee, which commenced operations in 1975, now has become well established. Major additions have been made in the Mattoon, Warsaw, Chicago, Glasgow, Willard, Crawfordsville, and Lancaster East Divisions. This expansion was capped by the acquisition of two very fine companies, which together represent slightly less than a five percent increase in our sales volume. We acquired an 85% interest in Interweb which specializes in quality magazines printed web offset and is located on the West Coast, where we have had sales offices but no manufacturing facilities. We also acquired Ben Johnson and Company, of York, England. This is an old established company with progressive and aggressive management. It produces a variety of printed products and has an effective sales force that covers the United Kingdom and the Continent. We are pleased and proud to have these two excellent enterprises as part of the Donnelley organization and see many mutually advantageous opportunities.

Early in 1978, two important technological capabilities came on stream: our Selectronic* gathering and Selectronic* addressing services. Selectronic

*Selectronic is a service mark of R. R. Donnelley & Sons Company.

gathering allows our customers to bind only those catalog or magazine pages that reflect the interests of each customer or subscriber. Selectronic addressing features the use of ink jet printing of subscriber name, address, and personalized message on the cover and inside the piece. Both systems utilize our computer-driven binding equipment.

We continue to expand our national sales coverage and, in the Chicago area, sales offices have been established in the Loop and at Oak Brook to serve our customers better.

At the beginning of 1978, we approved a capital budget that provided for projects totaling one hundred million dollars, far larger than anything previously dreamed of. While this confidence may seem foolhardy to some in view of a much heralded possible recession, it is based on a careful appraisal of plans of present and prospective customers. Since our projects take from four to six years from conception to full production, and we do not have the clairvoyancy to time our completions with an uptick of the economy, we have followed a policy of constant expansion consonant with our financial, technological, and human resources, and our evaluation of the markets we serve. To date, this policy has been successful and we expect to continue large appropriations. There will be expansion at present locations, but we hesitate to grow beyond a generally optimum size in any one division. Another book plant is being planned for Harrisonburg, Virginia, and a gravure plant is planned for the southeast. These two plants will give us better geographical coverage, and will increase our productive capacity to meet the growth of our customer requirements. Manufacturing, sales, and staff personnel are being developed in an effective and economical manner to keep pace with our growth.

Our Company is not without its problems. Shortages of energy and lightweight coated paper have not been solved and may intensify in spite of our best efforts. Inflation continues unabated, and is particularly troublesome in those areas that are labor intensive and where its effects cannot be offset by technological improvements as in the manufacturing operations. Like all businesses, large and small, we are burdened by a vast array of governmental regulations and overzealous regulators. When we realize that the bureaucracy is supported by the taxes of businesses and individuals, the burden on our economy and society is doubled. We pray for relief, for the benefit of all.

The success of our business is due to some true, tested principles. Quality, integrity, and service are watchwords to which we are all dedicated. We constantly strive for the best of customer, supplier, and employee relations. Currently, we are producing work for almost two thousand customers. To do this, we rely on almost six thousand suppliers, large and small, and they have served us well. The dedication, skills, and loyalties of our people continue unsurpassed. More than six thousand employees, or almost half the total, have been with us for more than ten years. To show our concern for these and all Donnelley people, we provide an outstanding program of benefits. During 1978, a dental benefit plan was added and our disability plan was improved for employees. Further improvements were instituted for retirement, life insurance, and medical benefits for everyone, including retirees.

We approach the future with a cautious optimism, and with great confidence in our customers, suppliers, and employees. Our hopes are that this will be mutual, and in this we include our seven thousand stockholders. To all, sincere thanks, and very best wishes for Christmas and the New Year!

THE PUBLISHERS

Christmas, 1978

CONTENTS

The Tongue River Country

THE TONGUE RIVER COUN

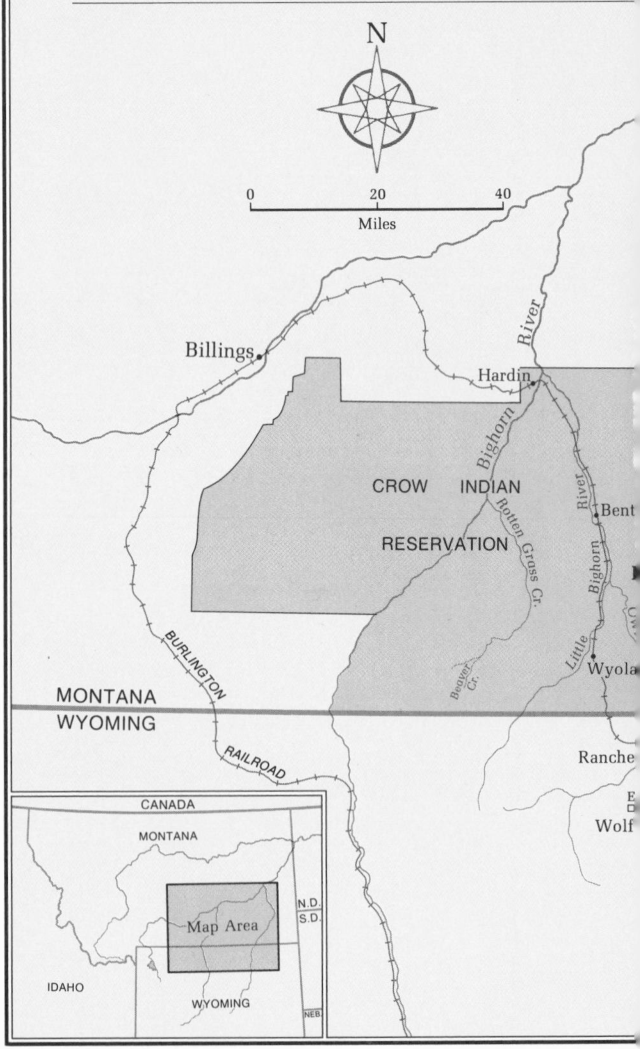

N

0   20   40
Miles

Billings

Hardin

River

Bighorn

CROW   INDIAN

RESERVATION

Bent

River

Rotten Grass Cr.

Little   Bighorn

Badger Cr.

Wyola

MONTANA
WYOMING

BURLINGTON

RAILROAD

Ranche

Wolf

CANADA

MONTANA

N.D.
S.D.

Map Area

IDAHO

WYOMING

NEB.

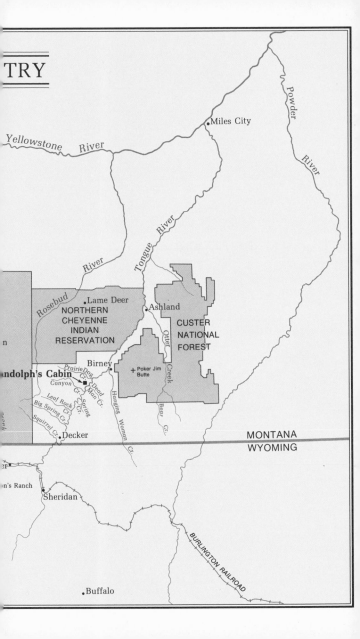

Powder

Yellowstone   River

River

Miles City

River

Tongue   River

Rosebud

Lame Deer

NORTHERN
CHEYENNE
INDIAN
RESERVATION

Ashland

CUSTER

NATIONAL

FOREST

Otter   Creek

Birney

Prairie Dog   Dead

ndolph's Cabin

Canyon   Cr.   Man Cr.

Poker Jim
Butte

Leaf Rock   Spring

Big Spring Cr.   Cr.

Hanging Woman Cr.

Bear   Cr.

Squirrel Cr.

Decker

MONTANA

WYOMING

Cr.

er

on's Ranch

Sheridan

BURLINGTON RAILROAD

Buffalo

ILLUSTRATIONS

All photographs are from the author's collection except the Model T Truck which is from the Ford Motor Company archives, obtained with the assistance of the Veteran Car Museum, Denver.

HISTORICAL INTRODUCTION

THIS LIVELY ACCOUNT of western life is set in the Tongue River country of Southeastern Montana, an area that remained an American frontier as recently as 55 years ago, when Edmund Randolph lived and worked there.

The area was by-passed by early American explorers. Lewis and Clark traveled the Missouri River far to the north while Zebulon Pike and John Fremont led expeditions far to the south. The rush for gold and silver in western Montana during the 1860s and '70s brought prospectors through the area, but the lure of riches meant moving on west to the mountains as quickly as possible. This activity touched off a decade or so of battles with various Indian tribes who roamed throughout the area. With the exception of the Battle of The Little Bighorn, which brought about the demise of General George Armstrong Custer and all his men in June 1876, the other encounters are not as well known and remembered: Tongue River in 1865; The Fetterman Massacre in 1866; The Wagon Box Fight and the Battle of Dull Knife in 1867; Powder River and Rosebud Creek in 1876; and Canyon Creek, Lame Deer, and Wolf Mountain in 1877.

This was the country that Edmund Randolph became so much a part of. Not only did he spend a substantial part of his life in this area, but more importantly, it seems always in the forefront of his memories.

The Historical Introduction in all previous books in *The Lakeside Classics* series has been the responsibility of someone other than the author, but since we are so fortunate to have a living author, it seemed most appropriate to ask Edmund Randolph to position his own story for us. Here are Mr. Randolph's words:

"The Birney area was a small pocket of the American frontier that flourished as late as the 1920s. At that time, it was a little known, thinly populated area of interrelated people oriented toward beef cattle ranching; all theoretically mutual friends more or less dependent upon each other for help of all kinds and under conditions sometimes even approaching the question of survival.

"Their nearest paved road was fifty miles to the southwest, at Sheridan, Wyoming. The approaches and all side roads were gumbo or red shale. Mail came three times a week when the roads were passable and the several creek crossings were fordable by the small mail truck from Sheridan.

"The telephone was of the old, hand cranked, dry cell battery type, with a single, iron wire connecting the ranches with the Sheridan operator. The subscribers were signaled by a series of long and short rings, with the longs coming first, all subscribers being able to listen in on each other's conversations. This did not provide privacy, but was fine for spreading news fast, or announcing an emergency.

"All ranches maintained strings of saddle and draft horses called cavvies which were far more used than their few automobiles.

"There has never been a telegraph office or a railroad in the Birney area. As a matter of fact, even though the name appears on many maps and the postal service has assigned a ZIP code, there is no formal town at Birney, even today, and there is no indication for a stranger to identify it, except for the name on the Post Office or the designation that it is at the junction of Hanging Woman Creek and the Tongue River. There are two stores, a church (non-denominational), a grade school and a few scattered houses.

It was within a twenty-five mile radius of the Birney post office that most of the events in this story took place."

Randolph finished this manuscript, originally titled *Don't Fence Them In*, while spending the winter of 1955 in Madrid. As he was London bound in a few weeks, he sent it unsolicited to William Heinemann, Ltd. That firm published the book and sold the American rights to W. W. Norton & Co., New York. The American edition, published the same year, was slightly abridged, had no photographs, and came out under its present title.

The author feels that his book is a simple statement of events that actually occurred, which he set down with a minimum of poetic license necessary to reconstruct the essence of long lost dialogue. The book includes events which took place before his arrival on the scene and after his departure from it as well as those which he experienced himself. He respected the privacy of personal names by harmlessly changing them and, in general, followed the standard methods of producing a reasonable continuity in his narrative.

He did not write the book with any intent of producing a work of scholarly interest requiring footnotes, but rather to set down events which he considered typical of the country, or unusual, or in some way interesting, and the people connected with them: data which he felt would otherwise go unrecorded, but shouldn't.

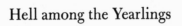

Hell among the Yearlings

I

Dude

IT DIDN'T seem so at the time, but one of the most propitious days of my life was when the Nassau Hall telephone operator was found in my clothes closet. This episode, although severely frowned upon by the Princeton authorities, did not—surprisingly enough—spell expulsion from college for either my roommate or me. But it was a move in the right direction. At the very least, it marked the point of departure that led eventually to my life as a Montana rancher.

The trustees who had inherited me along with my father's estate viewed my attitude toward college, and life in general, with some doubt. They had good reason. I had been rather a problem to them since they had taken charge of me in 1922.

When my father died, my life went through a sudden transposition from the fading glories of a passing era into something startlingly different. His three children (of whom I was the middle, and all of us then minors) now became problems of his estate. Guardians were appointed for our persons and trustees busied themselves with our financial affairs. We were called to Wall Street for conferences, perched at the head of a long, bare, fumed oak table

and consulted about what was going to be done
with our lives. We were advised on everything. My
brother and I were even advised about naughty dis-
eases by one of the trustees with experience in that
line. And no doubt, our sister was told a thing or
two on the side.

At one such conference it was decided that I
should go into Princeton University. Why, I shall
never know, except perhaps for the fact that Princeton was in a sense founded by our family, an early
member of which donated the original land. John
Randolph of Roanoke,[1] a great statesman and eccentric of the Federal period, was also a student
there in the eighteenth century, but, I think, was
invited to leave after nicking somebody in a duel.

Despite these ties of tradition, I could never get
enthusiastic about college life. Most of the time I
was sickly, behind in my work and bewildered by
my life, which did not seem anchored to anything.
I underwent several operations for a leg infection
and also developed a suspicious lung.

After the telephone-operator episode, my roommate (also my partner in crime) and I were given
short suspensions, which seemed lenient enough, as
they were to run concurrently with the summer vacation. We spent that vacation in Montana, where

[1]Though himself of the northern, not the southern Ran-
dolphs, the author here is referring to John Randolph of
Roanoke (1773–1833), a longtime member of the United
States Congress.

another classmate had wangled jobs for us in the forestry service of the Anaconda Copper Company. It was my introduction to the West and, after my first sniff of Montana, I decided that college life was not my forte. I submitted my resignation to Princeton and it was cheerfully accepted.

My next brush with the West came almost immediately when through some foggy process I found myself at Eaton's Ranch[2] in northern Wyoming, almost on the Montana line. At this "dude ranch" I soon learned that the word "dude" here had a special meaning: a friendly nickname for an Easterner while he is a paying guest at a western ranch, a good-natured term, devoid of ridicule, used by Easterners and Westerners alike as a simple, time-honored classification.

Probably the trustees sent me to a dude ranch instead of to a sanitarium to fool me about my lung. But I was not fooled, and suspected that I had been shipped out there to do or die; I didn't particularly

[2]Generally referred to as the first dude ranch in the West. The Eaton brothers, Howard, Willis L. and F. Alden, first established their ranch, the Custer Trail Ranch, near Medora, North Dakota. The first guest, W. W. Thayer from Milwaukee, signed their register on June 24, 1883. In 1904, the Eaton brothers moved their dude operation to the foot of the Bighorn mountains, west of Sheridan, Wyoming. The post office they set up is named Wolf, Wyoming. The Eaton ranch continues to flourish today, hosting the grandchildren and great-grandchildren of their early visitors. *Eaton Collection, Western History Research Center, University of Wyoming, Laramie.*

care which. The only thing I cared about was the prospect of having a little fun first, if I was going to die instead of do. I had been given a disheartening list of don'ts, including drinking, smoking, gambling, riding (in view of my bad leg) and girls. I wondered what else one did in Wyoming and groped about for some plan of life. As time slipped by, the invigorating climate and kindly surroundings began to take hold of me both mentally and physically. Day by day I felt healthier and happier, and I began to get ideas. One of the first ideas I had was to challenge the list of don'ts, thereby enabling myself to mix more freely into the activities of the ranch, know the people of the country better and perhaps turn up some prospect of an occupation.

I began by taking gentle rides, despite my supposedly fragile leg. First at a walk, next at a trot, then at a canter. There was no ill effect. If anything, my leg got stronger. Heartened, I took another don't by the horns and began mixing with the younger drinking set at the ranch. They invited me into their circle and shared their exciting bootleg liquor, all the more exciting for being forbidden fruit. In my case it was doubly forbidden, both by my doctor and by Prohibition. First I quaffed gently, in a modest test. Later I raised my sights for a higher mark, approaching the bounds of moderation, and still without ill effect. Before long I was a regular member of the younger drinking set and accompanied them on their trips to town for refilling of our jugs and perhaps a few hands of blackjack.

Sammy Doyle[3] was the town bootlegger and gambler, a small, pale man who carried on both his illicit operations in the cellar of a pool hall, reached by a trap door and guarded by a lookout and buzzer system upstairs. I went down the hatch on my first dive with a local cowpuncher. Despite his subterranean seclusion, Sammy was much in the public eye at that time, for he had lately found a man in bed with his wife, shot him and been acquitted. He was very proud of his marksmanship. From under the green baize table he then proudly produced the gun and patted it. "You can't beat an old single-action Colt," he stated modestly, giving the gun most of the credit.

At this time I took stock of myself and made a few decisions, feeling that I wanted to stay out west but not without an occupation. It was obvious that the moment had come for a change in my set of values. I had had the typical Manhattanite's narrow-minded attitude about the East in general and New York in particular: that the whole U.S.A. must pay homage to the East, all other parts of the country being, somehow or other, mysteriously inferior. But lately I had seen something of the vastness of our

[3]Fictitious name given to Andy Steil, a well-known free spirit of Sheridan (especially during the bootleg era), who hung out, more than occasionally, at the American Pool Hall, below which he ran his businesses.

country, and my eastern provincialism had gone quietly overboard.

Mines and forests of the Anaconda Copper Company, great stretches of range and herds of beef convinced me that I could assume a great deal more of this vastness and power than I was ever likely to see. The comparatively minute areas back home which I had been brought up to revere diminished in importance and retreated to a more sensible perspective where, being in sharper focus, they could better be appraised. The real power, after all, came from the vastness of the country. Wall Street was only a set of gears for handling it.

So I decided to stay, to find an occupation, to change my values and to learn how it was that many millions of Americans not residing in Manhattan managed to exist in what seemed to me like a fairly happy state, getting along with each other, earning livings, making homes and raising families.

Of course, the good life of the old West was nearly a thing of the past when I arrived out there, but its spirit was making a brave last stand, and still is. I have always felt that at least I caught the tail of an era which flowed along gracefully and naturally as a unique part of American history.

My position, therefore, with relation to the era of old, open-range, trail-herding, Indian-fighting days as against our modern times of motorizing everything—almost to the exclusion of the horse and cowboy—is a sort of spanning position. For, while I

cannot claim to have seen any of the real old times,
I have been close to them through many real old-
timers. I have seen, as it were, the softly glowing
sunset of those days just over the horizon, as it
turned into the harsh glare of our mechanical era. I
happened along at a unique time. If I were any
younger I would be like the present generation, unable to feel connected with the pre-gasoline days;
and if I were any older I might be short tempered
with today's modern young ranchers and oversym-
pathetic with the old school (who also had their
faults). As it is, I stand somewhere in between, and
on fairly good terms with both, neither condemning
nor extolling either but saying simply, "This is how
things were when I came along."

II

Tom Bryan

ONE DAY there appeared as a new guest at the ranch a tall, wiry young man in torn, faded blue jeans, scuffed boots, a blue cotton work shirt and, incongruously enough, the remains of what was once a smart, snap-brim fedora hat, battered almost beyond recognition but cocked at the subtle angle of one who really knows eastern hats. The hat alone, in comparison to the western boots, alkali-caked with runover heels, made the two ends of this individual so strikingly different that one couldn't help wondering about the middle. It turned out that Tom Bryan[4] had given lots of people plenty to wonder, and worry, about.

Tom had appeared from somewhere in that vague

[4] A member of that clan sometimes referred to as the "golden Irish," Thomas Fortune Ryan's (Bryan) grandfather came to Wall Street at age twenty-three with great ambition and little else. When he left Wall Street upon his death in 1928, he bequeathed an estate of more than $100,000,000, a wealth he had garnered by organizing the American Tobacco Company; saving the Equitable Life Assurance Company from financial disaster; developing, with the Guggenheims, diamond and gold mines in the Congo Free State, and various other ventures. Many of his children and grandchildren who were left his money led chaotic and disoriented lives. New York *Times*, November 24, 1928; New York *Post*, April 14, 1977.

11

and thinly populated cattle country to the north-east, knowingly referred to by natives as "the Tongue River country." Among the dudes, nearly all had heard of the Tongue River country, but none had actually been there. It was sort of like the Land of Nod, with boundaries vaguely described as "over the line, in Montana," or "down Miles City way," or the country between Powder River and the Rosebud which, on the map, seemed like a rather large, blank area to me. For one thing, there were no towns of any recognizable proportions. There was no railroad or telegraph and, of course, no electric service. There was reported to be a single-wire party telephone line working (when it worked at all) on dry cell batteries, and there was the dim outline of a dirt road which wound along the river valley from the Wyoming line toward Miles City. At a few points on this road, small settlements were indicated at the junction of the Tongue River and various creeks running into it, or near these junctions. Near the junction with Squirrel Creek there was a speck marked "Decker," and at the junction with Hanging Woman Creek, another speck marked "Birney," sandwiched between the Cheyenne Indian Reservation and the Custer National Forest. This, I learned, was where Tom Bryan hailed from. Further along, the river was joined by Otter Creek and there was another speck, marked "Ashland." Then there was the Cheyenne Indian Agency, at Lame Deer. Later I learned from personal observa-

tion that there was another town, not marked anywhere, called Jim Town,[5] consisting of one old
wooden building, a hitching rack in front of it, a
cast-iron, elbow-action pump behind it, and nothing else. The building was, of course, a saloon, conveniently (and once legally) located a stone's throw
from the bone-dry limits of the Cheyenne Reservation. Even before Prohibition, liquor was absolutely
taboo on Indian reservations and selling even beer
to an Indian, anywhere, a serious offense.

Eventually, I inquired about Jim Town because
of its morbid, futile atmosphere, and sought for
some clue to "Jim's" identity. Here I learned my
first lesson about the old-time idea of identity in the
West. For various and sundry reasons, it just wasn't
inquired into too closely, as people who went west
in the early days often did so with the hope of losing their identities and, therefore, the etiquette was,
simply, not to ask. There was no point in disturbing tranquil waters where all had come to enjoy a
common peace. Real old-timers developed a genuine and unaffected disinterest in the matter of one's
name. "Feller-goes-by-the-name-of _____" would
be considered sufficient identification among them.
They distinctly didn't like the formula, "What is
your name? . . . Answer: N or M." Rather, they
would ask you, "What name do you *go by*?" without

---

[5] Jim Towns, by that and any other name, were scattered
throughout the open spaces and sparse population of the
western landscape.

meaning the slightest offense to the person addressed.

Jim, of Jim Town, apparently fell into this category. The most definite information I could ever
get about his last name was: "Looks like nobody
ever reckoned he *had* a last name." Jim was just a
person who had a passion for going about the country founding towns and naming them after himself.
His idea of founding was to begin with the heart of
any good town, a saloon. But he never progressed
from there. His towns didn't progress beyond the
saloon stage, and Jim would move on elsewhere.
There were several Jim Towns in that part of the
West.

With the exception of a third-class highway, a
few ranches strung along it and the inevitable
barbed-wire fences, this country has not changed
much in appearance from the days of Lewis and
Clark, Washington Irving and Theodore Roosevelt,
all of whom mentioned it in historic accounts of
early expeditions and Indian warfare. As of 1955,
there is still no railroad or telegraph, and the same
single-wire, hand-cranked battery telephone is in
operation (on and off). The government REA electric power line is a newcomer. On the whole, the
district remains very much like what a recent New
York *Herald Tribune* editorial on the Cheyennes
called it, "a remote part of Montana." In the early
1920s, the beginning of my long acquaintanceship
with it, and before the automobile came into very
general use, this country seemed remote indeed—ex-

tremely so, compared to what I had known before.

People living in the Tongue River country were supposed to be a little different from other people. There was about them an aura of extra ruggedness, resourcefulness and individuality not generally surrounding townspeople, dude ranch people or the "mink and manure" set of wealthy Easterners who had gone into cattle ranching near the more populated centers. Tongue River people had more, and stranger, ups and downs, and cared less about them. They had, usually, less money, and cared less about that, too. They trusted to God and got what they needed. Or, if they didn't get just exactly that, then they liked what they got. And, if they didn't like it, they joked about its inadequacy.

The arrival of Tom Bryan from a well-known cattle outfit in the district was, in a sense, mildly extraordinary. But this was not the only extraordinary thing about Tom. He was more than passably good looking in a tough Irish sort of way, lean and wiry, with feline grace of movement. There was in his features no trace of that smooth, standard, well-bred look which Europeans call *racé*, and he wisely made no pretensions to birth. "Grandpa was a stableboy in Virginia," he would say, quite frankly and rather charmingly. "Walked into New York when he was kicked off a train for not having the fare. Flopped down in the lobby of a Bowery hotel, on one of those circular settees with a hump in the middle, and overheard a couple of crooked politicians planning a horsecar racket. So he made them cut him in on it, and that's how the whole shamboozle got started."

The shamboozle, incidentally, wound up some fifty years later as one of the greatest financial cudgels ever wielded in Wall Street, eventually paying off in the hundreds of millions and famed to the far corners of the earth.

Tom told me about this, squatting up against the rough corral, where he had been exchanging easy banter with cowboys waiting to take the dudes out riding. I was standing somewhat apart from them at first, trying to decide whether to go on one of the rides or hang around and fathom this strange jargon relating to doings on the nebulous Tongue River. Puzzling terms about pulling calves, sticking bloated steers, or rawhiding challenged my imagination and curiosity. I forgot about ordering a horse and moved up closer.

When the corral boys had gone off to their duties, Tom sidled over with a good-natured grin and a glittering twinkle in his watery blue eyes. He plucked the remains of a Bull Durham cigarette from the corner of his full-lipped mouth, ground it into the dust with the high heel of his scuffed boot and inquired, "Duding it here?"

The verb was a new one to me, but I told him that I was, and asked if he weren't going riding.

"Naw!" he answered, scornfully. "I'm a different kind of dude. Just a lallapaloosa from the Tongue

River. Anyway, I've got to hang around the white house. Waiting for a long-distance telephone call from New York."

"The White House?"

He snickered. "Isn't that a hell of a name? On a ranch, it's what they call the main house where the family lives."

I wondered, but did not ask, about the rest of his explanation, from which I got no sense, not knowing what a lallapaloosa was, or hardly anything about Tongue River, except that it was a district of odd names and words. I had learned of creeks named Hanging Woman and Dead Man, a butte called Poker Jim and individuals actually known as Shoot-em-up Jones and Hardwinter Davis. As I looked Tom over more closely, I felt that there was something remotely familiar about him and, to strike a common chord, I ventured, "New York . . . that's my home town."

"Yes, I know. Mine, too. How in the world did *you* get out here?"

I told him briefly and returned the question, to which he settled on his heels, western fashion. He pushed the battered, once-smart fedora to the back of his head, revealing masses of thick, curly chestnut hair, and squinted at the horizon as if trying to recall the events of eons ago, although he was only a few years older than I—possibly in his twenty-fourth year. He began telling me about the shamboozle that his grandfather had started, and many of its ramifications. He had the Irish gift of gab, all right, but his was slightly acid, especially where his family and upbringing were concerned. Before he had finished, I classified him as a remittance man from a family of millionaire mad hatters. I had heard of Bryans in many strange situations, but never of one being a cowpuncher, or whatever Tom was. His exact classification was still a little obscure to me and, as I pondered it, a fuzzy vision of him in tail coat, white tie, silk hat and kid gloves, arriving drunk at a Ritz Carlton débutante party floated before me, incredibly.

Tom had, moreover, a heritage which could have explained his being on Tongue River, or almost anywhere. I remembered that, not long before, there had been a famous cornering of a certain stock in Wall Street by one member of his family against another. Other members, in true Mad-Ludwig-of-Bavaria fashion, had built great houses and left them practically unoccupied. One piqued prankster among them was said to have caused alarm clocks, all set for different hours, to be placed in the walls of a relative's house to annoy him.

Tom's own father had a strange hankering for buying expensive things which he didn't need, in quantities of eleven, and then torturing the merchants who had sold them. On one occasion he bought eleven gold-handled umbrellas from a famous Fifth Avenue jeweler, on another, eleven jade elephants, transactions attended by startling public-

ity. But his masterpiece was the purchase of eleven
Rolls-Royce cars, all at once. In this deal, he first
tortured the salesman, whom he forced to inquire
about credit references (an entirely unnecessary detail) by telephoning Mr. J. P. Morgan, who had been
cunningly enticed from his bathtub, flaming in one
of the well-known Morgan bursts of temper. Bryan
sat back, chortling, while Mr. Morgan and the terrified salesman had their cozy little talk.

This frolicsome prelude was followed by the
main act: baiting the long-suffering Rolls-Royce
company. In due time after the cars had been delivered, Bryan announced that it was all just a bit of
fun, that he did not want the cars, could not use
them and would rather not pay for them (which he
could easily have done without even missing the
change). The company was invited to repossess its
property, the coachwork of which was all now ex-
quisitely monogrammed by Proudfoot, so they
would have something to remember him by. In the
meantime, he had hidden the cars in storage
throughout various parts of the country, and when
the company came after them, he sprang his surprise: he had forgotten where they were and there
would be a great Easter hunt. The hunt progressed,
with the aid of much expensive legal talent, until
everybody was satisfied, no one more so than Mr.
Bryan, who enjoyed every penny of it.

This, then, was the type of heritage represented
by young Tom Bryan, and as I eyed him ever more

closely, squatting on his heels and expertly rolling his Bull Durham cigarettes, I wondered whether he ran true to type. If so, it could have explained his plight. Obviously, there was a connection somewhere. It would be interesting to know what the connection was, how he came to be out there on Tongue River. I had already asked him the question. Gradually, he got around to answering it.

"You see, the family got damn well fed up with us kids. There were too many of us and we were pretty ornery, I guess, especially me and one of my kid brothers, Kimmy. Then, there's Irene, my pet sister. She won't stand tied, either. We always hung together pretty close, just like three little stinkers will, and the family were always pouring it on us. Grandpa, especially, hates my guts because I carry his name and I was always blamed as the ringleader, teaching the others to take a snort once in a while and have a little fun. Whether it was my fault or not, I always got blamed for what all the rest of them did."

"That makes it pretty tough," I sympathized.

"I'll say!" he agreed. "Getting blamed for a bunch of wild bastards like that's enough to get anyone down. You know, I have six brothers and four sisters, none of them angels . . . But all good kids," he mused affectionately. "Now, I never see them." His head lolled in his hands at the injustice of it all. "I was shipped west without a *sou marquis.* Now I pitch manure, down on Tongue River."

So, that's what he did. Pitched manure. "How long ago were you sent out?" I asked.

"About six or seven years. You see, what really got the old man wild was when I drove the Hispano-Suiza up on the putting green in the middle of a golf tournament out on Long Island. His name was coming up for this club at the next governors' meeting, and he was trying like hell to win the tournament and make a big impression. Then, all of a sudden—zowie! There was the old family Hispano, right up on the green, just as he was putting. A bunch of us were coming back from a wedding—plastered, as usual. Of course, I just happened to be driving, worse luck, and I couldn't make the turn coming up to the clubhouse."

"What happened then?"

"Well, of course, I was full of champagne and howling like a banshee, and didn't have any driver's license. So, the cops came up, and we mixed with them—gave them a damn good fight, as a matter of fact. You know how it is when a bunch of Irishmen get together. The old man missed his putt and lost the tournament. Then his name was blackballed at the governors' meeting, and the club sued us for damages."

"Sounds like a pretty good mess to get away from," I consoled him.

He threw up his hands in despair. "Well, anyway, here I am. No more Hispano, no more champagne, no more cash. I'm down to a knot-headed

cayuse and a jug of rotgut. Not a *sou marquis*. They
only send me fifty dollars a month. That just about
keeps me in liquor, tobacco and overalls." Laughing, he slapped his tattered levis.

I wondered how, in his straitened circumstances,
he could afford the luxury of a dude ranch. "What
do you do for the rest of your money?" I asked.

"Pitch manure, I tell you. No kidding. I work as a
hand for this outfit down the river. Do almost anything: chores, cow-punching, haying, wrangle the
horses, rock the baby, ice harvesting . . . anything.
Maybe you've heard of this spread, the White Cattle
Company?"[6]

I hadn't, and said so.

"They're old-timers from the trail-herding days.
Busted now, but that doesn't matter. Salt of the
earth."

There churned in my mind the strange jumble of
Tom's life pattern—a composition of manure,
champagne, rotgut and foreign cars—until I didn't
know what to say next. Finally, I asked, "Like it out
here in this country?"

"Sure. Finest country in the world! If you don't
go to hell here, there's no hope for you. And this
outfit—you should see it. Stretches for miles up and
down the river, around Birney and all over the
Cheyenne Reservation. They used to run lots of
cattle there, and on the National Forest land, too,

[6]The White Cattle Company was the author's name for
the Brown Cattle Company.

mostly up around Poker Jim Butte. Only, there aren't so many cattle now. Hard times, you know."

"Poker Jim Butte?" I asked. "Is that named for Jim of Jim Town?"

"Naw," he answered scornfully. "Entirely different fellow. This Jim was an old cowpoke who got wintered in with a couple of trappers in their cabin, when he was out rawhiding. You know, that's riding the range in late fall and winter, looking for beef steers or anything else missed by the fall roundup. Well, they got snowed in and played poker all winter, and Jim had pretty high hands all along but just not quite high enough, and he kept losing and losing. About the middle of March, when the snow melted, he'd lost everything he had: his homestead, all his horses, his saddle, his clothes, his bank balance and even his wages for about a year ahead. Well, finally he got up to go—pretty discouraged, of course—but he had a hunch to play one more hand . . ."

"The damn fool! What did he draw?"

"A pair of deuces."

"Too bad! Well, that's the way it goes, though. So, I suppose he shot himself?"

"No, they had his gun. He'd lost that, too. The poor old bastard was so desperate he bet on the deuces and bluffed the trappers out and won back everything."

"Pretty damn lucky, I'd say."

"Didn't do him any good, though. The shock was

so great it killed him then and there, and they buried him on top of the butte."

"Sounds to me like somebody's pipe dream."

Tom considered the matter awhile. "Oh, I don't know. I've seen things almost as cockeyed happen down that way, and old Jim's grave is up there on the butte, sure enough, just above where we pitch the roundup camp each year."

At this point he looked at his watch and excused himself on the grounds of his telephone call. I didn't see him again for a day or two.

In the meantime, everybody at the ranch seemed to have heard about the telephone call from New York, and many were the versions of its significance. Tom, as everybody knew, was there for a special reason. He was no ordinary dude, and he was expecting someone from New York to join him, who probably would be no ordinary dude, either. A woman, of course, but who? Some member of his family? A mistress? Or, as one version had it, a visiting nabob, perhaps Queen Marie of Rumania? Whisperings circulated among the women dudes, many of whom had secret leanings toward Tom, for he was gay, irresponsible, mysterious and, above all, had that fatal fascination: the fascination of being utterly worthless. He had only to make a droll face or engage in some senseless antic to make the ladies shriek with glee. I saw him delight a perfectly strange woman, parked in her dinky little Ford runabout on the main street of town, simply by inspecting the instrument panel, rolling his sparkling, watery blue eyes, cracking an alcoholic grin and saying sweetly to her, "Ampères . . . one of the very *finest* French cars, madam!"

When Tom's girl arrived, she turned out to be short, blonde, slightly older, gay, very rich in her own right and in the process of being divorced from a millionaire real-estate operator in New York. Everybody loved Dorothy Stett,[7] and from the moment of her arrival the ranch took on an added air of gay abandon. There were card parties in her sumptuous cabin where drinks flowed freely, and her great, open fireplace roared a welcome at all hours. Tom was ever present there, quipping with the dudes or talking cattle in strange lingo with the cowboys. There were trips to the drinking and gambling dens in town, where Tom and Dorothy would entertain on a princely scale all and sundry who came their way, whether known to them or not.

Thousands of silver dollars clanked over the baize between the couple and Sammy Doyle, and many were the recitations by Sammy of how he "shot that sonofabitch," each recitation tailored to fit the occasion, the number, sex and type of his clientele, for Sammy never offended anyone. He had a certain version for timid girl dudes whose sense of humor might still be untried, and that ver-

[7]Fictitious name given to Mrs. Henry Rea, then being divorced from her Pittsburgh steel magnate husband. She later married and divorced Thomas Fortune Ryan, III.

sion wouldn't shock the prissiest Sunday-school teacher. But gradually, with proper encouragement, he would fill in highlights and shady areas in the picture, until this gory scandal reached its full-blown maturity. Clients would continue gambling meanwhile, fascinated by the d'Artagnan in this pale little man who lived under the street, and waiting expectantly for the moment when he was sure to exhibit the old single-action Colt.

It was a sad parting when this gay ménage broke up. But it had to end when Dorothy's lawyers began to doubt whether the type of life she had been leading was helping her divorce case any, and advised that she return east, where already there were splutterings in the gossip columns. Tom also was wanted by his outfit for the fall roundup, and he invited me to come along, for at least a look at the Tongue River country. This suited me exactly, as I felt in good shape all around and was itching to find some sort of occupation.

"But what good could I do down there?" I asked, feeling terribly green.

"Maybe you can help me pitch manure. It's really not so bad, once you catch on to the swing of it. Come on and have a look, anyway," he said, as if he really meant it, which decided me on my next move.

III

The Events at Soup's On Creek

IT TOOK US a few days to get Dorothy Stett packed
off on the train for New York. Tom had to cele-
brate vigorously, both before and after her departure, following which he could not stay at the ranch
any more, out of sentiment. So we hung around the
town of Sheridan a few days, preparing to take off
on the expedition down Tongue River.

In those days, Sheridan was a cozy little town to
hang around, still unspoiled by the big commercial
rodeos that were just coming into vogue then, by a
hankering for big-city status, which it later developed, and by billboards, traffic lights, air travel,
neon signs and parking meters.

It is still about as cozy a little town as ever stood
on its tiptoes and called itself a city. Then, almost
everyone knew everyone else and the old-time atmosphere of genuine friendliness prevailed. There
were, of course, automobiles and even a few miles
of paved road extending north and south of the
town, but yet ranchers did not feel too conspicuous
coming to town on horseback and knew that they
could always find a livery stable to look after their
ponies. It was easy to find friends or be found by
them, to deliver messages or receive them through

27

certain natural centers of information, or merely by speaking to people on the street.

One day, in the depths of Sammy Doyle's, after it had been decided that I should go back with Tom, the thought occurred to me that, possibly, the White family should be let in on this news, as they might have something to say about it themselves.

This theory Tom dismissed with a wave of the hand. "What the hell?" he explained. "They'll be glad to have you. I'll fix it up." After a moment's hesitation, he added, "It might take a few days, though. I can't go to Al White[8] direct. He's kind of down on me. Sent four messages in to town, to get me out there and help gather the beef. But, *you* know goddam well I couldn't make it."

Trying to show a sympathetic attitude toward his plight, I asked, "What do we do, then?" Actually, I was not too keen about barging in on a family uninvited, not one member of which I had ever even met, and I mentioned this to Tom.

"Never mind," he reassured me. "I'll fix it up so you meet Al White. He'll be coming in to town in a few days, to flush me out. But remember, I'm not speaking to him."

"On account of hanging around town so long?"

"That and a few other things." For an instant, he frowned mysteriously, then brightened up and added, with an air of finality, "I'll send a message out to

[8]The author's longtime friend, and partner, Albert G. Brown.

Betty[9] about it. That's his wife. She can fix anything."

"What's she like?" I asked.

"A redheaded Dixie lady. Full of southern hospitality. Salt of the earth, but a pretty peppery temper. She can romp all over you when she gets mad."

"Let's not get her mad, then. It's bad enough to
have Al White mad at you."

Tom passed over the point lightly. "She won't be
mad if you go out there. As for Al, why, that
doesn't mean a thing, because he's always mad at
me, anyway. It's just his natural state of mind. He
can't help it."

It occurred to me that Tom's life at the ranch was
not a bed of roses as things were, and that I
shouldn't make it any worse. "Maybe this would be
the wrong time for me to go out there," I suggested.

"Hell, no. I tell you, I'll fix it up."

We climbed up through the trap door into the
pool hall and went out into the weak afternoon sunlight. "Hope you come out all right at the ranch," I
said when we reached daylight.

"I always do," Tom answered, smiling, breathing
deeply and looking around him, as if he'd just seen
the town for the first time. "God, I feel a lot better
now. Well, so long. I've got a date."

The finishing touches to our arrangements with
the ranch were carried out by laborious telephoning; we did a little outfitting at the local stores;

[9]The gentle, but steely, wife of Albert G. Brown.

Tom had his gallon jug replenished with moonshine, and presently we were ready to leave town.

Aside from luck in catching a ride (which we
didn't have), the only available method of transportation to Tongue River was the Birney mail stage,
which made the 60-mile run three days a week. It
was a broken-down Model T Ford truck with an
open wire cage mounted behind an enclosed cab.
Its skipper, Ole Hansen,[10] an importation from the
Norwegian peasant class, was a hard-bitten ex-cow-
puncher who had turned to government service
when advancing age and the gradual fencing up of
the open range had curbed his activities. Ole was
the only individual I ever knew or even heard of
who actually believed that Uncle Sam was a real,
live person living in Washington, wearing red and
white candy-striped pants fastened under the in-
step, a star-spangled blue tail coat and a red, white
and blue beaver topper. He had an unholy terror of
Uncle Sam, who could "do any goddam thing he
wanted, even rustle cattle, if he wanted to," with
immunity, and to whom Ole always referred as
"vun *hell* of a big feller."

At any rate, Ole could and did carry the U.S.
mail against all odds. He also carried an occasional
passenger going to one of the ranches along the

[10]Fictitious name given to Pete Salveson, whose Norwegian
family immigrated to the Wyoming-Montana border area
where they settled in the late nineteenth or early twentieth
century.

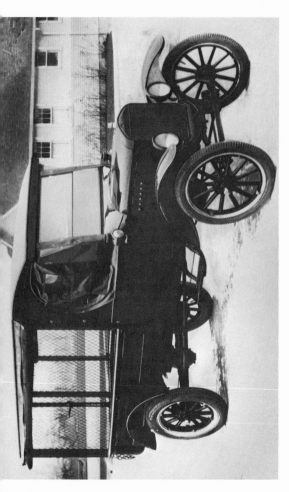

A Model T Screen Panel Ford Truck, similar to the one on which the author made his ill-fated journey with the mail carrier, Ole Hansen.

Courtesy of the Ford Motor Company Archives, obtained with the assistance of the Veteran Car Museum, Denver

route, at the rate of about a cent a mile, or Indians
going to or from the Cheyenne Reservation, for
about half a cent. For the comfort of his passengers
he had rigged an old tarpaulin over the cage, which
in rainy or cold weather was lashed down all
around. Although the passengers were thus somewhat protected from the weather, they were unmercifully exposed to all smells that the Indians and
the old Ford together could produce, as they sat
huddled in murky gloom. There were no seats, passengers being expected to make themselves comfortable among the mail sacks and not to sit on the
lock-sack, containing registered and insured mail,
which was supposed to be kept handy in case of
emergency. His truck was equipped with a special
compound gear shift, which always baffled him
more or less, since he was something of a tippler
and nothing of a mechanic. Ole was still further
equipped with a well-worn but still usable .30-.30
Winchester carbine.

November had rolled around before Tom and I
met Ole at the post office, at a little before six
o'clock of a frosty morning. Tom's knees showed
blue through the rips in his levis and he shivered in
his thin leather jacket, loading his gear, which consisted of an old worn-out suitcase and a gunny-sack
containing a gallon jug of moonshine protectively
padded with hay. Ole had on a long horsehide coat
with two rows of five buttons down the front and a
battered cowpuncher's hat, in sharp contrast to

Tom's little fedora. I was the Beau Brummel of the trio in my Brooks Brothers chesterfield, with its velvet collar, and a dark-blue woodsman's cap with a flap of scarlet wool which pulled down around my ears and the back of my neck.

Ole had a big load of mail and packages, a great deal of which he piled in the cab beside him, making room for Tom and me with our bags in the rear compartment, where he was careful also to leave some unexplained extra empty space. This space he filled up after we got started, by making several surreptitious stops around town to pick up forbidden cargo. Explosives and combustibles were taboo with the Post Office Department, but anyway, we took on a 55-gallon drum of high-test gasoline for the Coleman lamps along Tongue River, and rolled it up to the front end of the cage. While that was being loaded, Ole telephoned the owner of a hardware store to come down to his place of business and open up, as we needed several cases of shotgun shells very badly. We then went to the brickworks, where the town magazine was, and added to our load two kegs of blasting powder.

The cargo began to get cumbersome. Tom and I shifted around among the parcel post packages and the mail sacks, while Ole could hardly get in and out of his cab, so crowded was it with objects that fell out when he opened the door and so hindered was he by his long horsehide coat and the Winchester, which kept jabbing him in the ribs. Finally, he threw the gun in the rear compartment with us.

By the time we got all our illegal cargo aboard and began heading for the sagebrush, it was after eight o'clock. A light snow had set in the night before. Now it began to come down more heavily and a bitter wind whipped the old tarpaulin, keeping it slapping against the wire cage, admitting gusts of whirling snow. The ancient truck, once it left the pavement, made an incredible noise. Everything on it was loose and rattling. The engine backfired and spluttered. The body creaked and groaned from abuse and overload, while Ole, happy as a lark, clashed away at his gears and fought the wheel against an increasing tendency toward swerving and skidding as the snow got deeper. Our cargo shifted, especially the gasoline drum, and Tom, fearing that it might crash into his jug of moonshine, lashed it in one corner with a throw rope which he took from a saddle inexplicably mixed up with the mail.

At the first steep hill we had to put on chains. This was a major operation, as Ole had forgotten where the chains were, although diligent hunting finally revealed them at the bottom of the mail pile. The chains themselves were broken in several places and had to be patched up with barbed wire, which Ole cut from the surplus on a gatepost, with good-natured cursing and repeated assertions that "nothing holds up Uncle Sam's mail," although he himself had held it up about two hours in collecting his illegal cargo. After the chain hunt, we piled the sacks back in again and Ole looked over his load appraisingly. "O.K. Vall, I tank we go now," he remarked. "Got the lock-sack all right?"

"Right here, on top," Tom reassured him. "Just where Uncle Sam wants it."

"He's vun hell of a big man! Ve got to guard his mail good. Now ve put the padlock back on. Coming to Decker post office pretty soon." And he snapped the lock on the cage door. The padlock was a formality which he used especially whenever he arrived at or left a post office.

The Decker postmaster gave us some hot coffee, bread and jam, and Ole insisted on hanging around, helping him sort the mail, as he enjoyed glancing over the postcards. Altogether, we must have whiled away between one and two hours, so that it was past noon when we got on our way again. To the bracer of coffee, Tom and I also added a few swallows of moonshine, but Ole, although he loved it dearly, would not take any in the presence of the postmaster. He and Tom always stopped for a sip later on, at a certain creek about halfway, which Tom had nicknamed "Soupçon Creek." Ole called it, "Soup's on." Its real name was Leaf Rock Creek, derived from fossils of prehistoric leaves found there, and it had good water for a chaser.

As the daylight began to fail, my body ached from the chill and the uncomfortable positions we were forced to hold hour after hour, and I began to anticipate with pleasure the little ceremony at

Soupçon Creek. Tom, expertly appraising our position in the wilderness from various landmarks and scattered ranches, had just announced that Soupçon Creek lay beyond the next ridge and was casting longing glances at his jug, safely nestling in its hay-padded gunny sack, when my nose caught a suspicion of smoke.

"What did you do with your cigarette?" I asked.

"Flipped it out the back end, long ago."

"Sure?" I sniffed about the sacks. "Thought I smelled smoke just now."

"Probably a leak in the muffler, coming up through the floor boards."

But presently there was no doubt about it. A haze of acrid, white smoke was emerging from somewhere beneath the mail sacks. We shouted to Ole that something was wrong, but he mistook our shouts. The rattling of the truck, the thickness of the rear window and the fact that he was fairly deaf from the old cowpuncher's universal remedy, quinine, did not help matters any. To improve the situation, and as the smoke was becoming quite stifling, I took his carbine, smashed its butt through the window and, already fancying the flames licking at my buttocks, shouted above the din, "Fire, you damn fool, let us out of here!"

Dumfounded and dim-witted, Ole jammed on his brakes going down a winding hill and looked back over his shoulder to inquire, "Fire? Vat you mean, fire?"

The truck skidded, lurched and slid into the ditch with a mournful groan, the down-side door flying open and admitting to the cab a blast of snow and icy wind which poured through the broken window and provided a perfect draft for the smoldering flames. A small tongue of yellow fire licked up from the hay around Tom's jug and he beat at it fiercely with his fedora. From somewhere below came an ominous, crackling sound.

Ole got down on his hands and knees and peered stupidly about under the car. When the fact that we were afire dawned on him thoroughly, he went into a panic, shouting desperately, "Yesus, boys, save the lock-sack!"

"How about saving us first?" I suggested, fairly well out of patience.

Ole ran around to the back of the cage and started fumbling about his person in heavy cotton work gloves, searching for the key to the padlock. His horsehide coat had huge pockets stuffed with all sorts of objects which came tumbling out into the snow: rusty nails, kitchen matches, an unbelievably soiled handkerchief, wire cutters, a can of Copenhagen "snoos," an orange, some nuts and bolts, a penknife. But no key. He couldn't remember where he had put it. I felt that we were as doomed as Marie Antoinette in her tumbril.

"To hell with the goddam lock-sack!" Tom bellowed. "Bust that door open and let us out!"

"Get a wrench and twist the hasp off," I yelled.

"I got a file somewhere," said Ole.

Then Tom had a brilliant idea. He grabbed the
.30-.30, pumped a shell into the chamber and
shouted at Ole, "Get away from that door. This
Irishman's coming out!"

The rattling old doors hung loose on their hinges
and we pried them apart enough to get the muzzle
of the Winchester between, just behind the hasp.
One shot was enough to free us. Tom jumped out,
rifle in one hand, jug in the other, and I right behind him. He promptly removed the jug to a safe
distance.

Once free, the danger did not look so great. The
fire was somewhere under the middle of our load.
The rear sacks were unharmed. The explosives
were up forward and the wind was blowing back.
Ole started pawing the mail bags madly, looking for
the lock-sack and whining pitifully, "I'm done for if
we don't find it. I gotta pay back every penny to
Uncle Sam!"

He was reduced to a groveling state, almost in
tears, for fear of what the powerful Uncle Sam would
do to him. The lock-sack should have been on top,
but just wasn't, and I tried to console Ole that we
would soon find it. But both the consolation and
the search were in vain, and Ole beat his little round
bullet head in despair. The anguish he displayed was
really touching. He was trying to pray to Uncle Sam,
but didn't know how.

I said to Tom, as we dug for the powder kegs to

throw them out, "Wouldn't you think he'd let up on the horseplay about Uncle Sam when the mail is burning?"

"That's not horseplay. He *really believes* it." And as I looked back at Ole, his arms flailing, his hat knocked off and blowing away over the snow without his even missing it, the awful truth dawned on me: he really *did* believe it.

"Ole!" I called back, trying to comfort him. "Don't worry about Uncle Sam, he'll understand it wasn't your fault. We'll explain it to him, won't we, Tom?"

"We sure will, Ole. We'll say it was all our fault. We'll take the blame. He can't do anything to us."

We could see that this worked like magic as he answered, "T'anks, boys, t'anks. You won't tell on me? You won't say we had gas and black powder with the mail—and them shotgun shells? I didn't mean no harm. Yust got to make a living, somehow."

"Of course, we won't tell," I reassured him. "We'll even say we were smoking. That's probably what caused it. Lucky thing you don't smoke. You just chew that goddam snoos. That's what'll save you with Uncle Sam. I'll write him a long letter, all about it, and explain everything."

He picked his can of Copenhagen out of the snow and packed a little more of the stuff between his front teeth and upper lip, which seemed to relieve him greatly. "I ain't no good at writin' letters, boys.

All I know how to do is haul 'em." And he returned to his search for the lock-sack.

"Tell you what I'll do, too," said Tom. "I'll have my grandpa talk to Uncle Sam and tell him what a good driver you are. He knows him, personally."

It wasn't long before the gasoline tank of the truck, under the front seat, blew up, wrecking the cab and starting a new blaze forward, with the wind whipping it back. Obviously, the stage was now a lost cause, with flames on both sides of the remaining sacks, the shotgun shells and the drum of high-test gasoline, which latter began to produce low, warning "pong" sounds. Instinctively, we all retreated to safety, waiting for the drum to explode, as the whole front part of the truck was now enveloped in flames.

Ole, between Tom and me, was a picture of dejection, eyes glued on the rising flames, absolutely beaten. "Goddam!" he whispered, and hung his head. We watched in silence for a while and then there was another "pong" from the drum. At this, Ole looked up, and his little steely eyes returned the challenge of the flames. "She's gittin' ready to blow," he said, "but I t'ank we got time for one more try," and he dashed from us toward the wreck, mumbling about the lock-sack.

We caught him on the rear step of the wreck, just about to climb in, dragged him back a safe distance and sat on him, for he was by then on the verge of hysteria. As we did so, there was a muffled roar and the gasoline exploded in earnest. A column of black smoke shot upward and the little truck became a veritable holocaust, in which the banging of shotgun shells punctured the frosty atmosphere with its irregular staccato. The truck seemed to crumble in all directions at once and, in a matter of a few minutes, there was nothing left of it but the engine, fenders and a red-hot frame writhing in a circle of melting snow. Shells in the hot ashes continued to pop off for some time afterward.

With the fireworks over, we let Ole up. He had returned to something like normal and told us, "Ve got to notify the post office in Sheridan. I'll walk back over the divide to Halsey's ranch, where they got a telephone. Someone's got to guard the mail, so you boys take the gun and stay here."

Tom and I set about destroying traces of our illicit cargo. With a stick we pushed the remains of the gasoline drum out of the smoldering wreckage and over a cut bank, where the postal inspector would not see it. Then we took the jug of moonshine some distance up the side of a hill, first, however, filling an empty pint bottle which Tom had with him. We knew that, since it was by then snowing rather hard and several hours would elapse before the postal inspector could show up, our tracks to the cache would be covered.

"When the pint's gone," said Tom, "we can heave the bottle over the cut bank without leaving any more tracks, in case they search us." We returned with our pint, to sit on the pile of mail sacks.

By that time it was quite dark and cold. We were getting hungry. The chill air certainly sharpened one's appetite. I thought I had never smelled any air so fresh and clean. It was dead still except for the occasional yapping of coyotes—hungry, too— and a few shotgun shells which continued to pop off from time to time.

Tom looked over the burned and battered sacks, from which a few boxes had tumbled out, and asked, "Do you think there could be food in these?"

"What good would it do us?" I answered, getting up and scuffling about among them. "We couldn't steal it from the mail."

"Some of these packages will never get to where they're going, anyway . . . busted up and charred so you can't see the addresses." He turned over a box with his foot. It broke open and something rolled out. He stooped over it and lit a match. "Look here! Just what we're after!" He held up oranges, a tin of smoked turkey, candies, and a jar of guava jelly.

"Who's it for?" I asked, bending beside him.

"Goddamned if I know. The label's burned off."

"Who cares? Let's pretend it's for you." And we fell to, devouring the contents.

"You know," said Tom reflectively, "I was just thinking. We're supposed to be guarding the mail." He tapped the .30-.30, munching away happily. "But what we're really doing is robbing it."

"Yes, I know," I admitted guiltily, scraping out another knife-load of guava jelly, and reaching blindly into the battered box to feel what else was there. My hand came upon a small envelope. In it was a card addressed to Tom, with love from one of his sisters.

Tom studied the card affectionately. "From Irene, my favorite sister. You know, the one I told you about, who used to raise the most hell."

It must have been about nine o'clock when Ole got back to us, in a Dodge pickup, with the postmaster and an inspector. By that time our tracks to the cache were snowed under, and Tom had thrown his empty pint bottle over the cut bank when the headlights first appeared.

The inspection went off smoothly and there was no question of anything but an accident. Ole got lots of sympathy, lost most of his gloom and immediately started planning on a loan from the local bank to buy a new car. Fortunately, no shotgun shells went off at this stage.

A local rancher put Tom and me up for the night. Ole went back to town, reappearing next day with a hastily improvised mail truck, wreathed in smiles. It was a horrible-looking wreck, but he loved it and all the world. He had been exonerated by the postal authorities and the bank president had granted him a loan, so he was back in business again and full of optimism. This increased to boundless joy when he later found the lock-sack, which he had left at Decker by mistake. It had nothing in it anyway, except a small package of cattle vaccine.

The sun blazed in a cold, blue sky and the country, dazzling white, sparkling with untold billions of diamonds, looked a lot more cheerful as we proceeded merrily on our way, not forgetting to stop at the scene of disaster and revisit our cache on the hillside. "Not a track anywhere," said Ole gratefully. "You boys sure done good by me. T'anks."

These, then, were the circumstances that enabled me to remember, more or less clearly, my arrival at the White ranch, which we reached that afternoon.

IV

Al White

A<small>L</small> <small>WHITE</small>'s bloodhound face drooped in dreary
creases from beneath an olive-drab Stetson of
the fuzzy type, which had definitely seen better
days, as he rocked beside his living-room fire, reading a thick volume of Civil War history. At first, I
didn't think that he seemed at all glad to see me, as
he explained, "Tom said you were coming out," in
a way suggesting that he, himself, had no part in the
invitation. But suddenly the creases resolved themselves into a smile and the kindly brown eyes twinkled as he said, "Welcome," and I knew he meant it.
He had just been riding beside Stonewall Jackson,
and it had taken him a little time to come out of the
past. That momentary, faraway look never bothered
me again, as it did some people, nor did I ever cease
to wonder at the contrast between it and the man's
naturally sunny disposition, clouded though it was
by misfortune.

Al was a short, heavy-set man whose whole shape
was out of proportion to the broad-brimmed Stetson which he wore almost constantly, even in the
house. He seemed to cling to it as he clung to his
history of the Civil War. They were his escapes
from the presently morbid ruins of his cattle outfit

into a more glorious past. As he spoke to me there, before the fire, interminably rolling Bull Durham cigarettes, taking a few puffs from them and absent-mindedly throwing them into the grate, I realized that this man was no ordinary rancher. He had practically no contact with the present, only with the past and the future. I had a hint of his youth, in a southern military institute where, apparently, he had developed the roots of his lifelong admiration for the Old South. He gave off the feeling that the Old South was not so very far away from him, al-though actually he was only in his mid-forties, a fact hard to realize if he were to be judged by physical appearances alone.

Along with this dream life of the past, Al had his dream life in the future, and this revolved about the coming of the railroad along Tongue River. This railroad had actually been started, years ago, and abandoned. A considerable amount of grade had been completed, the ghosts of which could still be seen: long, straight mounds of earth, now eroded by wind and water, pointing, like wrinkled old fingers, along the path of disappointed stockholders' shat-tered dreams, down through the string of five ranches owned by the White family. Some flimsy old iron bridges had even been put across the river, to accommodate the trains that never ran, and these now served to carry the rudiments of a highway. There were known to be great deposits of lignite coal under all the White ranches, and the railroad had been dickering for this coal at the time of its demise—had, in fact, even made some small down payments on contracts. Therefore, as Al pointed out modestly, it was easy to see that the railroad was coming; and, when it came, that they would be rich once more. Even as he spoke, a certain very clever promoter, a Mr. Bushby,[11] a fine southern gentleman, was working day and night on the resuscitation of this noble project and that very week was having an important conference with some Atlanta bankers. The bankers were sure not to turn Mr. Bushby down because his demands were so modest. The required sum was forty-six million dollars, but Mr. Bushby, because of his fine sensibilities, was only asking for sixteen at this time. Of course, he would ask for the rest later but, in the meantime, with this sixteen million, the coal contracts could be closed. Al was absolutely convinced that the railroad was coming. I am sure that, on clear days, he could even hear the whistle blow.[12]

There was also an oil scheme mixed up in Al's future. Some promoter had come along the river,

[11] A promoter of the proposed "North-South" railway to connect Sheridan with Miles City, a never-ending dream of the Brown family.

[12] Ironically, today this northern Wyoming—southern Montana land of Albert G. Brown and his neighbors is one of the richest coal areas on the globe. In fact, many of the author's former neighbors are "coal millionaires." Although subject to heated debate there are approximately 1,524 billion tons of coal hidden under the sagebrush of sixty-three counties of the northern Great Plains.

pronounced oil present, set up a little wooden rig
on one of the White ranches and peddled stock
throughout the countryside.[13] He pecked a little
hole in the earth, but soon gave up. Al's hopes did
not disappear with the driller, however. The driller
only thought there was oil on the place, but Al
knew it. That driller would be back. His departure
was only a stall, to buy up the land for nothing.
That was the way big oil companies worked.

At nineteen, this all sounded very wonderful to
me and I had already begun to see a way of making
my fortune. Al indicated to me that, since their financial crash in the Hard Winter of 1919, they no
longer had any cattle to speak of, but that his company intended to buy up a big string of cows with
the coal and oil money. "And, just imagine the advantage of having your own railroad running right
through the outfit, for shipping!" he beamed.

I imagined and imagined. If the Whites were going to own this railroad, I imagined that it would be
good to get in with them on the ground floor. I even
imagined myself puffing into Sheridan in a private
car, perhaps with my own engine, just as father told
me he had once been obliged to do in Florida when
he was in a hurry to go somewhere for dinner. I
would have a picture taken of myself on the rear

[13]Although Birney has never been the site of significant
petroleum discoveries, promotional hearts were set aflutter
in southern Montana by Samuel Gary's opening up of the
Bell Creek oil field in the early 1960s. "Sam Gary," *Rocky
Mountain Oil Reporter* (September, 1965) XXII, pp. 6–8.

platform of this private car which would be called the "Rangeland"—and send it back home to the trustees, just to impress them. Al's enthusiasm was, indeed, contagious.

He led me about the house with a funny little shuffling walk, explaining that it was originally a log house, covered over with boards and enlarged. He showed me his little collection of Indian relics, some geological specimens indicating coal and oil, his father's old sidearms used in the Civil War, photographs of beef shipments in the old days, when dozens of carloads of fat steers rolled down the tracks each fall, bearing the White brand, and fat checks rolled from Chicago, Omaha or Kansas City in return. "Those were the days!" he sighed, as the rundown heels of his scuffed western boots shuffled about the darkening and now quite chilly house. He apologized for the temperature and threw another log on the fire, explaining, "There hasn't been anybody around here to stoke the furnace in a long time, and I'm just not very good at it." Again he smiled his beguiling smile. I almost said something about Tom, as the "Chore man," staying away so long, but suddenly remembered that they weren't on speaking terms and that Al had deftly avoided mentioning Tom's name in showing me around the house and pointing out the room he planned for me to share with him.

Not only were the radiators stone cold, but we had no electric light. This became painfully evident

when Al snapped on a lamp, which glowed faintly
for a few moments and then faded out. "Batteries
must be run down," he said unconcernedly, giving
the bulb a disgusted look and then dismissing the
subject as something entirely out of his orbit. It certainly was out of his orbit, being one of the present
problems of the ranch. He simply had almost no
connection with, or interest in, the present, and the
mechanical problem of starting the ailing light
plant to charge the batteries was such a hopeless
one for him that it did not concern him in the least.
He alleviated the situation by lighting an oil lamp,
several of which were scattered about, since the
light plant, apparently, never worked properly
while Tom was away.

I wondered about Mrs. White and asked where
she was.

"Oh, I guess they're out in the corral, with the
milk cows. Ought to be in any moment, now."

The pronoun I took to include Tom, on whom
depended our light and heat. I couldn't do anything about the furnace, but I did have a fair knowledge of engines and told Al I would try to start
the light plant, so that his wife could have light
when she came in from milking. "That would be
a great help." He beamed at me, turning back to his
book. "The engine room's that little house just outside the kitchen door. You go down several steps,
so be careful." Then he added, as a sort of afterthought, "It's a sorry place, that engine room."

I found that he had described it correctly. It was a dreadful place. And I *did* go down several steps, skidding down on my backside and landing in a pool of murky, greasy water with steppingstones placed here and there in it. My candle, inadequate to reveal the full extent of the hazards anyway, had snuffed out, and I went back to the kitchen for an oil lamp. On my second trial, the full extent of Al's meaning became apparent. The engine room was, indeed, a sorry place: a small, foul-smelling cubicle extending five or six feet underground, so the batteries wouldn't freeze. It contained an old-fashioned one-lunger gasoline engine with a damp magneto and a bent crank which, by being held at a certain uncomfortable angle, was used to spin its massive flywheel with the effect of producing wheezing noises, supposed to develop (if all went well) into firing. But this did not always happen.

I began to think, after an hour or so of toiling with improvised tools, that Al was fairly smart in his preference for oil lamps and candles. But then the unexpected happened. The engine started uncertainly, with a series of ear-splitting reports from its unmuffled exhaust pipe which, for some mysterious reason, was pointed at the trunk of a cottonwood tree not three feet from the side of the engine house. This caused a combination of bangings, reverberations and echoes inside the little building, while flames and the sickening smell of exhaust fumes leapt from the inner portion of the exhaust pipe. I beat a hasty retreat up the steps, practically into the arms of Tom and Mrs. White, who were just returning from the corrals.

"Why, you're the most useful guest we've ever had around here," she exclaimed by way of welcome, in a curious mixture of southern drawl and western heartiness. She was obviously delighted at seeing the house lights go up, through a series of faltering, rosy tints to a final, steady banana-yellow brilliance, and I felt that my very first effort at being a good guest had been a success. "Glad to have you. And just go on in and take it easy. I'll have supper ready right soon. Tom'll show you where your room is."

"I've already moved in, bag and baggage. Hope I'm not putting anybody out."

"Nobody in there to put out, only Tom," she laughed gaily, "and we've been trying to put him out for years."

"Come on in," said Tom. "Let's have a snort."

Betty White gave him a sharp look over her shoulder, making me feel slightly guilty, then went about the business of her milk pail.

Tom walked ahead of me through the house, stepping lightly and clowning, making a sour face as we passed behind Al's back. Al had not moved from the fire, was buried in his book and never turned around. He was still reading by the oil lamp, apparently not trusting the electricity. Tom then produced a jug from the closet and over it we fell to talking for a half hour or so, taking an occasional hearty pull. Then we heard feminine feet tap quickly down the corridor and our door suddenly framed Betty standing there, her arms akimbo, addressing the Chore man.

"Tom, I'm agoin' to take that jug. Abbit says you've been asuckin' on it all day, he can tell by the way you walk, and we don't want any more nonsense like the last time you came back from a trip with that shootin' man, and blood asplatterin' all over the parlor. . . . No reflections on Mr. Randolph, here, of course." She smiled at me, apologetically, then pursued her point. "Now, give me the jug. I'll dole out a pint every night after work, and no more."

Tom surrendered the jug meekly, and she was out the door as quickly as she had come in. I marveled at her efficiency. Here, it seemed, was a small-boned, well-chiseled and smooth-skinned southern belle in whose mouth one might think that butter wouldn't melt until she opened it. Then she had all the assurance of General Lee himself, leading a cavalry charge. It was the type of courage a young, gently reared southern girl needed to marry into a Montana cow outfit, move out there to live, in the horse-and-buggy days, stand the rigors of winter, drought and financial reverses, while doing all the housework, bringing up three sturdy children, keeping her pluck and also her looks. I felt that I was definitely on probation as an unknown crony of

Tom's and, even worse, a possible blood splatterer.

I withstood the probation period successfully and was finally told, by both Al and his wife, that I could have whisky in my room at any time, and that Tom was being moved to another room, as he would have to get up earlier to do some extra chores. I expressed relief at not being classified as a blood splatterer, and Betty sweetly explained that she hadn't meant to say that, but it just came out. Then she went on to elucidate.

"You see, here come this tall fellow, Cliff Stanley,[14] some cowpuncher friend of Tommy's, in the middle of the night. He was reeling around from moonshine. Said he was looking for Tommy, which sounded natural enough. I got out of bed and talked to him in the kitchen, but I didn't ask him in the house because it was so late and he was so drunk, and he had a six-shooter stuck in his boot top. I told him that Tommy had just come back from one of his trips, full, and was asleep over in the bunkhouse, and that he could go over there and sleep, too. . . . Well, sir, I hardly got back to bed when I heard a shot. So, I woke up Abbit and I says, 'Abbit, get up and go over to the bunkhouse. Cliff Stanley's shot Tommy.' But Abbit, he just rolls over and says, 'What of it?' . . . Well, the next thing, here comes a pounding on the door. Seems like Cliff thought he'd shot Tommy, but Tommy, he was

[14]Fictitious name given to Joe Lewis, who passed through before the author's time.

drunk and had rolled under the bed, so the bullet just went through the bedclothes. But Cliff thought he'd killed Tom, and he'd figured on killing himself rather than hang, so he'd come over to tell Abbit about it. But, all he said to me was, that he wanted to see Abbit. So, I rushed back to the bedroom and I shook Abbit again, and I says, 'Abbit, Cliff's out there in the yard with a gun, and he's shot Tommy and now he wants to see you, but don't go out!' And Abbit—you know Abbit—he says, 'Why not?' And Abbit insists on going out. So I says, 'You don't want to get yourself shot, like Tom, do you?' And Abbit says, 'Cliff didn't say he wants to shoot me. He says he wants to see me.' But still, I told him Cliff had a gun, and Abbit had better take his, too."

All this time, Al was reading *A History of the Confederate War*,[15] from which he would look up once in a while and smile tolerantly.

Disregarding him, Betty went on with her narrative. "Well, Abbit couldn't find his gun, and said he didn't know whether he had any shells for it, anyway. So, I gave him my little one and filled it up with shells for him, and had it all cocked and ready. But then he had to get dressed. So we lit the oil lamp (as the engine hadn't been running while

[15]Civil War buff Brown was probably absorbing the prose of then popular George Cary Eggleston's *The History of the Confederate War. Its causes and its consequences; a narrative and critical history* (New York, 1910).

Tom was away) and Abbit gets fully dressed. He even insists on putting in his new set of teeth. Then he puts on a bow tie and a coat. All this time, we could hear Cliff crunching around out in the yard, and Abbit was making a perfect target for him through the window. Now I ask you, wasn't that a silly thing for him to do?"

Here Al looked up from his book and offered an explanation in defense. "I hadn't ever been mixed up in a Montana shooting before, but in the academy, down in Virginia, they always taught us that a gentleman wears a necktie to a duel."

"Well, anyway," Betty continued, "out he goes, with my little gun all nice and ready. It was only a twenty-five caliber, and I saw Cliff's was a forty-five, so I was kind of worried about that and also because Abbit isn't too good with a gun, anyway. So, I wanted to come out with him, to see he had a fair chance, but Abbit wouldn't hear of it. He walked out alone, just as calm as could be, and I sat down here by the fire to wait. Pretty soon, I heard another shot, and I knew it wasn't my twenty-five. So, I began to think of what a good husband Abbit had been, even if he did set the barn on fire and let the pipes freeze up once in a while. And, when I thought of him lying out there in the snow, with his boots on, and his bow tie and his new teeth that weren't even paid for yet, all of a sudden I got mad. So, I grabbed our old shotgun that I knew still had shells in it from hunting prairie chickens that morning, and I headed for the yard, to finish up Cliff myself. But when I got to the kitchen, here comes Abbit in at the door. He wasn't even mussed up. 'What happened?' I asks him.

" 'Cliff shot himself,' says Abbit, calm-like.

" 'Good Gawd!' says I. 'What're we going to do?'

" 'I'm going back to bed,' says he, and starts taking off his bow tie.

" 'What?' says I. 'With two dead men on the ranch? Don't you know, we've got to call the undertaker to come out and haul them off?'

" 'No dead men on this ranch,' he says. 'Cliff didn't kill himself. He's weaving around out there, in pretty fair shape. He didn't kill Tom, either. Tom's just dead drunk, that's all. I went over to the bunkhouse. He'd fallen under the bed, but I know he's alive, all right, 'cause when I kicked him he cussed me. Just a few holes in the blankets, that's all,' says Abbit."

Betty White, it seems, had then taken to cranking the old battery telephone with a will, until she raised the hospital in town and had an ambulance sent out for Cliff Stanley. Al had poked up the fire and settled down to read, while the ambulance came. Cliff Stanley had staggered in and collapsed in a chair facing him, spouting blood from a chest wound. When Betty emerged from the broom closet (where the telephone was) she had come upon this fireside scene and now recalled it.

"There they were, asetting face to face, Abbit

reading about old Stonewall Jackson and Cliff just
splattering blood all over the chair, and it was running down the leg of the chair onto the floor. Cliff
was feeling kind of glum, all right. Too much
moonshine in him, and not enough blood, and he
was mumbling something to Abbit about Tom being dead and himself going to die soon. Abbit
doesn't even look up from his book, but says, 'No,
you're not. Men like you and Tommy just go on
and on. He's not dead, either. Maybe you both
ought to die, but your kind never does.' Abbit acted
real disgruntled with them both for still being alive.
Cliff, he just groans on and off and says a little
something once in a while, and Abbit shuts him up
so he can go on reading his book. Cliff groans, 'I
always said I was going to kill myself,' and Abbit
says, 'Well, you haven't done it, yet,' unconcerned-
like. Then Cliff, he groans again and says, 'Gawd,
what'll I do now?' and Abbit, he tells him, 'Far as
I'm concerned, keep right on shooting . . .' Well,
sir, I thought that ambulance like to never have
come. Finally it did, though, and the doctor fixed
Cliff up all right and took him in to the hospital. He
was out again in about a week."

V

The Outfit

I HAD a genuine desire to be of some use around the ranch and, at least, try to earn the food and lodgings which, week after week, despite their strained finances and with unquestionable warm-heartedness, the Whites urged upon me. I didn't know what to do in return for it, so made a point of getting up at five-thirty every morning and going with Tom on the rounds of his chores. In the cold dark before breakfast, we would start out for the corrals, where we had kept in a couple of stake horses when turning out the cavvy the night before. These we would saddle up and, leaving the corral gates open, go out to wrangle.

The cavvy was small, consisting of about six gentle saddle horses—two of which were the children's transportation to school and the other four fairly good cow ponies—a team of grays and a team of chestnuts, an eccentric old black gelding named Badheart (which was alternately, and unpredictably, both the quietest and the meanest horse imaginable), two brood mares with colts and three or four green broncs, which were slated for breaking as soon as the family could afford, or otherwise obtain, a bronc twister. These horses might be found on either side of the river and, generally speaking, within an area of about seven thousand acres fenced off, so that less than an hour of riding was usually sufficient to round them up and bring them in. I always enjoyed this hour, as the stake horses were fairly good riding themselves and often we would have a little sport on the side, a shot at a coyote or a bobcat, since we usually took a rifle along. Sometimes we would take a small-bore rifle and, being more after food than sport, knock down a few prairie chickens from their roosting places in the bare branches of tall cottonwoods. We also shot cottontails which, in those pre-rabbit-disease days, formed a delightful part of the ranch menu. In the fall there were great flights of duck at which we banged away, wading our horses after those that dropped in the river. And for just plain target practice there were always prairie dogs, sitting up straight above the entrance to their warrens, flicking their tails with each chirp and having the tantalizing habit of falling into their holes when hit, so that it was next to impossible to retrieve a dead one. That winter I learned to trap for coyotes and used the dead prairie dogs for bait. On these morning rides I would also ride my trap lines and got several coyotes that way. A good coyote hide was nice to mount and, in those days, would also bring a few dollars on the market. They were then plentiful, and we could always hear them barking when we went out to wrangle.

Breakfast over, we would rope out the two children's ponies for them to ride to school. Tom showed me how to handle a lariat (always called a throw-rope, however) with a fair amount of dexterity, so that I could at least catch a saddle horse in a corral, although I never did go in for roping cattle on the range. That first year, we would saddle the children's horses for them and keep them apart from the others, waiting for the starting signal, which was the passing of the spinster schoolmarm, Aggie Lester,[16] through our corrals on her way to the school, five miles upriver. Aggie was a kindly, middle-aged soul; no great beauty, but pleasant, hard-working, long-suffering and meticulous. She was tall, angular and prim, and the old black mare she rode was just like her. Aggie and her mare could always be counted upon to show up jogging through the lower meadow just before eight o'clock. She took a short cut through the Whites' corrals, giving Tom and me a pleasant word as we opened the gates for her. As she was a strict Prohibitionist, we would sometimes kid her by offering a nip of moonshine on a cold morning, and we always enjoyed her mild admonitions.

The Whites also had a fine stallion, kept in a separate paddock, back of the corrals. This paddock

[16]Fictitious name given to Mabel Spracklin, schoolmistress of the little Canyon Creek school on Brown Cattle Company land. Later, Miss Spracklin married a Sheridan resident.

had no water, so we watered the stud twice a day in the main corral when the other horses were out. Sometimes, on really cold days, we fed him his hay and grain in the somewhat dilapidated barn opening onto the corral. This stud was a constant threat to Aggie's mare and Aggie was terrified of him, even though we always shut him up in the barn or put him in a little round corral when she came through. But one morning, when Aggie's mare must have been ultra attractive, the stud just couldn't restrain himself. He burst through the flimsy barn door and, with wild whinnyings, took in after the mare. Three or four times, they went around the main corral, Aggie (who was not a bad rider) crouching down in the saddle, screaming for help and desperately hanging on to a sheaf of examination papers, the old mare's heels lashing out savagely at the stud which, from time to time, got his fore feet on her rump, baring great, yellow teeth and emitting blood-curdling love calls. It seemed that every time Aggie looked around in her wild race from love she looked right down the stud's throat and was more determined than ever to remain a virgin. "Help, help!" she screamed. "Get him away from me! Do something . . . open the gate!"

There was no point in opening the gate, as the stud would only have pursued her all the way to school. Nor was there any way of handling him in his frenzy, without even a halter on him. Tom grabbed his rope, threw a neat loop over the stud's head, and we both lay back on it, the stud dragging us around the corral almost without seeming to notice the difference. When he dragged us near the snubbing post in the center of the corral, Tom worked enough slack in the rope to get a couple of dallies around the post, and we had him, rearing and snorting, but perfectly helpless, at the other end. "Now, open the gate and let her out on the next time around!" said Tom.

I did so, and the passage of Aggie and her mare through that gate was much like the finish of the Kentucky Derby. "Don't be late for school!" Tom shouted after her, as she thundered away from us and over the hill, not once looking back. Both Aggie and the mare retained their virginities for some time thereafter, but eventually both fell prey to the wiles of nature.

Kidding Aggie was a form of diversion with us, as no one was ever born with a more strait-laced nature, and her aversion to alcohol fascinated us. One afternoon we were driving an empty sled down the river past the schoolhouse, having taken a load of salt or oil cake out to the cattle. Aggie was dismissing her little pupils for the day as we came along and stopped at the schoolhouse to joke with the children. The idea of a sleigh ride being of universal appeal to children, we took on a load of them, the ones going home on horseback leading or driving the others' ponies before them. We begged and implored Aggie to come along with us which, after a certain amount of coy resistance, she finally did.

The sled was just a wagon box mounted on the running gear, and in it there happened to be a stone crock of horse liniment, which could easily pass for a little brown jug of moonshine. Tommy and I pretended to be drinking from this, acting wilder and wilder, and poor Aggie's terror mounted accordingly. The team needed no urging, but we whipped them up, anyway, and went in for a little fancy driving, switching the lines and the jug back and forth, one driving while the other pretended to be drinking. Occasionally, we would pretend to drop the lines or not know which one of us had them. We made a swing or two off the road into the sagebrush, at one time plunging into a creek bed and up the other bank with considerably more speed than we had figured on. Aggie shrieked at us to have pity on the innocent children, but the innocent children urged us on with shouts of glee, especially when we began captioning our various maneuvers: "Dead Man's Curve," "The Devil's Leap" across an irrigation ditch, "The Great Mississippi Steamboat Race" and other nonsense.

Aggie pleaded to be allowed to get back on her old mare, which loped along behind us, showing good speed after her practice race with the stud, reins tied up, but faithful to her mistress's voice. Our heartless answer was that we *couldn't* stop. We galloped over a treeless flat across which ran a line of scraggy cedar poles supporting the lone iron wire of the party telephone line and around which we cut several figure eights, explaining that this would help get the horses winded and under control. Finally, there loomed up a closed gate to one of the pastures. Aggie had one last twinge of fright as we shouted back, "Everybody duck down, we're going through the gate!" But, miraculously, we pulled up just short of it. She lost no time getting out of the sled, taking her brood with her. She didn't hold her grudge against us very long. First, she gave us a good piece of her mind, but later brought us some chocolate fudge she had made. Actually, I think she liked us, and we were really very fond of her.

When Al would send Tom off from the ranch, either on some errand or in disgrace, I would do the chores alone and, although not too efficient, I could harness and handle a team, at least. I had also learned the furnace and lighting plant routines, could feed hay to cattle wintering at the ranch and was tireless at riding around with an ax on my saddle, keeping the watering holes in the frozen river chopped open. I felt better, in that all these little things were steps in the right direction toward earning my keep.

That first winter I helped put up the ice harvest, during which neighbors would congregate and help each other. The Whites' ranch was one of the more favored meeting places, both because the harvesters were always treated very cordially and also because the river there provided a good, natural ice field. Icing is heavy work, but well worth the aches and pains, frostbite, weariness and other drawbacks, which were soon forgotten during later days of sweltering summer heat, when the ice was such a comfort.

The Whites used their own coal, from a crude mine on the ranch. This was just an outcropping of lignite coal in the washed-away bank of a creek bed about five miles from the house. Whenever the coal bin in the furnace room got low, Tom and I would hitch up a team to the old wagon and head for the mine. We bored into the solid bank of coal with an auger about six feet long, making a hole possibly two inches across. It had a T-shaped handle, which we would take turns at twisting, laboriously. At the proper depth (which was when we got tired of twisting) we withdrew the auger and put in a certain unmeasured amount of blasting powder, varying in each case with our feelings at the moment. One time it might be a pint, the next time a peck. We really didn't care. But we usually put in enough to make a pretty good explosion, which was fun. We tamped and wadded the powder in, then drove the wagon off to a safe distance, where one of us would hold the horses while the other would light the fuse and run. After the explosion, we would load up our coal and start for home.

Tom was seldom silent during our chore duties. He rambled on and on, in a charming strain of Irish wit, but with a certain negative acidity, tearing down everything and everybody in the country, except Betty White. His talk smacked of inferiority complex: he could never reconcile the lush surroundings of his youth with what he, and I, were doing. Yet he seemed to love what he was doing and took great pains in tutoring me as his helper. But he lived in a haze of golden anticipation, waiting for the day when his testy old grandfather would die and at least a few of the Bryan millions would trickle down to him; perhaps even enough to buy up all the debts of the White Cattle Company, take over the outfit, do Betty proud and show Al who could put whom off whose ranch, and when.

But through the haze of Tom's biased harangues, and from my own observations, I could piece together the general situation of the White family. They were second generation cattle kings from the early 1880s. By that I mean they were rated at over a million dollars when the sum represented gold. Their range—owned, leased and otherwise acquired—covered probably between 150,000 and 200,000 acres. They had come up from Texas in the last days of the trail-herding era and had flourished until the famous Hard Winter of 1919. Into that winter they plunged with about 10,000 head of cattle, coming out with less than 1,000, which later fell off about 60 per cent in value. Notes, carelessly signed in the lush days, came due and couldn't be met. The banks had taken over their cattle, ranch equipment, personal belongings, life insurance policies and practically everything movable. The family subsisted in great part on what they could get out of their garden, the few staple groceries which their credit would still buy, and game, which was abundant. The bunkhouse was deserted because there were no longer any cowhands. Friends helped them run the remains of their mortgaged cattle, and there seemed no way out.

None of this did I learn from the Whites themselves, except for a few casual, joking references to the fact that they had taken a beating, along with many others, in the Hard Winter. I learned it all from Tom, grumbling over his chores or gurgling in his cups. Whole chapters of detail came out on various long winter rides up side creeks to visit his moonshining friends.

That winter Tom had a message from Dorothy Stett. She was in Paris and simply couldn't do without him any longer. The cable, sweet and raucous, was telephoned over the party line from the telegraph company in town. Tom was somewhere up a side creek at the time, but everybody told him about it on his way down. Excitement was terrific. One thousand dollars was being transferred to a bank in town, earmarked for the purpose of bringing Tom to New York in the style to which, lately, he had not been accustomed. In New York additional funds would be waiting, with which he was to secure a suitable wardrobe and first-class passage on a luxury liner to Cherbourg. There, Dorothy's Rolls would meet him and convey him to Paris like a gentleman which, she hoped, he would try to be or, at least, imitate as closely as possible.

The shock was too much for Tom. He couldn't even milk next morning. His train reservation was secured and he champed at the bit, waiting for the great day to arrive. Everybody catered to him. Betty sewed patches on his blue jeans and borrowed an overcoat from a friend, for him to wear on the train. In Sheridan, he was to put on his town suit, made by a good tailor in New York many years before and still fairly presentable, except for pressing and a few missing buttons, which details Betty White looked after. I contributed a good Brooks Brothers suitcase, as he had no luggage, his original bags having been stored in the coal shed and eaten by mice, so that his recent short jaunts about the country were carried out with the aid of a gunny sack or two. He was to have outfitted himself thoroughly with smart luggage in New York and left my suitcase there. But, of course, and according to Betty's predictions, I never saw the suitcase again. However, there was something unneighborly about the idea of letting poor Tom arrive at the Grand Central Station with a gunny sack when I had an extra bag lying around, even considering that this was exactly the way his grandfather had arrived in New York some fifty years earlier.

Even Al was touched by the festive spirit aroused by Tom's forthcoming adventure and brightened up perceptibly. They were on speaking terms again, and Tom even volunteered to discuss the Second Battle of Bull Run one morning at breakfast. Tom had dropped his morning milking chore and some of his others. He still ran the engine, fed the chickens and saddled the children's horses, but was prone to stretching out on the window seat, writing letters and waiting for telephone calls. Al cheerfully overlooked this shirking of duty, undoubtedly considering it necessary to Tom's plans for making a departure. And the thought of Tom's departure was a welcome one to Al. The separation would be pleasant and—Al hoped against hope—permanent.

This state of dither around the ranch lasted five or six days and was shared by neighboring ranchers, who came to call, say good-bye and ask leading questions. Most of them were well informed as to Tom's telephone calls, telegrams and cables, having listened in on the party telephone line, which was well monitored to catch the latest events. If some busybody decided that she had missed out on one of Tom's cables from Paris-France, for instance, she would call up her cronies and immediately be advised from their memories and imaginations, the former usually shaky and the latter fertile. All were interested in Paris-France and secretly yearned to know what Dorothy Stett—after the third day, simply referred to as Dorothy—was like, whether she was one of those women in France who sold their bodies, and what Betty White thought of the whole situation. The White children were delighted that Tom was going on an exciting trip, although they had no definite idea what it was for. They plagued him with various questions about France from their geography books. He answered them with superb nonsense and promised to send them letters with foreign postage stamps which they could exhibit in class. Aggie Lester called and brought some of her homemade fudge. She indicated shyly that she had heard all about Tom's forthcoming trip, and blushed a little to prove it. She asked him if, as a great favor, he would send her a postcard of the Eiffel Tower, to tack up in the schoolhouse. "Dearie, I'll send you a postcard every day, for this fudge, and bring you back a bottle of champagne!" he answered her. She cast her eyes down modestly and blushed again. "Oh, Tom, I'm afraid Dorothy wouldn't like that."

Tom went in to town with Ole, on the mail stage, and the ranch quieted down to normal, or, I should say, actually, subnormal, for he left a definite vacuum behind him, into which we were all drawn, somewhat dolefully. Everybody had some kind of fault to find with Tom and, although we all agreed that he was the most worthless of human beings, yet we all—even Al—admitted missing him. Occasionally one of us would murmur, half consciously, "I wonder what Tom's doing now?" Or, a passer-by would drop in to ask, "Heard any news of Tom Bryan?"

We were not long without news, however. Tom had gone directly to Sammy Doyle's underground emporium. There he had royally treated the local riffraff in his accustomed manner, except more so than ever because they were all informed of his financial windfall, and laying for him. He lost a good portion of his capital to them at blackjack, got drunk, spent the night in jail and so missed his train for New York. It was two days before he got out of jail, sobered up, but with only half his capital left. He still had his ticket to New York, and the judge had arranged to salvage his Pullman accommodation. He went back to Sammy Doyle's to recoup his losses, but failed. When his remaining capital had shrunk to about $150, he got nervous and asked Sammy for advice.

"Why, if I was you, Tommy, and had a gal *that* rich nuts about me and offering to ship me all the way to Paris-France, I wouldn't worry at all. My advice would be to keep right on playing. She'll send more when she gits to missing you bad enough."

"She might send money for me to show up over there, Sammy. But will she send any more if I *don't* show up?"

"How do I know? Try her out, that's what I say. Women are awful goddam funny, sometimes. They do the silliest things. She might be silly enough to send you more. You can't never tell about women."

"Suppose she's not silly enough, Sammy, then what will I do?"

"Take it easy, kid, you're sitting pretty. Even if you wasn't, your credit's always good with me. Here, take another stack," and he pushed the chips over to Tom. "Your luck's bound to change sooner or later. And, besides, you got money waiting for you in New York, ain't you? Why don't you have the bank back there wire you some?"

It was an idea, better than trusting to the uncertainty of a woman's whims or the much greater uncertainty of a player's luck changing very much for the better in Sammy Doyle's place. There was cash already deposited for him in New York, and there was more waiting for him in Paris. For two hours more he played on, keeping about even and waiting with bated breath for the buzzer from the pool hall, upstairs, to announce that Western Union had a message for him.

At last it came. But Dorothy had turned out to be smarter than they thought. The bank had instructions from her to pay Tom only at their main office in New York, and in person. Sammy let him win a last hand, just to show that his luck was changing, and analyzed the situation. "Yes, sir, looks like you got a smart woman there, Tom. She's scattering bait all along the line, but not too much in any one spot, so you got to keep moving. I guess she wants to make sure you really git there."

Tom finally boarded the train, with just enough money left to see him to New York. Sammy Doyle, some of his riffraff and the policeman came down to see him off and wish him well. The newspaper sent a reporter and ran a humorous article next day. Then there was a long silence before we heard from Tom again.

VI

Party at Bear Creek Schoolhouse

WITH TOM gone, Al White grew more sociable, and we became better friends. He trudged about with me amiably but, for the most part, silently as we did the chores, sometimes with his younger daughter, who was just past the toddling age, tagging along, their devotion to each other being very touching. Occasionally he broke his outer reserve and showed a warm glow of humor beneath.

Betty White had not been off the ranch for a long time and, having the true feminine instinct to gad about and catch up on the local doings once in a while, she developed a keen interest in a forthcoming dance at the Bear Creek schoolhouse. This was slightly out of horseback range on a winter night, being some twenty-five or thirty miles across country. So urgent was her desire to attend this function, however, that a kindly neighbor came to the rescue, offering us the use of his little four-cylinder touring car, in which we could be reasonably protected from weather by putting up the side curtains, such as they were. The car itself was of ancient vintage, but had fairly good tires on it, a set of chains and one headlight.

Al dearly loved the idea of driving an automobile, although he had practically no knowledge of how to do so, despite the fact that he had owned the first car in that country, an old Haynes, and several others in better days. The mere act of driving seemed to lift him from the gloom of his troubles into a different world, a world which, once he clutched the wheel, made him forget all principles of mechanics and rules of the road (if, indeed, he ever knew any).

The main attraction of this dance for Betty White was the rumor concerning the local wolfer and his mysterious wife, whom nobody had ever seen. The profession of government wolfer has now, I think, passed into history and, even then, was a fast-disappearing curiosity.[17] Relentless war and handsome bounties by the cattle- and sheepmen had succeeded in driving wolves from that country before my arrival there, the bounties being sometimes as high as $100 on the head of a wolf from cattlemen, plus the government and state rewards. For a number of years, wolfing had been a lucrative profession for those few who had the unique qualities required to pursue it: a love of hardship, lonely places and cold weather, inexhaustible patience and a lot of practical knowledge of nature in general and wolves in

[17]The wolf, like its fellow generic neighbor the coyote, has been the subject of folklore, history, ecological challenge, and Congressional debate. For a brief, basically accurate account of predator control in the West of the past, consult Stanley P. Young, *The Wolf in American History* (Caldwell, Idaho, 1946) pp. 117-133.

particular. For this wily killer had a reputation as the cleverest of all animals and the most difficult to trap or shoot.

As a wolfer, Charlie Gorrie[18] had everything. He knew wolves as intimately as he had known his mother. He even looked like one and, some people said, smelled like one. He had been at the profession for twenty years during the heyday of wolfing and was a fount of information on this obscure subject. All this time he had been collecting a salary from the government, generous bounties on the side from livestockmen, money from the sale of hides and even for secrets of hunting and trapping. The secrets he would sell at a price if he were in the right mood or he would part with this information in such a way that it would not do the recipient much good, or interfere with his own business. He might, for instance, take $50 to explain why you are using the wrong kind of trap for a certain animal, and what kind you should use. Then, switching over to the trap he recommended, you might find that your luck was still no better and apply to Charlie for more information. Another $50 would educate you on the fact that you were using the wrong kind of bait, and what bait you should use. But it would require an additional fee to learn how to set the trap. Even when you had mastered all this,

[18]A fictitious name given to Charlie Florrie. In the 1960s the author ran into Charlie in Sheridan where the two old friends recalled with glee the incident at Bear Creek.

there was still room for improvement since, for instance, the knowledge was useless unless you knew *where* to set the traps. "Can't catch fish in a haystack," Charlie would explain. And, for another $25 you might learn that coyotes did not ordinarily pass where you set your traps, but favored a well-worn trail on the other side of the ridge.

After the wolves were driven back into Canada, Charlie's main source of income dwindled, but he still did a fairly good business in coyote, bobcat and beaver. I had trapped and shot a few coyotes, but had never bought any of Charlie's information or, in fact, ever seen him except on the one occasion of this dance at the Bear Creek schoolhouse, when he gave me a few tips, gratis. Practically nobody else ever saw him, either, for he lived in a remote cabin away back up in the hills, was pretty well snowed in all winter and subsisted on game, bacon, canned goods and simple staples, rations not calling for much contact with stores. He claimed that coming down out of the hills too much and hanging around where people lived made one absorb the smells of civilization, the man-scent which, dragged back to the hunting grounds, stunk up things and kept the game away.

Charlie, now well past middle age, had always remained a bachelor, until that time. This fact and the general knowledge that he must have a certain respectable sum of money hidden away somewhere always fascinated the women of the countryside.

They thought that they should marry him off, so that there should be, even if no children, at least someone to spend his money. This money was supposed to be in the form of silver dollars which he had well hidden somewhere in the hills, having no use for banks, or "folding money," and never going to town if he could possibly avoid it. The women couldn't bear the thought that he might die leaving the whereabouts of his cache a mystery, and there was even a report that several wilderness adventuresses had tried to live with him in order to locate it. But until now Charlie had evaded them all. His theory was that a man who lives with a woman eventually absorbs the woman-scent and cannot get rid of it, a thing which drives wild animals farther away from traps than anything else. He also bewailed the fact that a woman insists upon getting to where there is some civilization every two or three months, coming back loaded with the fatal scent of civilization.

Someone who "had it for certain" told Betty White that Charlie Gorrie was going to be at the Bear Creek schoolhouse dance. This, in itself, was a curiosity occurring about as frequently as an eclipse of the sun. But the fact that he had taken a wife and was going to introduce her to society at this event made the prospects irresistible for Betty.

We started for the ball one evening after supper in our little car, with Al White fighting the wheel, the tattered rain curtains flapping noisily about us, but effectively warding off a good part of the near-zero breeze, and all bundled up to our noses. Al wore his woolly chaps, for extra warmth, and Betty sat in the front seat beside him where, wrapped in all available sweaters and a mackinaw, she could benefit a little from the engine heat. I sat in the back seat, ready to hop out and open gates, very thankful for a long, handsome muskrat and beaver sleighing coat which I had inherited from my father. This Beau Brummell effect looked slightly out of place with my Pendleton pants sticking out below and my woodsman's cap above, but it was certainly handy for the occasion.

We rolled merrily down along the river, then turned up side creeks and started climbing over divides. There was only a slight skiff of snow along the river bottoms, but higher up it became a real problem and we had to put on chains. Betty kept venting her amazement and curiosity about Charlie Gorrie's wife and throwing herself into a frenzy of expectation. Every once in a while, through the whistling of wind and the rattling of rain curtains, I would get the thread of her queries to Al ". . . But what do you suppose she could *look* like? . . . And where in the world could she *come* from? . . ." and, "I just can't imagine what she'll *wear* . . . How do you suppose he ever *got* her?"

It appeared that, among the ladies of Tongue River, several conflicting theories were rampant. Some had it that Mrs. Gorrie was just a squaw old

Charlie had taken up with because she knew a lot about wild animals and liked to live like one. Others ventured that she was the daughter of an old mountaineer he had shot messing around his traps, and that he had promised her his cache of silver as hush money. Some said that she was a madwoman escaped from an asylum. But the general consensus was that he had come by her legitimately, through a heart-and-hand bureau, just ordering her right out of a catalogue and having her shipped to Miles City, timing her arrival to coincide with an order of traps and ammunition.

As to why Mrs. Gorrie had never been seen, there was also a wide divergence of opinion. One theory was that she had turned out to be an old woman in a wheel chair and that he had sent her right back from Miles City. Someone had heard that she materialized as a floozie with perfume that ruined his traps, so that he had traded her off to a blind hillbilly for a box of .30-06 shells. Someone else was sure that she had been recaptured and taken back to the asylum. One even said that she had been eaten by a bear. But Betty was inclined to believe, along with some of her more skeptical friends, that there never had been any Mrs. Gorrie at all and that the whole story was a crazy piece of fiction dreamed up by Charlie himself to keep the women from pestering him, or perhaps because his mind was failing. "Why, they say he's gone plumb silly," she explained, in support of this theory. "I've heard he howls at the moon like a wolf and won't eat anything he hasn't killed himself."

"I even heard that he has a peculiar way of going to the bathroom," Al admitted shyly, "a little here and a little there, all over the woods."

"Now, yawl know, no woman's going to marry anything like that, even if she *does* come out of a lunatic asylum," Betty answered. Her logic had a sound ring to it, and I couldn't wait to see Charlie Gorrie. She wagered that no wife would be there.

I didn't have to wait long, for Charlie was in the schoolhouse when we arrived. I had no difficulty picking him out, for he was the cynosure of all eyes, sitting on the long bench up against the wall, with the women waiting for invitations to dance, an empty space on either side of him. Charlie didn't like to be crowded, and everybody knew it. Besides that, there may have been other reasons why the women didn't want to edge up too close. He wore a hodgepodge of old work clothes, faded sweaters and "beat-up" western boots, the whole color scheme being strangely neutral and shapeless. He was short, spare and muscular, with a weirdly canine face in which the eyes were deep-set under bushy eyebrows, the nose straight, the forehead sloping back, the chin receding. His hair was gray and he wore it long, frontier style.

Alternately, Charlie sat on the bench and walked about the room restlessly. He would stand first against one wall and then suddenly, as if someone had called him, cross the room to another, or work himself into a corner, as if suspicious of anyone standing beside him, or more particularly, behind him. In walking about, he had a graceful, slinking gait and looked furtively to either side and occasionally behind him, as he went. "What do yawl reckon he's looking for?" Betty asked. "Must be looking for his wife, just like all the rest of us," someone answered. "No! I tell you, he hasn't *got* any wife," said Betty. "That's all just gossip. Yawl know there aren't such things as wives that nobody ever sees and that a husband just can't find . . . Look! Where's he going now?"

Charlie, with wolflike grace, had slunk out the door into the anteroom. I thought that, perhaps, he had caught the Gunther-scent of my muskrat coat and was going to investigate. He had, in fact, taken it in, as I learned shortly. "Maybe his wife's one of those women sitting on the horses tied up outside," Al suggested.

Queries went back and forth in the little knot that had assembled around us and various explanations were ventured as to what Charlie Gorrie had done with his wife, the explanations getting more and more ridiculous as they developed into a sort of game. Everybody was expected to make a suggestion. Someone suggested that she broke a leg and Gorrie had to shoot her. "Maybe she fell down with her head under her and couldn't get up," said an old cowpuncher. When it came to my turn, I said,

"Maybe he used her in an emergency for wolf bait."

A thin voice spoke up behind me. "No, I ain't used her for wolf bait."

I turned around, and there he was. He had been listening to us for some time and his gimlet eyes bored through first one and then another of us. They were brownish yellow, like the eyes of a wild thing, and I felt sure that they would light up in the dark. His nostrils twitched slightly, as if he were getting our different scents. There was about him a faint odor of the zoo.

Then he burst into a cackling guffaw at our obvious discomfort. "If it's my woman you're alookin' fer, you ain't agoin' to find her."

Betty gave me a knowing nod of satisfaction and then asked, kindly, "But, Mr. Gorrie, where is she? We're *so* disappointed!"

"Left her back up in the cabin. She don't feel too good. Got the belly cramps."

"Is there anything we can do for her?" another woman asked.

"Hell, no. She's all right. Just fixin' to whelp some time next month."

So, at last, there was a prospective heir to the Gorrie silver! This information seemed to give the good ladies some relief. They broke up gently and turned their attention to the dancing.

This was a rather dull and graceless performance, shuffling about to the strains of a piano thumper (afflicted by a dearth of chords), a fiddle scraper and an unimaginative drummer. The rhythm was in waltz time, but much too slow, and the dancers knew nothing about dancing.[19] They just walked slowly back and forth after each other in a bewildered sort of way. But about once an hour a square dance would be called, and then they were much more vivacious, especially the older people, who knew all the words and calls. A certain drinking element was obvious, with jugs cached outside in the sagebrush or bottles in saddlebags. About half the men came on horseback and had their horses in the small corral which the school children used. Anybody would give you a shot of moonshine, whether he knew you or not, and I had a few nips from the various jugs. Several babies were bedded down in the anteroom, dozing and drooling happily among overshoes, spurs and oil lanterns. I scraped around the floor a few times to the music with Betty and was beginning to wonder how long these things lasted when I found myself face to face with Charlie Gorrie again. We were both backed up against the big potbellied stove, the fluted, curved underside of which glowed a soft, dark red. Once in a while Gorrie would open the stove door, study the burning coals within and then spit mightily from the copi-

[19]Many have been the commentators on the Saturday night dance scene in a western dance hall. Sometimes known as "stroke your fiddle, shake your partner." Those of us who have survived or observed a western dance can attest that this institution of western culture is alive and flourishing in many small communities of the West.

ous and, apparently, ever-increasing supply of tobacco juice with which his whole being seemed to
be charged.

Finally, he looked sideways at me, in a sort of
half-pitying, half-derisive glance, and said, "Well,
young feller, it's easy to see you don't know nothing
much about wolfing."

"I guess I don't, Mr. Gorrie," I had to admit,
sheepishly. "Looks as if you had cleaned all the
wolves out of the country before I got here."

"I've cleaned out a hell-slew of 'em," he suggested modestly, "and them that's left ain't worth goin'
after, with no bounty any more. Coyotes and bobcats is all that's left to bother the stockmen now."

"I've just started doing a little trapping myself,
this winter."

"Say . . . you're the new dude feller from the
Whites' ranch, over on Tongue River, ain't you?"

"That's about it, Mr. Gorrie."

"That your fur coat out in the anteroom?"

"Yes, that's mine."

"You trap them muskrat and beaver?"

"No. I've only gotten a few coyotes."

"I figured that. . . . Sure looks like a store-bought
coat. . . . How many coyotes you got so far?"

"Only three. Trapped two and shot one. Somehow, they don't seem to like my bait."

"Bait? What you use for bait?"

"Mostly prairie dogs, but sometimes I set traps
around an old carcass."

He considered awhile, then told me to try smoking my traps and set more of them around the tail of the carcass. "Coyotes always start eating at the tail end," he advised.

We were getting along famously. I acted very humble in the presence of the great maestro, which seemed to please him and draw him out. He was fascinated by the fact that I came from New York, and asked me if it was really true.

"Sure," I admitted. "Born and raised there."

"I heered that, awhile back. Called the feller a goddam liar."

I didn't know which way to take that, as I noticed him eyeing me up and down, carefully, and tried to look as relaxed as possible. "Well," I asked, hoping to sound casual, "why?"

"You're the wrong color. I heered you was our color, and y'are."

"What color should I be?"

"Kinder puddin' color, near as I can figure it. You know, when I was back east, long years ago, I learned that folks gets whiter and paler, futher east you go. Course, I only got as fur as Omaha, but I asked about it from a feller in the stockyards, and he told me, way back east folks gets real puddin' color."

"That's just because business keeps them indoors. You'd get the same color if you worked in an office and rode in the subway." And, in return for his trapping information, I told him about the sub-

ways and the Woolworth Building. He listened,
agog, spurting his tobacco juice into the coals from
time to time.

"Railroad trains arunnin' under the ground, huh?
And people livin' hoisted away up in the clouds!
Why don't they stay on the ground, like us regular
folk? What the hell's the matter with 'em? Ain't
they got enough land?"

"That's what it looks like, Mr. Gorrie. You see,
the whole island has only got a little more than
twenty sections of land in it."

"Aw, hell! Then 'tain't even worth botherin' with
at all."

"Not much for all those people, over two million
of them."

"Holy cats, boy! Must be just like crowdin' cattle
into the cars." He shook his head sorrowfully. "The
poor sonsabitches! . . . No wonder you quit the
herd and come out here. Two million people where
there's only room enough for a couple of dozen!
And, back up in my hills, a man can ride twenty
sections all day long without scarin' up enough fellers fer a poker game. . . . Two million people!" he
repeated, in an incredulous gasp. "Say, boy, how
many people *is* that, anyway?"

"Well, Mr. Gorrie, a million is a thousand times a
thousand. So, two million is a thousand times two
thousand."

"Holy cats, boy! You know what you're sayin'?
Why, that's—Aw, hell, I just ain't had enough book

learning. . . . But it's a hell-slew, anyway, and they ought to move 'em off on a reservation somewhere, like they did with the Indians."

"The trouble is, Mr. Gorrie, that they don't want to move. In fact, more people keep trying to get on the island every day."

"Well, I'll be goddamned!" said Charlie meditatively; then asked, "How about your folks? They out here too, now?"

"No, they couldn't come."

"That's what I call real unselfish, to send you out here when they can't come themselves. What I always say is—just like your folks—it's the youngsters that should be given all the advantages. Well, now, young feller, never mind. Times is bound to git better, and maybe they'll be able to scrape up the price someday."

"They might be able to scrape up the price, but they just wouldn't want to come, anyway. You see, they're the kind I was just telling you about, the kind that think the island is a great place to be."

"I don't savvy it."

"It seems kind of peculiar to me, too," I agreed.

He opened the stove door and let fly another terrific stream upon the coals. "You know, son," he continued sympathetically, "I had some kin that was a little bit peculiar, too. It might happen to anybody, specially in them big cities. Somethin' in the water, I reckon . . . although, pussonally, in regards to my own folks, they come from Arkansas and always had plenty of good mountain water, so we never found out what the trouble was. Humans is like stock, I say. Some of 'em can go loco just from eatin' something, like a horse eatin' the loco-weed. But that don't affect the others in the same family that ain't et it . . . see?"

I followed, vaguely, and said, "I guess you're right, Mr. Gorrie."

"What I mean is . . . just because there may be a few locos mixed up in our kin, that don't say *you* or *me* is peculiar, does it?"

"Hell, no!" I hastened to reassure him, wondering at the same time whether I might possibly look as peculiar to him as he looked to me.

"You git yer folks to come out here like you done, and I'll wager they gits cured of them peculiar city ideas. All they need is a change of pasture and a little fresh air, and somethin' different to do fer a while, like trapping. It's done a heap of good fer me, and I'd be glad to show 'em some tricks of the trade, if it'll help 'em to git normal agin."

This astounding offer was the only one he ever made, so far as I knew, and the stark reality of it floored me. I wondered if old Charlie had a jug cached somewhere, to account for this expansiveness, and could answer only, "Oh, thank you, Mr. Gorrie!"

"Course, you know, I don't usually tell things fer nothin'."

"Yes, I know."

"But in your case," he went on, "I figger your folks must be pretty decent people and not the kind that would go back there to New York City and sell my information about how to catch coyotes."

"I'm sure they wouldn't do that, Mr. Gorrie."

"And the same goes fer you, young feller. . . . Well, I got to git moving." He slunk out into the anteroom and, with a long stick, used as a pointer by the schoolmarm, removed his boot overshoes from a nail high on the wall where, clasped together, they had been suspended out of reach of the mob. I trailed after him, watching him struggle into his sheep-lined coat and clap a fur hat on his head. I was thinking over his generous words about the trapping information. Here, I decided, was a golden opportunity to improve my coyote-trapping technique, while old Gorrie was in his "noblesse oblige" mood. So, I asked him boldly, "Mr. Gorrie, what do *you* use for coyote bait?"

"Well, son, most of the time I don't bait a coyote trap at all. Of course, a dead prairie dog staked down in the trail near yer trap is all right fer young'uns. But, nowadays, old coyotes is on to that. They'll push a stick around till they spring the trap, then steal the bait. Ever have that happen?"

"Four or five times. Never could figure out what happened or why I only catch pups."

He laughed his dry, cackling laugh. "They'll do it nine times out of ten, especially if you don't smoke yer settin'. Now, an old coyote—them with the good pelts—you got to remember, is close kin to a wolf, and you got to treat him like one. Bait at the trap ain't the main thing. A real trapper uses a lure."

"What's that?"

"Oh, it kin be lots of things."

I had a feeling that he was edging away from his offer, and was determined to pin him down before the moonshine, or whatever caused his mood, wore off. "What kind of things?"

"Oh, it could be some kind of unfamiliar scent that he can smell but don't see: something buried in the ground. Or, it could be something he kin see, but don't savvy, like a little piece of red string waving from a tree. Don't have to be near the traps, either. Sometimes a quarter mile away is all right."

This sounded like more evasion, so I pursued relentlessly. "What good does that do?"

"Young feller, when a wolf—and a coyote, too, fer that matter—can't figger something out, he gits so curious it just burns him up. Then he starts to circle around it and look it over, or smell it over, from all sides. He never goes straight fer it. So, you put yer traps where he's goin' to circle."

"How do you know where he's going to circle?"

"Well . . . that's where bein' a good wolfer comes in."

This sounded like a dead end, and a hopelessly vague one. But I made a last appeal to his generosity and his recent promises. "Mr. Gorrie," I said, "is

that really *all* you can tell me about lures? I
thought you said you would give me some real information that would *help*. Isn't there something
definite, something *special*, that you can show me?"

He hesitated a moment, and then admitted,
"Yep, there is. But . . ."

"But what?" I felt another evasion coming.

"But the women won't like it. We'll have to go
outside."

We went out to the little corral, where his horse
was patiently waiting, with cinch slacked and no
bridle, munching a few wisps of hay. Charlie unbut-
toned his sheepskin coat, plunged one hand inside
and fumbled deep within the recesses of his costume, finally coming up with a little medicine bottle, tightly taped around the cork. He handled it as
carefully as if it had been nitroglycerine.

"What's that?" I asked, as he untaped the cork.

"Best lure in the world. And nobody's got it except me. Here, take a whiff." He handed me the
bottle.

It is impossible to describe the acrid stench that
assailed my nostrils. It was the most horrible thing I
have ever smelled and, despite coming from such a
small bottle, was offensive to a nauseating degree
even at arm's length, where I quickly held it as I
turned away to get a whiff of the clean, icy night air
and restrain my heaving stomach. I know of no
words to describe a smell of this kind. "Putrid" or
"retching" does not begin to convey the mildest

description of what it was like. It was simply THE END. Nothing like it has ever been devised, I am sure—or, at least, I hope. All I can say is that, even today, after thirty years, the mere memory of it makes me ill.

"Oh, God, Mr. Gorrie!" I wailed, dancing about the corral with the bottle stuck out behind me, to keep to windward of it. "What in *hell* did you make that out of?"

"I didn't make it," he cackled. "A coyote made it. And, look out, don't spill that bottle! That's valuable stuff. It took me *months* to get that much!" He tagged after me frantically, while even his horse, getting a whiff, wheeled in its tracks and snorted disapproval.

He had his treasured bottle back again as quickly as I could hand it to him. He put the cork back in and taped it up, lovingly, remarking, "Pretty stout, ain't it? That's why I said we better come outside. Womenfolks sure goes wild when I open it indoors. But that's the real stuff, worth its weight in gold. It sure gits 'em!" Tenderly he placed the bottle back somewhere inside his strange costume, adding proudly, "I wouldn't sell that bottle for anything."

I almost expressed my thoughts aloud: that nobody would buy it for anything. But, instead, I asked, "How can you stand keeping that thing in your pocket?"

"Oh, it ain't so bad when you get used to it." He smiled. "And, taped up around the cork, like that, not much smell comes out. Main thing is, to keep it at body heat, or a little over, until right up to the time you use it. That's why I carry it on me. It works much better that way. Standin' up agin that stove, tonight, sure helped out a lot. I figgered on ridin' my trap line and makin' a few settin's on my way home."

This, I thought, explained the vacant space on either side of him when he was sitting on the ladies' bench.

"Mr. Gorrie," I said, as he bridled his horse and tightened the cinch, "I want to thank you for that valuable tip on trapping. I shall never forget it, but I shall never use it. That stuff's too strong for me."

"Well, young feller, you stick to your prairie dog bait, but you'll never get rich on it, like you will with this lure. Why, a prairie dog's got to be right near the trap, and even then it's no good after it's been froze up a few days. But this here stuff! Why, you kin bury it two feet deep in the right place, upwind from yer traps, and fan 'em out half a mile away, and it'll stay O.K. for two months!"

"As far as I'm concerned, Mr. Gorrie, you can bury that stuff two hundred feet deep, downwind from me, a hundred miles away, and it will be O.K. forever."

He swung up into his saddle and rode away, chuckling to himself, his pony's hooves crunching the powder-dry snow and his carbine in its scabbard flapping against the horse's side. He looked like an old bundle of rags disappearing in the moonlight amid little puffs of smoke, as the clear, icy atmosphere showed up the breath of both man and beast.

Back in the schoolhouse, I found things pretty hot, both literally and figuratively speaking. The stove had been stoked up to full capacity by some anemic old ladies and blazed away with drafts open, red hot all over. A square dance had been called and shook the little building to its rafters with the stamping, the monotonous rhythm and the clapping of "Turkey in the Straw." Demon rum was obviously present, having escaped from the various jugs and bottles cached outside in haystacks and under saddle blankets. Old and young swirled about crazily, caught me and drew me, against my better judgment, into the melee, there to educate me (somewhat inefficiently) in the various complicated steps and figures. Before I knew it, my boot heels were clicking along with the rest, although not in the best Arthur Murray tradition. A friendly wrestling match was in progress in one corner of the schoolroom, adding to the tumult. The only quiet area was the anteroom, where the children still snoozed and drooled peacefully. An American flag quivered above the scene and blank blackboards, temporarily forgotten, bore silent witness to education in the raw.

Along toward one o'clock the party began to break up, from sheer exhaustion. Babies were sorted out and bundled into wagons, sleds or dinky little cars. In the anteroom, two cowpunchers were betting as to whether one of them could gently pull his chaps out from under a sleeping child without waking it. Spurs were strapped on and jingled over the snow. Horses whinnied, sensing their owners' approach, and lithe figures swung up on them, cursing and joking, prancing and clowning, finally jogging off, in twos and threes, to distant beds which many would not reach until it was time to get out of them again and go to work.

In our own case, Al sprang behind the wheel of our little car, Betty settled down beside him and I, in the rear compartment, muffled myself in my store-bought coat, preparatory to the take-off. But Al's stamping on the starter button brought forth only a diminishing series of little groans, soon followed by complete silence, since the battery had been discharging all evening with the ignition switch left on, and lacked the ambition necessary to turn over the well-chilled motor. Then we remembered that I had drained the water out of the radiator. A bucket of water was drawn from the school pump, warmed in a kettle over the stove and fed to the thirsty engine. Two cowboys, eager to display the prowess of their favorite rope horses, hitched on to us with their throw-ropes and towed us downhill until the engine started, and we were off.

The moon had set and the predawn cold was intense. Al's driving was exciting, but that was about all one could say for it. We slid about from one side

of the road to the other, in and out of ditches, and
raced down little gullies to make sure of enough
speed to get up the other side. Dozing was difficult,
but I managed a few winks between gates. We sailed
past forks in the road and turnoffs which I could
have sworn that we should have taken, but every
time I mentioned this, or questioned the route, or
could not remember some particular gate, Al would
be right there with a comeback. He had a detailed
explanation of exactly where we were, on what part
of which ridge, and between which creeks, and it
always seemed that he had ridden over that particular spot in the cowpunching days of his youth, with
a string of cattle, under unusual circumstances.
Later on I found out that this was all perfectly
true. But that country, at night, in the snow, and
with the after effects of the Bear Creek schoolhouse
rumpus still upon me, looked all alike to me. There
was not a sign or a habitation to go by. One simply
took his direction from creeks.

In one place, we seemed to balance along on a
narrow ridge, which I was sure that I couldn't remember. The one headlight of the car, fed by an
almost dead battery and running mostly on the generator, in fits and starts, was not readily conducive
to the picking out of landmarks, and I had been
vaguely keeping track of our position by the old
gate method: four gates behind us, three to go. It
was somewhere along in here that our headlight
flickered out. Al claimed that the road was like an

open book to him even in the dark, and vowed that he could go on, anyway. But Betty, who was terrified to drive with him, even in broad daylight, screamed at him to stop.

"Let's have a try at it, anyway," Al argued calmly. "You know this road. It's the old freighters' road to Powder River we used to take, years ago."

We staggered along for a while, in Stygian darkness. Then she screamed again and knocked his broad-brimmed nutria Stetson down over his eyes. That settled it. We stopped then and there.

It was a bleak and wind-swept divide where we came to rest, lulled by the familiar sounds of a cold Montana winter night: wind sighing through a few scraggly pines and the distant wail of coyotes. I wondered whether Charlie Gorrie might be out there somewhere, getting them all stirred up with his vapors.

"What yawl expect us to do now?" Betty, excited, demanded of her spouse.

Al pulled out the makings and quietly began rolling himself a cigarette. "I guess we might as well bivouac here for the night. There isn't so much of it left, anyway."

The question of mechanics suggested itself to me, in connection with the possibility that we might be forced to bivouac there much longer unless something was done to keep the car from freezing up. Dawn was a good four hours off, and the thermometer could not have stood much more than ten above zero. Al estimated that we were some four or five miles from the nearest water, the scramble for which, through snow and darkness, would not pay. Furthermore, we had no container in which to carry the water or to salvage water drained from the radiator. So, draining the car was out of the question. We considered keeping the engine running, but had no idea of how much gasoline was in the tank.

"I'll have a look," said Al, reaching in his pocket for matches.

"No, you won't, either!" Betty screamed loudly. "Hyah—give me those matches!" She took them away from him and added, exasperated, "He's already blown up two cars doing that."

"But, Betty," Al pleaded, "I'll be careful not to drop the match *in* the tank again."

"Yawl ain't dropping matches anywhere near this cyar," she answered, flustered momentarily out of her upbringing. "We got enough trouble right now without you starting any fiahs. If you want to start a fiah, start one out yonder in the sagebrush, that'll keep us wahm."

It seemed to me that our salvation might lie in running the engine slowly, for a few minutes each half hour until dawn, although running it at under the generator's charging speed might also exhaust our battery and sound taps for the ignition system. With no gasoline gauge and no ammeter, the problem of how fast to run the engine, and how often, and for how long, began to take on a challenging aspect, and absolutely forbade the use of the self-starter. I found, to my joy, that there was a crank in the car, which would save us a lot of battery waste, so I got it out from under the seat and put it in position for use. Then I suggested that we run the car to the next steep downhill slope and stop it there, blocking the wheels, with the brakes off, so they would not freeze in the "on" position, as I had seen happen before.

Betty would not hear of Al's driving the car in the dark another inch, so I took the wheel, freely admitting that I could not see a thing. She and Al walked ahead, scuffing about in the snow for little canyons, into which, she was sure, the car would, otherwise, plunge at any moment. After a few minutes of this, we came to the brow of a steep hill and perched there, putting a large rock ahead of each rear wheel. With mixed feelings of hope and trepidation, I turned off the engine.

"Now," I said, "at least, if the starter doesn't work, we have the crank. And, if that doesn't work, we can coast downhill and crank on momentum."

"Maybe," Betty qualified my statement.

"Anyway," said Al, unconcerned, "I know where there's a ranch only five or six miles from here, where I can go and come back with horses to get home. We can drain the car and send someone back for it."

I thought that he was not without foresight, to have worn his woolly chaps.

"I don't care how we get back, long as the kids don't go hungry," said Betty.

"They won't go hungry," I tried to reassure her. "We'll be home for breakfast, all right." To make it sound more convincing, and also to satisfy my own curiosity, I gave the car a trial crank, while it was still warm, and the engine started beautifully.

Betty was still skeptical. "That's all right *now*," she said, "but how do you know it won't freeze up before you try that again?"

There was only one other thing I could do to reassure her. I had bought a gallon of white mule from one of the moonshiners at the dance and now produced the remainder of it. "This," I said proudly, "tests one hundred proof guaranteed," and, thinking that a little of the Sir Walter Raleigh spirit might raise her morale, I drained some water from the engine to make room for the moonshine and poured it down the radiator spout. "That," I predicted, "will make anything kick over!" After all, it only cost eight dollars and although, in those Prohibition and pre-antifreeze-solution days, drinkable alcohol was considered far too valuable for radiators, I still thought it was a good investment. For if the high-test moonshine helped save the situation and our friend's car, it was certainly worth eight dollars; and if not, at least one had the satisfaction of trying to be a gentleman. In either case, it could not have done more harm in the car's pipes than in our own. "Now," I beamed at Betty, "aren't you glad you gave me permission to have whisky on the ranch?"

"Yes, and I reckon that's about the best use you could find for it."

The problem of firewood was acute. We scraped together a few little branches and lighted them, but got only a second-rate fire, which kept us running for more branches all the time. Al said that he knew of a gully not far off, where there had always been lots of good pitch pine chunks. He offered to get a sample for us, and then disappeared into the night.

An hour passed and he did not show up. In the meantime I had cranked the car twice, raced the engine a little, tooted the horn, stoked up the bonfire, shouted and waved firebrands around on the edges of all the cut banks I could find, thinking that he might somehow have gotten down into an exceptionally difficult gully and lost his bearings.

"If it were anybody else, I would worry," Betty said. "But Abbit doesn't lose his bearings."

"How does he do it?" I asked.

"He's just uncanny, that's all."

"What do you suppose is the matter?"

"That's just what I'd like to know. When Abbit doesn't come back, something's wrong."

I took another firebrand and followed his tracks. They went to the edge of a bank and stopped. I leaned over the bank, straining my eyes to pick up the tracks again below, but the flickering light was not strong enough to show me any signs of Al. I shouted a few times more, cupping my hands over my mouth and turning in all directions, but there was no answer, so I went back to the fire. I didn't tell Betty where the tracks had led, but remarked casually, "I guess he'll be back any time now. He's got matches, and can always light a fire if he wants to be found."

"But I took his matches away from him!" she sniffled guiltily. "Poor Abbit, he *is* so careless with them."

"Oh, I'll bet he's got lots more, in other pockets," I said cheerily.

"One thing, though," she consoled herself, "Abbit never gets hurt. He just *never* gets hurt. He's been run over by cattle, and dragged from horses, and turned over in cars, and fallen through the ice, and blown up twice. He just *never* gets hurt."

This seemed like such an impressive safety record that I could remark with conviction, "Well, then, he must be safe enough down in that little gully."

When it came time to crank the car again, I went to the edge of the cut bank and shouted some more. This time there was a faint answer, from somewhere far down in a canyon. "Are you all right?" I called.

"Absolutely," came the faint reply.

Now that the tension was relieved, I got another firebrand and waved it from the jumping-off place, to give him our direction. Then I threw the firebrand into the dark abyss. It went down, down,

down, in flaming swirls, almost out of sight, then landed, with a shower of sparks, on some rock far below and fizzled out, like a Fourth of July rocket in reverse. I gasped at the idea of anybody's having survived such a fall.

But Al had survived it, all right, and before the next cranking time came around, he strolled casually up to the fire, grinning broadly under the Stetson, which was now mashed down over his ears. In his arms were several sturdy pieces of pitch pine, which he threw on the fire, apologizing for the delay. His clothes were torn and mussed, but he was otherwise unruffled.

"Why, Abbit, *whatever* happened to yawl?"

"Oh, nothing, dear. I just had to go down there further than I expected." He sat down quietly, rolled himself a cigarette, then turned to me and asked, "How's the car?"

"Doing fine. The moonshine seems to have gotten churned around all through its system now, and our patient has thrown off the chills."

"I kind of wish we had saved some out for ourselves, now. I could do with a little nip."

He did, indeed, look tired, and stretched out gratefully by the fire, which now blazed as if it might develop into a three-alarm affair. We let him sleep for three more crankings, then, at the first faint glow of dawn, he awoke. The fire had about died down and was not worth rebuilding, so we stamped it out and abandoned our bivouac.

The car started easily and I took the wheel to give Al more rest. After opening two gates, he went to sleep in the back and Betty, not wanting to wake him up, insisted on opening the last gate herself.

When we reached the ranch it was nearly breakfast time, and the two older children were having a field day getting breakfast together. They couldn't both leave the baby, and were drawing lots to see which one would stay home from school.

Al and I were a little late getting through our chores that day.

VII

Sheep, Bobcats and Beer

IT WAS time for me to be getting serious. Being a chore boy was all right for a while, to learn a few fundamentals of ranch life, but beyond that it did not offer any satisfactory, tangible return. I knew that Al White could not afford to pay me anything and, even if he could have afforded it, I would not have taken Tom's job away from him. This job was ideally suited to Tom, who treated it as a joke which would last only until he came into his inheritance. He had no idea of making anything out of it or of creating any sort of constructive life for himself in the West, whereas I yearned to get away from the idle, stereotyped life of the East and try my hand at some active venture. I reasoned, therefore, that I should continue with the chores only until Tom returned and that, in the meantime, I would decide what to do thereafter.

There was only one active, outdoor business to be in: livestock. Everybody seemed to have lost his all on cattle at that time, and for a short while I entertained the idea of going into sheep. This idea was first broached to me by an old Spanish-American War veteran, whom I met working on the ice harvest.

Henry Lunk,[20] lived a few miles up one of the neighboring side creeks, where he had a homestead claim and a neat little stone house, practically the only stone house in the country. He worked his homestead under deplorably inadequate conditions and, with his wife, Lena, otherwise eked out an existence by doing odd jobs. In the winter he would help harvest ice; in the summer, hay. Or, he worked as a roundup cook in the spring and fall, while Lena was a good ranch cook and much in demand, although her circle of patrons was small because of her physical handicaps: she was born both deaf and dumb.

Despite these unfortunate handicaps, Lena was the most cheerful of people. She did not mind at all, being deaf and dumb, nor did Henry, or anyone else. She was not dumb in the sense of being totally mute, for she could make sounds. But never having heard language spoken, she had no idea what sounds to make. She would read your lips and imagine from them what the sound might be like if she could hear it. Then with fantastic imagination and initiative together with a certain spirit of gay festivity, she would undertake to make sounds in answer. If you could understand these sounds, or persuade her that you did, she would do a little dance of glee,

[20] Fictitious name given to Henry Funk, a Spanish-American War veteran, who homesteaded on Canyon Creek about six miles from the 4D ranch of the Browns. Occasionally, he sought employment with the Browns.

pointing one finger up in the air, cocking her head from side to side and grinning broadly. Everybody at the ranch understood Lena's language and I soon learned it, too.

Henry also had language difficulties, but of a different sort. His affliction was incurable profanity. He was practically unable to construct a simple sentence without it and, after a few drops of booze, was completely unable to do so. It wasn't that he was ill-tempered or trying to shock anyone. He cursed simply because he could not speak without cursing; it just didn't come natural to him. Everybody understood this and nobody held it against him any more than they held Lena's affliction against her, although strangers were likely to raise their eyebrows a bit at Henry's unexpected and unnecessary broadsides of Billingsgate on all occasions, and even ranch mothers would scurry their curse-hardened children away from his withering volleys of blasphemy.

Henry and Lena were actually a most devoted couple, but this fact was obscured from view most of the time, especially to the uninitiated, by the fact that they never could speak to each other with any degree of normality. The first time I heard them speaking together in what they evidently considered normal conversation, I thought they must be going to jump at each other's throats. Lena, making groans as if mortally wounded, shifting about from one foot to the other and waving a frying pan to illustrate some point, while Henry was shouting at her and calling her "a splay-footed old bitch." I reported my fears to Al White, who just laughed and said that it was their normal way of speaking. "She can't translate those things," he explained, "and Henry gets some kind of relief by letting them off, so there's no harm done."

Henry pointed out to me that the sheep business had great possibilities, that he knew a lot about it and that his homestead would make fine range for a few bands. All he lacked was money, and he suspected that I had some. If so, it seemed that we could combine forces and make a killing in the sheep business. He invited me to spend the night at his homestead and look the situation over. So, I rode up there one afternoon, thinking that, at last, perhaps I had found a way to make my fortune.

But doubts arose as I neared the homestead and there floated down the trail to me a stream of blasphemy that seemed to pollute the crystal-clear air and make even my horse shudder. This was interrupted from time to time by such grunts and groans as would lead one to conclude that a backwoods murder was in progress, if one did not know Lena's language. To me, it meant that Henry and Lena were having a little light afternoon conversation preparatory to welcoming me into their home, and that they were preparing a surprise for me. Upon my arrival, they acted as coy and kittenish as a bride and groom bursting with the secret of their first blessed event. Lena was jigging around in a state of excitement—I thought, once or twice, none too steadily. Then I noticed that Henry, too, was a bit flustered and goggle-eyed.

The surprise turned out to be some green beer which they had just made and, I was sure, had just been sampling, in my honor. Henry produced a few bottles of this, which he kept hidden under the floor. One bottle exploded before he could open it. Then he poured me a glass of the liquid, which was white and oily with a somewhat offensive odor having nothing whatsoever to do with beer. I tasted a little, cautiously. It bit my tongue and gave me the vague feeling of wishing to throw up. I pretended to sip it with great admiration, while the alcohol seared my throat and made me wonder how I could ever finish the whole dose, to say nothing of the bottles he had in reserve. I ventured the opinion that the brew had quite a kick to it.

I persuaded him to let go the beer and show me around his place a little, so that I could learn why it would be good for sheep. We went out to the corral and he saddled an enormous bay work horse, aboard which he climbed laboriously, being somewhat afflicted by arthritis in addition to the green beer, and we started off up the creek, toward the head of his place.

There was in all, probably, a section of good range, another section of questionable range mixed with shale hills, timber and scrub growth, plus the possibility of leasing a third section adjoining. This would give a maximum of only just over 1,900 acres, or a somewhat shaky basis for a very small sheep operation. Perhaps we could have handled 300 head with no chance of expansion, which did not seem to me like a worth-while proposition.

The house itself was small, but comfortable and immaculate. It had only a bedroom, living room and kitchen, but they were neat and uncramped. A large coal stove in the living room and a coal range in the kitchen kept up a comfortable temperature. Floors were scrubbed, windows washed and hung with freshly laundered white curtains. The oil lamps did not smell, their chimneys sparkled and the wicks were trimmed. From the kitchen came a delicious aroma of baking, for Lena made her own bread. Just outside the kitchen door was a well with its aged plunger pump. This, when sufficiently primed with a half bucket of water, and upon having its handle worked furiously enough, would respond with a series of snoring sounds followed by weak belches of water. In the fading glow of twilight, the soft, warm glimmer of lamps and the sturdiness of the walls around us gave off a feeling of snug security from the elements outside, the falling thermometer and the wind sighing through the tall pine trees.

The living-room table was cleared and set for supper beside a window next to the front door and overlooking a very pretty view up the creek. On it,

Henry proudly put two bottles of the green beer, as I was afraid he would. But strong, bracing air and our ride up the creek had swept all the fumes from our heads and we were ready to resume the attack. He had an old-fashioned, fumed oak coverless portable phonograph and a few ancient records, mostly cracked, which he sorted out on the table under the lamp, finally selecting one which he recommended highly. Just then, animal noises came from the kitchen and Lena emerged, with a glass.

"No, goddam you, I say, no!" Henry screamed, grabbing the beer bottles and holding them above his head. "After supper, I tell you, but not now." He waved her back to the kitchen, explaining, "The old woman gets drunker than a fiddler's bitch, so I can't let her have any more till after supper."

An eerie whimpering came from the kitchen, indicating hurt pride, but sounding like something from Mars. He drowned it out by putting on the phonograph record he had chosen. It screeched "The Whistler and His Dog" in wavering tones, bringing back shades of my nursery days and all kinds of mixed feelings. Lena poked her head into the room again, all smiles, and let out a terrific grunt.

"She likes that one. It's got a swing to it, and that feller sure is a whistling bastard, ain't he?"

"How does she know it, if she's deaf?"

"She just feels it. She feels all kinds of things, like if I'm sick in the middle of the night. Gets right up

and knows right what to do for me. Why, I wouldn't
trade her for a dozen of these jabbering women!"

They set so much supper before me that I
couldn't eat it all. There was soup from good, rich
meat stock kept permanently on the back of the
range and periodically replenished. Then came a
generous pile of fried chicken from their own
plump, grain-fed flock, supplemented by mounds of
beans and preserved beets from the root cellar, a
great platter of nicely browned potatoes and at least
three small loaves of steaming homemade bread. As
a further caution against malnutrition, there followed large slices of pie with jam to go on it and
quantities of steaming, black coffee. All was in su-
perabundance, with several helpings of each urged
on me in almost cruel hospitality.

After supper, Henry let Lena have another bottle
of beer, partly in appreciation of the good meal she
had put on and partly as an added entertainment
for me. "Come on, boy," he said, winking, "we'll
spell her off and do the dishes while she gets in
gear." And we went into the neat little kitchen,
where two buckets of water were already simmering
on the stove, waiting to be dipped out into the
clean dishpan.

Lena got in gear rather quickly and was humming
along nicely by the time we finished our chore. I am
sure that no gourmet ever enjoyed a vintage champagne more than Lena enjoyed that beer. She had a
record on the phonograph, which she studied in-

tently, beating remarkably good time with her foot and laughing gaily at what must have been my obvious surprise that she could do so. After a while she was seized by the ballet instinct, clapped Henry's fur hat on her head and cavorted clumsily about. It was an old, homemade beaver hat made from skins he had trapped down on Tongue River and sewed together, with ear flaps. The ear flaps swung up and down as Lena whirled around, cocking her head from side to side and pointing up in the air.

"She sure loves to dance," said Henry. "Especially, when I give her some beer. I believe she'd dance all night if I kept pouring it to her. I've had her going for hours."

"Doesn't she ever wear out?"

"Not as long as there's any beer left."

"How about next morning?"

"Funny thing, it don't seem to hurt her a bit."

When the ballet was over, they produced snowy cotton sheets and warm, clean army blankets, bearing the imprint of the Quartermaster Corps, issue of 1918. With these and a couple of immaculate pillows, the living-room sofa was transformed into a very passable bed and I retired, a lamp and caddy of matches hard by, as a precaution against the rousing effects of the beer. Henry and Lena cursed and grunted in the next room—with the door left open for heat from the living-room stove. Presently all was quiet, except for the inevitable wailing and yapping of coyotes.

Some time before dawn, there was a great shaking of grates, which roused me from my torpor to a sort of semi-drowsy state in which I perceived the bulbous form of Henry in his long-handled drawers, unbanking the stove and range, loading on fresh coal and adjusting the drafts. His grotesque figure was silhouetted by an oil lamp which he carried in one hand during the operations, casting eerie shadows about the walls and ceiling. Then he slipped quietly back to bed and I dozed off again.

The next time I awoke, windows were tinted with orange and gold, lamps twinkled cheerfully in the kitchen, where Lena padded about in slippers, getting breakfast ready. Muffled curses came from Henry, on his way in from the well with two buckets of water. When they saw I was awake, they closed the kitchen door to insure my privacy.

It was not long before we renewed our attack on the commissary. Quarts of preserved fruit were opened up. There was piping-hot Scotch oatmeal and an assortment of standard breakfast foods, with milk and very heavy cream fresh from Henry's own cow. Then came stacks of pancakes with both syrup and melted butter for them; eight or ten fried eggs, sausages, hot bread, toast and corn muffins with, of course, a dependable supply of jam, honey and coffee. This was piled, in a smoking array, on the little table by the living room window. Lena gave a series of groans, indicating that she hoped it would be enough, and Henry added reassuringly, "Eat hearty, boy, there's plenty more in the kitchen." I did the best I could, which seemed a disappointing performance to them but made me ache inside and wonder how I could get back on my horse.

Henry and I were reviewing the sheep situation, from which I was seeking a graceful exit, when our discussion was cut short. Suddenly he leaned toward the window and stared out at the snowy valley, where there was just beginning to be enough light to distinguish moving objects clearly.

"What is it?" I asked, straining to follow his gaze. Something graceful was coming down the trail toward us.

"Sonofabitch of a big tom bobcat! I thought I seen his tracks around the chicken house yesterday." He eased the window open and a blast of frigid air, straight from Saskatchewan, enveloped us unmercifully. "Now, just lean back a little there, boy." He reached above him and took a .250-3000 from the wall.

I quickly vacated my seat and retreated from the area of the muzzle blast as he pumped a shell into the chamber, took an elbow rest on the breakfast table and drew a bead.

Lena jumped up and down in childish excitement. "Gobollom, gobollom!" she cheered him on.

There was a deafening crash. China rattled on the shelves, the lamp went out and a warlike smell of smokeless powder was wafted back into the room on the breeze from Saskatchewan. A little geyser of snow flicked up just beyond the bobcat. My ears rang as if I had been clubbed soundly on the side of the head.

"Just a *little* bit high," Henry remarked, adjusting the sight. He was calm for once, intent upon his feline prey.

Lena didn't hear the shot but, apparently, enjoyed the concussion. "Gobollom!" she egged him on, as he pumped in another shell.

I opened my mouth this time as he trained his aim on the bobcat, which was now on the run, an almost impossible shot. There was another ear-splitting report, followed by an equally shocking salvo of curses as the bobcat disappeared into thick underbrush.

Henry ran a cleaning rag through his rifle and replaced it on the nails. "Been losing a lot of poultry around here lately," he said. "Guess I'll have to try setting some traps."

"What do you use for bait?" I asked.

"Prairie dogs are about as good as anything."

Here was a chance to show off my newly acquired learning. I considered the matter awhile, scratching my head knowingly. "That may be, Henry. But, of course, I've always thought there's nothing like a lure."

"Yes, but that stinking stuff's hard to come by."

"Oh, I don't know. Why don't you get Charlie Gorrie up here and let him make a few settings for you?"

Henry looked disgusted. "Why, I'd rather have the coyotes and bobcats around here than that spooky bastard!"

I could see what he meant. After all, he had lots of poultry.

With the sheep and predatory animal questions thus disposed of, I went out to the corral and saddled up my pony, despite the polite pleadings of Henry and Lena to stay longer. The pony, I found, had been treated with a largesse comparing very favorably with that dished out to me. He had been given hay, grain, salt and water in abundance, and was perky almost to the point of being a problem. He threw a hump in his back as the saddle landed on his withers and blew up his belly against the tightening cinch, so that I, in my distended physical condition being not too limber, felt it the part of wisdom to walk him about cautiously before stepping on, and then to do so in the corral. He danced out nimbly when Henry opened the gate, but soon settled down to that slow, steady jog which is the traveling gait of the western horse. Thus I left the strange, but generous hospitality of the Lunks.

Henry and Lena waved me off down the creek, with gruesome sounds and woeful blasphemy. I wondered what the future could possibly hold for this aging, childless couple, with their physical and mental handicaps, their practically total lack of education and what would ordinarily be considered the darkness ahead, illumined only by the kindly light within their simple souls. "Lead, Kindly Light, amid the encircling gloom." I thought of the old hymn. And, somehow, I suddenly felt that there was really no such thing as gloom, that it was all a matter of viewpoint. As I turned in my saddle, waving back at them, I could see only the dazzling light of sun, sky, snow, and the twinkling in their eyes.

I gave up the idea of sheep and decided upon cattle ranching as an occupation. The situation of the practically defunct White Cattle Company was ideal, if not made to order, for me. Here were the remains of an important ranching enterprise going to ruin for lack of capital. The Whites were short on cash but long on practical experience, while my situation was exactly opposite. We needed each other's help.

For us to go into business together could not, I thought, prove too disastrous to me, since prices seemed unlikely to go much lower with beef selling at between six and seven cents a pound. Cows and calves, with their relatively high consumption of hay in that northern climate, were a drug on the market, particularly since hay was then scarce, due to a recent drought. But someday hay would not be so scarce. If cows and calves were not a buy then, the chances were that they never would be.

It seemed a perfect setting. The White family and I were congenial, as we had already proved. In return for my capital, I wanted a home and a business in the West. Al had provided the home so generously that I, with my means, already had felt embarrassed at living there on a non-paying basis. I had approached Al with the suggestion of working for him, saying that I wished to stay indefinitely and learn something about ranching. But his innate sense of southern hospitality would not allow him to let me work for my bed and board, and he would not have me working for nothing. Since he could not pay me anything, and I was not worth anything, anyway, this sally of mine had led us only to an impasse.

I had realized that it was an impasse when, one evening by the fireside, Al tilted the old nutria Stetson to the back of his head, rolled another cigarette, smiled his sweet, sad little smile and said calmly, but with tremendous reassurance, "Why, hell, Ned, you're plumb welcome to stay on here as long as you've a mind to." The tone in which he said this was the tone of a lord in his manor dispensing, as a matter of course, largesse to a visiting nabob. Our muddy boots and rough work clothes faded away in the flickering firelight as he said it, and suddenly we were lounging comfortably, in silks and satins, on the pillared veranda of a spacious plantation in the Old South. (It was at about this time that he had discovered a rather distant family connection between his god, General Robert E. Lee, and myself.) I spoke my appreciation with what I hoped would be suitable decorum, and silently concluded that a salaried job for me was beneath both our dignities.

The howling of a blizzard, the need for stoking the
dying furnace, and a failure of the light plant just
at that moment, brought us back from dreamland to
our proper selves.

For a while, I had catered to Al's humor, knowing that it was the only way in which I could please
him. I emulated the southern gentleman a bit, although born a "damyankee" in New York City and
not especially in sympathy with the lounging tactics
generally attributed to gentlemen of the Old South.
But I tried. I rode and hunted and made guarded
references to life in the *haut monde*. In the evenings
I sat by the fire with him and encouraged him to
expand on topics he liked. I learned of reckless
spending in the days of the bovine barons. I saw
him as wagon boss of the White cattle outfit, whose
stalwart cowpunchers rode again, but in shadowy
forms, through the firelight. I rawhided and
"repped" with him over vast distances between famous roundups of the old days. Mile after weary
mile we rode, until we had watered our strings of
ponies in every river and creek from the Belle
Fourche to the Yellowstone and I could almost feel
myself becoming exhausted. Then we would drop
back a hundred years or so, to the Old South. We
spoke of fine families, heraldry, and dueling. We
made hot toddies out of side-creek rotgut, dignified
with the good name of bourbon after we had col-
ored it with burnt sugar, and drank toasts to the
Old Dominion, Jefferson Davis, Stonewall Jackson

and (rising) to the great Lee himself, not even forgetting his favorite horse, Traveller.

All this attempt at being a good visitor, however, did not for long soothe my conscience in the matter of overstaying my welcome at the White ranch. But each day I felt less like leaving and my sense of guilt mounted until I had to do something about it. I told Al that I wanted to build a little room or cabin for my own use, on his property, so that he would eventually own it while, in the meantime, it would ease the burden on their living quarters. To this he agreed genially and then added, as an afterthought, "Perhaps I have a better idea. Why don't you file on some land of your own, and build on that?"

Up until then I had never heard of the Homestead Act,[21] but Al explained it to me. In those days there was still considerable "original public domain" land in the western states: land which had never belonged to anybody, title still being vested in the United States Government by virtue of its sovereignty, through treaty, purchase, discovery or cession. This was the remainder of the vast area (nearly one and a half billion acres) of government

[21] Passed by a Civil War Congress in 1862, the Homestead Act, superimposed on an incongruous land system, nevertheless did accomplish part of its stated purpose—specifically, luring the Easterner west to gamble his later life on a 640-acre plot. By 1914, 718,819 entries had been made for 96,495,030 acres under the Homestead Law. Paul Gates, *History of the Public Land Law Development* (Washington, 1968), pp. 393-399, 493.

land offered for settlement just after the Civil War, including all states north and west of the Ohio and Mississippi Rivers, except Texas, and, therefore, including Montana. A patent could be obtained on these lands by any individual who filed a claim and was able to "prove up" on it within three to five years.

Proving up was a comparatively simple process if one did not actually have to depend upon the land for his living. The main requirements were a "habitable dwelling" (which could be very simple), a fence and minimum improvements of something like $1.25 an acre. If you could meet these requirements and prove that you had lived on the land for at least seven months out of the year for three successive years, the land was yours (up to the area of one "section," or square mile) with the compliments and blessings of Uncle Sam.

This idea fascinated me. It was a challenge. Fundamentally, Uncle Sam was betting a claimant $1.25 per acre that the latter could not live on his land for three years. I had the New Yorker's conception of fabulous prices for land and wondered what kind of land it was that Uncle Sam offered practically as a gift, by making such a ridiculous wager. I investigated and found that, for my purposes, it was not bad land at all, although, of course, the best land (from the standpoint of earning a living) had been taken up long ago. By 1905 roughly a hundred million acres of the best "original public domain" were in private hands. Thereafter, up to my time, in the early 1920's, available areas dwindled at the rate of from three to ten million acres a year. But there was still a good slice left when I came along, although it was mostly land inaccessible to water: hill and grazing land, covered to a great extent by sagebrush, natural range, pine and cedar. The big grab was over. But the little grab seemed not at all bad to a Manhattanite accustomed to hearing land values described in thousands of dollars per front foot. I was charmed at the prospect of buying 640 wild and aromatic acres at $1.25 first hand, to have and to hold for my very own. It was like being given Central Park without the smells, just for my personal sleeping place. I didn't care about water rights, irrigation or raising crops. I didn't want to be a farmer. I just wanted a place to get out of the family's hair at the ranch, and I thought that a square mile of sagebrush would answer nicely.

Al White pored over a huge map on which he had plotted the company's holdings and surrounding country, showing me where there was a section on which I could file, right near the ranch house. In fact, one corner of it—which he himself had long planned to acquire, before the hard times—came to within a few hundred yards of the house. This was a most unusual opportunity and he suggested that I grasp it, which I did, and filed. The coup also protected Al's interests to the extent of preventing some unscrupulous person's getting wind of the situation, acquiring the land and cutting White cattle off from a part of their range where there was good water.

Al had thus elected to take a chance on me, with no questions asked, by tipping me off to the homestead claim and taking me on as a neighbor in this somewhat ticklish location. And, so, I decided to take a chance on him. I would honor his salute gun for gun, in the finest tradition of the Old South. I grasped my pen firmly and, after a little correspondence with my Wall Street mentors, was able to lay $10,000 on the line. Al and I were partners in a new cattle venture.

One side of this partnership represented the practically defunct cattle corporation of the White interests, controlled by that family with only a few shares of stock outstanding, and that of no market value. Somehow or other, they had a thousand acres of land that, through some miracle, was not mortgaged, and this they contributed to the new company, valuing it at $10 per acre, to balance my capital investment. On the other side of the partnership I stood alone, with my $10,000 and a firm determination to learn something about cattle ranching. I learned plenty.

We located a bank in western Montana with a bad loan secured by cows, calves and a doubtful hay supply. As a result, my newborn outfit was soon the proud owner of some 300 cows and calves, bought at the ridiculously low price of $37.50 per pair, with a few thrown in at $35 and a 15 per cent cut-back. This meant that we were allowed to reject up to 15 per cent as unfit to command the agreed prices and deal for them separately at a lower rate. They were Durham cows, in poor shape, but with characteristically big, rangy frames. The herd was slated for spring delivery and, at the time we made the deal in the musty little board room of a small bank, with sleet beating dismally on the windows, and after a chilly, mud-sloshing inspection of the cattle at a nearby "Tobacco Road" type of ranch, I must say that my heart fluttered at the prospects. It looked like a rank gamble to ship them from where they were, in western Montana, to the Tongue River country. But when the time came we got away with it, and they were delivered to us off the cars at a ranch within forty miles of home. During all this time Al showed not the slightest concern about the safety of these tottering beasts. He rolled about as many Durham cigarettes as we had bought cows, manipulated the old olive-drab nutria Stetson from one side of his head to the other with gestures of utter confidence and unconcern, juggled his false teeth about in the usual manner and voiced not a word of dismay.

VIII

Chinook

THE SLUSHY midwinter weather which we had en-
countered to the west, much to my amazement,
persisted for some time and slowly moved eastward.
We arrived back at the ranch in the teeth of winter
again, but after a few days this warmer weather
caught up with us and it was as if the breath of
spring had suddenly gone haywire and decided to
blow over the Tongue River country in January. To
me it seemed uncanny, and I mentioned this to Al.

"Nothing uncanny about it," he answered reassuringly. "It's just a chinook,[22] that's all. We have

[22] A Smithsonian scientist and member of the Red River
expedition of 1860, Dr. A. J. Thibode jotted in his diary,
"April 1st. Pleasant, warm weather, high winds from the
S.W. They call it the Chinook wind." H.S. Brode, ed., "Diary of Dr. Augustus J. Thibode," *Pacific Northwest Quarter-
ly* (July, 1940) XXXI, p. 347.
  Alvin T. Burrows described the peculiarities of a Chinook
wind, "In the dead of winter it blows down from the mountains and high plateaus, where ice and snow are supposed to
predominate, as a hot, dry wind upon the foothills and val-
leys below. It's effects are striking. The snow at these lower
elevations, at first blown hither and thither by the increasing
wind velocity soon becomes moist and heavy under the influence of the blasts of hot air, and in an incredibly short time
may disappear. The temperature rises with astonishing ra-
pidity and the whole aspect of nature is transformed . . . A
rise of 20° to 40° in ten or fifteen minutes frequently occurs,

these every winter. A warm wind from the Japan Current that sort of gets deflected somehow and crosses the Rockies into this part of the country. It's usually good for from three days to a week."

The offhand manner in which he tossed me this information gave me the impression that the whole subject was terribly old hat, and I refrained from comment. I did marvel secretly, however, at the spectacle of snow melting in a matter of hours and an overwhelming influx of balmy air which suggested that the prairie lilies were about to pop up any minute, smack in the middle of January. I noted it mentally as an oddity to be investigated, and held my silence while Al expounded.

"You know," he said, "when we start running these new cattle we're going to need a lot more horses. The cavvy's getting pretty small now. Just the kids' ponies, a couple of wrangling horses, the

---

although the change is not always so great . . . The Chinook aids the railroads in keeping the tracks clear of snow, enables the stockmen to bring their cattle safely through the winter, and stores up water for future use, making irrigation in the summer possible. It is an ever-welcomed guest whose coming is indicative of good, and whose absence would be of momentous evil."

Alvin T. Burrows, "The Chinook Winds," *Yearbook* of the United States Department of Agriculture, 1901 (Washington, 1902), pp. 555–556.

Charles Russell's famous painting on a postcard, "Waiting for a Chinook" (or "The last of the 5,000") depicting one bewildered, emaciated steer standing in encrusted snow, with leering wolves circling it did more to dramatize the effect of a hard winter than any prose.

teams and a few others. Nothing much that we can use on the roundup."

"Yes, I know," said I. Of course, I knew nothing about it, except in the vaguest way.

"I've been thinking," he continued. "The White Cattle Company still has fifty-three head of mares somewhere over on Beaver Creek."

"Beaver Creek . . . ?"

"Yes. That's over on the Crow Reservation, about forty-five miles from here, maybe a little less."

I couldn't help smiling inwardly at this. Here was an asset which, like the miraculously unmortgaged thousand acres, had slipped deftly through the dragnet of those coldhearted city bankers who had foreclosed the White outfit. Fifty-three mares would be an item unlikely to be overlooked by a banker turning down the screws to squeeze the last possible dollar from his fading investment. Yet the mares were still around. "How in hell," I asked, "did they get over there?"

"Oh, it was four or five years ago, or more," he said vaguely, "on a breeding deal. Anyway, we'd better be getting them home with their foals before long. Should be some pretty good horses there, about ready to break . . . yearlings and twos."

So, there it was, the same tactics for self-preservation that many an old Wall Street wolf had used, except in sagebrush version. When the pressure got too unreasonable, these mares had just taken a vacation across country, on a breeding deal. The vanished assets were now about to return, and with good dividends.

"Let's go after them while this chinook holds out," he suggested. "No telling, we might not get another break in the weather like this before our new cattle are delivered."

"How do we know how long it's going to hold out?"

"Three days to a week. Always does," he reassured me. "Plenty of time to ride over there and back."

"Who's got them?" I asked.

"Fellow by the name of Dan Hawkes."

I sensed that the weather was not Al's only motive, as Dan was known far and wide for, shall we say, fast changes in the ownership of livestock through his wizardry with rope and running iron: that little metal ring which could be carried so inconspicuously, heated so easily and used so conveniently, for making (or "adjusting") any brand, whether calling for straight or curved lines, by the simple method of cutting two green branches and crossing them through it, for handles. It was an old art of the "lone prairie," practiced (one could not help feeling, from the pulse of the country) by the founders of many famous and respectable outfits and, therefore, rating a certain amount of etiquette when being discussed. There was no doubt about it, Dan Hawkes loved his art and practiced it—in both mediums, cattle and horses—with such gusto that, at least on one occasion to my knowledge, it had earned him an invitation to tarry awhile as a guest of the state in a fine, strong stone building where he was well protected.

Notwithstanding this failing, Dan was a very lovable and popular fellow. His sunny disposition and ready wit made him a great favorite with children. He was sympathetic, kindly and generous. He had a legendary, Robin Hood type of reputation, with an aversion toward preying on the poor, the struggling, the ill, or anyone needing a helping hand. It was hinted that such unfortunates sometimes found an extra calf branded for them, or a fine quarter of beef hanging up in the barn, around Christmastime, garnered, presumably, from more affluent sources where they would never be missed. Except by accident, he was supposed never to include the ponies which children rode to school and, when an accident occurred, had been known brazenly to return such ponies, with some joking explanation to the children.

"Well, if Dan's handling your mares, perhaps it's too late even now," I said.

"Oh, no . . . I don't think he'd operate on us. We've been broke too long."

I agreed that we should make the trip to Beaver Creek, not so much from anxiety over the mares as from youthful excitement over the prospect of meeting Dan Hawkes. It was almost like being introduced to Jesse James. In this prospect, however, I was disappointed at that time, although I did meet him later and was completely captivated. Moreover, I subsequently met several others strongly suspected of practicing this occult art of the range and, to my horror, found that I was profoundly impressed by their unusual charm and sterling qualities in all other respects. These fellows were not at all the coldhearted, shifty-eyed desperados which movies would seek to foist upon us. Nor were they the sleazy, present-day type of cattle thief who operates from the lonely stretches of highway bordering cattle ranges, with disguised trailer trucks fitted up as butcher shops inside, and all modern conveniences, adding the stench of gasoline to his already dismal profession. These were hard-riding, long-suffering, jolly good fellows who lived with animals and loved them. Often, they were legitimate cattlemen themselves, or top hands working for big outfits, not at all seeking to make their living as rustlers but only occasionally succumbing to some weak streak of character which compelled them to look longingly at an unbranded calf. Offenders of this sort, when caught, purged and returned to society, were usually welcomed back. The tendency was to forget old scores and help them start anew on the right track.

When we left for Beaver Creek, Al and I (at his suggestion, based on long experience with chinooks) did not overburden ourselves with warm clothes. I remember, particularly, deciding against

two valuable items—a sheepskin coat and overshoes—as too bulky to tie on my saddle and too
ridiculous to wear in that balmy spell. We each had
light leather jackets and cotton work gloves, ordinary, broad-brimmed Stetson hats (Al's, of course,
being his old olive nutria), with no protection for
face or ears and, fortunately, chaps. Al wore his
black angoras, and mine were a pair of very heavy
bat-wing chaps which had recently been made to
order for me by a little old-fashioned saddler in
Sheridan. We rode good, quiet, solid horses, but
took no extras with us, as Al felt sure that there
were some good saddle horses among the mares,
which we could ride back.

We had a pleasant, uneventful ride, leaving the
ranch before dawn—against admonitions by Betty
White for not taking warmer clothes—and reaching
the Hawkes ranch around six o'clock, or in time for
supper, which was, also, long after dark. Even in the
dark hours, the thermometer must have stood at
around 50 degrees, and during the sunlight hours
we were so uncomfortably warm in our light leather
jackets that we tied them behind our cantles and
rode in shirtsleeves. Winter was in the short hours
of daylight, all right, but not in the air, which was a
fresh, warm breeze that had melted off practically
all snow. At noon we lounged on a creekbank and
lazily munched some sandwiches which Betty had
made up, almost drowsy with spring fever. We had
to ride across the Cheyenne Reservation (a tract of

nearly 445,000 acres[23]) and part of the Crow Reservation,[24] adjoining it, during all of which distance Al astounded me by his knowledge of the country and how to get around it, knowing exactly where gates were located in the few fences then existing, without any roads, signs or buildings to guide him. We went up and down creeks which all looked very much alike to me, just miles and miles of rolling range grass, gulches and gullies, up this coulee, down that draw and along some divide. But for every place where I questioned him, he had a name and, usually, a few words of interesting comment.

When we arrived—to my great disappointment— we were told that Dan was off somewhere on a business trip, but that he was expected back next day. There were some cowpunchers just finishing supper in the mess house, so they took us in and fed us a good, hearty meal. The ranch was somewhat on the skimpy side as to accommodations, and there wasn't any spare room in the main house, so we slept in the bunkhouse with the boys. There was a sort of annex to it, as I remember, an old part which was used for storing odds and ends of ranch equipment, and in which the chinking between the logs was missing, so that wind blew through rather perceptibly. In there we bedded down, early, being tired

---

[23]For the boundaries of the Cheyenne Reservation please see the map.

[24]The area of the Crow Reservation is indicated on the map.

from our ride, and as we did so, I noticed that the erstwhile warm wind had chilled off considerably. The cowboys sat around, smoking and kidding each other for a while, then noticed the cold, too. They were rattling and stoking up the old potbellied stove when I dropped off to sleep. During the night, Al and I were awakened by snow on our faces and wind whistling through the logs. "Looks as if our chinook has folded up on us, Al," I said. "Aw, hell," he answered, "it's probably just shifted around to the other side of the divide for a while. It'll shift back in the morning," and he burrowed deeper down under the bedclothes. I stuffed some newspaper into the crack that was giving us the facial spray, after briefly viewing the situation by matchlight, threw my chaps over the lower part of our bed and went back to sleep.

By morning, we found that the chinook had certainly shifted somewhere else, all right—where, we didn't find out, but it was never seen again. In its place was a raging blizzard, and the thermometer outside the bunkhouse door stood at 20 below zero. "I don't understand it," said Al, scratching his head, then putting on his hat and rolling a cigarette. "I never saw anything like this before."

"Must be one of them new regulations from Washington," a cowboy shouted, derisively, pouring more coal on the fire. "This whole goddam country's changing, I'll tell you."

"Specially, this Reservation country," came a

higher, thinner voice answering him. It was from a last-generation cowboy with pale-blue, watery eyes, tired-looking from forty or so strenuous years on the range, but still lean and wiry. He had a magnificent white, tobacco-stained walrus mustache which showed to great advantage against his red flannels, as he stroked it thoughtfully and announced, "You little pistols just don't know how much times have changed. Not the half of it!"

I had heard them call him Harry the night before and noted that he was, apparently, an old-timer, some friend of Hawkes' who was bunking in there for the winter months, more or less silent and unobtrusive and out of his era. I hadn't paid much attention to him. But, now, he was a commanding figure in his long-handled drawers, blazing red. I had always heard red flannels joked about, but he was the first person I ever saw who actually wore them, and they now seemed to have a certain flare that went with his nature, besides being a striking backdrop for the mustache.

"Giving these goddam copperbellies citizenship!" he continued, disgusted. He seemed unable to express his disgust verbally against the new government policy, so he just opened the stove door for an instant, shot a stream of tobacco juice through it and slammed it, with terrific stage effect. "Why, when I was a kid, less'n fifty year ago, they was runnin' around here plumb wild, ahootin' and ahollerin,' naked as the day they was born and with their backsides painted every color in the rainbow, shootin' up Custer's outfit, right over the hill, here." He jerked his thumb in the general direction of the Little Big Horn River. "Citizenship . . . hell! There'll be no holdin' them in their places now, with their fancy new idees. Look what's happened already. When I was a young pistol like you fellers—and that was just a little while back—you could have any young squaw for two bits. Now it costs two dollars and a half and next, you'll have to get a permit from the U.S. Government!" That, apparently, was the last straw, and he was waving one boot over his head in indignation at the thought of such a development.

"Take it easy, Harry!" someone shouted at him. "Them young squaws won't be upsettin' you much longer. Who the hell do you think you are, anyway—Rudolph Valentino?"

We quickly braved the short distance to the mess house in the swirling snow, Al again expounding that this freak of nature could not last long. Actually, after breakfast, it did clear up and the sun came out for a while. We got talking about the mares and foals with Hawkes' foreman, Hank, who had just left his boss in Hardin, the county seat, and ridden in during the night. Hank told us that only a few of the mares were near the ranch, the rest on some distant lease, where it would take a couple of days to gather them. He said that he expected Dan back in the next few days and that, if we wanted to hang around, we were "sure welcome." In the meantime, he would send the boys out to wrangle the mares nearby, and also some others he wanted to run in. We settled down to poker, gossip, smoking and discussing the weather.

At about two in the afternoon, the boys came back, red-nosed and hungry, with a great clanking of spurs and rustling of chaps as they all headed for the stove, where some food had been kept warm for them. They had been able to pick up only eighteen of the mares out of about twenty-five they had expected to find, before having to start home while the daylight and their weary horses lasted. These were being held in a small pasture back of the barn overnight and would be run into the corrals next morning, for our inspection.

Al and I dragged our bed nearer to the stove that night. The following day there was still no sign of our missing chinook, but Al still felt sure that it would return. A fresh blizzard was apparently shaping up, and the thermometer then stood at exactly 40 below zero. However, it cleared off again during the morning, the sun came out and it warmed up to 20 below. This, of course, though very cold, was, in that dry climate, not unbearable. And so we all saddled up during the heat of the day and ran in the horses, including, besides our mares and colts, the few head of Hawkes' stock, which latter we cut out and put in a separate corral.

Al decided that, among his own mares, there

wasn't anything especially good for us to ride home. And, since none of them had been ridden for so long, anyway, the question of how they would behave was not worth taking a chance on, under the circumstances. He thought it wiser to make a second trip in better weather, when we were sure that Dan would be back home, consummate the deal by dividing the foals, and get all the mares at once. Getting bucked off on the way back across the Reservation, with your horse and saddle lost in a blizzard, was a possibility to be avoided at all costs. Therefore, it seemed that the best thing to do was to borrow a couple of gentle horses to ride home, leading or driving our own, and return them on our next trip.

We discussed this plan with Hank, the foreman, who told us to take our pick of anything on the ranch. "There's some mighty good little cowponies in this other corral, that we just cut out," he explained, "and we won't miss any of them. Matter of fact, I know the boss would be glad to sell some real reasonable. We got more than we can use."

At that time I owned only one horse and had long intended to buy one or two more. Dan Hawkes[25] was known for his good horses, and I thought this might be a chance, so I asked Hank,

[25] Fictitious name given to Oll McKinley, famous for his expertise with a long rope. Despite his shortcomings and rumors of such, Oll was well liked by all. The author never knew Oll personally, but rode to his ranch on that famed day.

"Got anything I can ride? Something good and gentle, more like a dependable dude horse."

"Dude outfits have bought up about all the real dude horses we've got, but all these horses is gentle enough for you to ride. Two blacks in there, especially. I'll show you, son." He picked up a throw-rope, stepped into the corral and let fly a quick, sure California loop[26] around the neck of a big black gelding, which he led prancing out the gate and turned over to me. "Throw your saddle on him and get acquainted."

He was a beautiful horse, of some breeding, considerably taller than a cowpony, with good conformation, and showing a mouth of about five years. He was black as Erebus, except for a little fleck of white on the pastern of one forefoot, full of life, but apparently gentle and used to being handled. I liked everything about him, including a trick he had of throwing his head away back to avoid the bridle, about as high as I could reach on tiptoe, at which Hank smiled and remarked, "That's the only fault he has, boy. He's hard to bridle, for anybody not as tall as you. Dan's wife been riding him about two years, now, and he's just too big all over, for her. Dan wants to sell him, and if he ain't worth seventy-five dollars, I'm a sonofabitch."

"I wouldn't want anybody to think that, Hank."

"Price all right?"

[26] A wide, oval-shaped loop thrown with an expertise based on years of use and practice.

"Sure. What's his name?"

"Sunday."

I saddled Sunday without any trouble, and stepped up on him. After a few turns about the corral, it was easy to see that Sunday was everything Hank claimed for him. So, I unsaddled him and called it a deal, asking, "How about a bill of sale?"

"Sure enough," said Hank. "We'll fix you up one. He's got a V quarter-circle on the left jaw, I think. We'll include that, too."

I had never seen a jaw brand before, but looked on Sunday's jaw, and there it was.

"How about another, son? Make you a good price."

"That depends."

He took his rope, and went into the corral again and came out with a second black, much smaller and chunkier, and very nervous, with long, luxuriant mane and tail, an even better looking horse than Sunday. This one was really rather small, but powerfully built. He snorted like a steam engine in the crystal air, great puffs of vapor coming from his nostrils in fitful blasts. I noted that Hank did not offer to let me saddle this pony, and had some trouble doing it, himself. "Playful little cuss," he grinned, "full of beans. Gentle as a lamb though. Dan's young daughter rides him." I guess he must have thought I wondered about this, for he added quickly, "I'll just step up on him and show you how gentle he is." He took up short on the near rein, pulling the horse's head well around toward him, grabbed a good handful of mane with his left hand, the saddle horn with his right and swung lightly— despite his two hundred pounds or so—into the saddle. My stirrups were a little smaller than standard and Hank, with his big feet encased in overshoes (although they were the boot variety, and properly shaped), missed the right stirrup as he settled in the saddle, and began fishing for it with his toe. At that point, the pony broke into a dead run and started bucking. Hank, taken by surprise and with only one stirrup (which is worse than none), was caught off balance and thrown. He landed with a sickening thud on the frozen ground and, had there not been a slight protecting cover of snow, could have been badly hurt. He came limping back, saying that he had sprained his shoulder. Actually, he had cracked a collarbone and two ribs, as he learned on his next trip to town.

After sitting down for a moment, he said he felt all right again and, when one of the boys had re- trieved Tar Baby—for that was the pony's name— and led him back, Hank got on him again, galloped him about the corrals, swinging him this way and that with no effort, wheeling him on his hind feet and generally trying to prove how "well broke" the horse was.

I was greatly impressed by the flashiness of this young horse, yearned to own him and was inclined to believe Hank's reassurances that there was nothing wrong with him "only, he ain't been rode enough, lately."

Hank loped Tar Baby around to where we were standing, set him back on his haunches smartly and, with a grin of satisfaction, stepped off. He dropped the reins on the ground, slapped Tar Baby on the belly and, when the horse never moved out of his tracks, grinned broadly at me. "See what I mean? . . . Now, step right up on him, son. He ain't agoin' to buck with you. If he does, I'll eat my hat. Just watch him a little when you get on."

I had long known the western trick of leading a horse a few paces with your back to him, then turning quietly and mounting without any fuss, so I took the reins and started walking (toward what I thought looked like the softest snowbank in the corral). He led very quietly, and I knew then that I was not going to have any trouble with him, which I didn't. But as a precaution, I sat well back on him and held his head up.

"He ain't agoin' to buck, I tell you," Hank shouted again, from the sidelines, whence I could feel curious eyes viewing the performance with sympathetic interest. "Give him his head and let him go!"

I did, and off we went, through all the same maneuvers, at a good clip. Only once did Tar Baby seem to gather himself together for a little trouble, and a couple of sharp licks on the flanks with the loose end of the reins got him over the idea. For a fleeting moment, I felt like the kid in the cartoon

"Once in a Lifetime."

The asking price was $75. "Of course, he's a younger horse than Sunday," Hank explained, "and he's going to be more of an all-round cowpony in the end. But he ain't broke to rope off of yet, so I figure ten dollars less."

"Chances are, Hank, I'll still have to pay someone to work with him a little bit more, before I can be sure of him. You know, I don't pretend to be a cowboy, just an eastern dude."

"That's all right, you done fine with him, just the same. You won't need nobody to top him off for you. Not if you ride him every day, you won't."

"But I can't ride him every day, and you know how it is over on Al's outfit. We don't have too many boys around. Fifty dollars."

Hank rubbed his aching shoulder and smiled. "All right, then, fifty-five. And if you can't get along with him, bring him back on your next trip. He won't cost you a cent."

We settled on that basis and went into the house to fix up the papers. Hank had the other horses turned out, keeping in only the four which Al and I were taking back with us: our own two and the new ones. "Put 'em in the barn for tonight, boys, and give 'em some hay and grain." For we had decided to start back in the morning, unless Hawkes showed up by nightfall. He didn't.

During that night the logs of the old bunkhouse popped and cracked from time to time, like so many pistol shots. "What the hell's all the racket?" I asked, being waked up by one of them, and old Harry answered drowsily, through his handlebars, "Gittin' colder, boy. When you hear that, you know the mercury's sure huntin' its hole."

In the morning, the first boy to light the lamp and get dressed took it over to the window, where it gleamed on the thermometer outside.

"What's she say, Shorty?" someone asked.

"Forty-five below and holding steady."

"Must be getting warmer," said Al. "I think we've seen the worst of it."

"What you mean is, it's just gettin' colder slower," one of the cowpunchers answered wryly.

"That's a good sign, anyway," Al defended his point. "It's got to get colder slower before it can get warmer."

"Say, Shorty," another voice asked, from beneath a mound of sheepskin coats and saddle blankets piled on a bed in the far corner, "how far down does that thermometer go?"

"Forty-five. That's the end of the line."

"Hell, there you are. Can't tell nothing by that," said the first cowboy. "That don't prove whether it's gettin' colder or warmer."

Our dash across to the mess house convinced us that it was considerably colder than the day before—the still kind of cold, without a breath of air or a cloud in the sky, and the stars all seeming oversize. The snow squeaked instead of crunching and the air made your nostrils tingle with frost as you sucked it in. I wondered whether Al still intended to ride back that day. In view of this possibility, I crammed down my gullet as much breakfast as I could manage. It all tasted good and, after I had my usual fill, I forced in a few extra wads, almost to the point of pain, against whatever trials might lie ahead. And luckily enough, for breakfast was hardly over before we groped our way to the corrals and saddled up. Al had decided to go home and return later for our fifty-three mares. We picked them up the following summer.

The boys had decked out each of us with an extra pair of long-handled drawers and an extra woolen shirt. Now we put newspaper between our shirts and in our boots, as added insulation. They also gave us leather mittens to put on over our cotton work gloves, and bandannas, which we tied over our faces, like masked bandits, and around our necks, to keep the snow out.

I saddled up Sunday and hoped that Al would choose one of the horses we had ridden over, so that we might at least have no equitation problems at the start, after which the danger would become progressively less as the horses played out. But no. He had to hang his loop on Tar Baby.

Now Al was short and heavy-set, somewhat past his prime, encumbered by angora chaps, extremely full of breakfast and not, in any state, particularly nimble to begin with. I dreaded the consequences if

Tar Baby should blow up out on the uncharted Indian Reservation, shed Al and disappear, saddle and all, into the swirling storm—or, worse yet, drag him. Apparently, I was not alone in my thoughts, for Hank, the foreman, noticing how Tar Baby fought against being saddled, sent one of his boys out to help Al by topping off the little black. The boy was a good bronc twister and soon had all the kinks out of Tar Baby, which he then turned back to Al, in considerably meeker mood. Al scrambled up on the horse with his usual unconcern for danger and the corral gates were thrown open for us. With a few words of good cheer and ribald remarks, the men waved us off on our way back across the Reservation.

For sheer physical pain and discomfort over a protracted period, I have never, before or since, known anything to equal that ride and I cannot conceive of anything much worse, short of actually freezing to death. Our ride lasted all day, with two breaks which, almost certainly, saved us from perishing. More than once, I thought over Betty White's words, "Abbit gets into the *worst* fixes, but he always gets out of them." Besides the two lucky breaks, we had the great advantage of full stomachs. This went a long way toward saving us from the ghastly fate of others—including one rather recent tragedy—who had frozen to death trying to cross the Reservation in winter.

Riding along doggedly behind Al, I could not

help having a few vague misgivings when, after a reasonable time, no sun appeared and the skies became increasingly leaden. Just about then Al announced cheerfully that it was "fixing" to snow and I wondered about finding our direction. I had marveled at his piloting on the way over, but that was in clear, balmy weather. How good would he be if a blizzard closed in on us?

In educating myself on this point, I had not long to wait, for within an hour the snow was so thick that I could barely make out his horse ahead of me, and closed up the distance for fear of losing him. I watched Tar Baby anxiously for signs of misbehavior, but Al kept him on a steady, brisk trot which seemed to take all the playfulness out of him. After a while I drew up alongside Al and asked what he thought of turning back. But he just smiled his quiet, knowing little smile and said that, since the snow was not coming directly out of the north, it would blow around and clear sooner or later—almost certainly before we got to the Rosebud, and that, from there on, the worst would be over.

I dropped back into line only partially reassured, because I could not see how it was possible to tell where north was, and somehow saddened by a sneaking suspicion that my suggestion was perhaps not a very brave one. Nevertheless, I could not see the point of dying out there when it would not prove anything, and in such an uncomfortable manner. I thought of the man in the buggy, whose horse had pulled him into an Indian camp a frozen corpse; of the poor devil whose body was found with a broken leg after his horse had fallen with him; of the four-year-old steer that was found frozen solid in his tracks. Occasionally, I would ride again beside Al, just for the feeling of reassurance it gave me.

Our first break was at a little cabin serving as line camp for some outfit with leases on the Reservation. In it were two partially frozen cowpunchers, struggling with numb hands to build themselves a fire in the range, their only heating unit. One of them tried to make the best of the situation by remarking, "The worst thing in the world for us right now would be a lot of heat. If you think freezing up's hell, wait till you try thawing out too fast."

The stove finally got going (without any danger of our thawing out too fast) and in due time we all had coffee. Several cups of it and some bread, with plenty of sugar and jam to give us energy. As our gloves toasted on the stove-rail, we fell to talking about the cold snap, speculating as to how cold it really was. One of our friends told us, "Feller over on Owl Creek, where they got a telephone, said he talked to Hardin this morning and the Weather Bureau said fifty-five below."

"What's our own thermometer say?" the other fellow asked.

"Can't tell," said the first one, strolling over to the window and scraping the frost off a pane. "Ours

only registers down to thirty below. This here must
be a tropical model."

Our friends had no extra clothing to give us, but
they did the best they could by parting with their
dish towels (which were the usual sugar and flour
sacks, cut open) and some gunny sacks. The dish
towels we tied over our heads, hats and ears, knot-
ting them under the chin, while the gunny sacks
were affixed to our stirrups with binder twine in
such a way that they afforded our toes some modi-
cum of protection.

As we left the line camp, the sun started to come
out. Thus cheered, with our gloves dry and warm
and more food in our stomachs, together with the
hot coffee, hope sprang up anew within us as we
faced our ordeal again. Everything looked perfect.
Al even had a nice, small round corral as a safe
place in which to mount Tar Baby, an added bless-
ing. It must have been about ten or eleven in the
morning when we waved good-bye to the boys and
headed, I knew not where.

A sharp wind blew the snow clouds away, the
bright spot in the sky got brighter and, before long,
the sun came blazing forth in icy glory. The snowfall had been about a foot, loose and powdery, not
enough to hinder us, except by its incredibly dazzling brightness. I yearned for a pair of dark glasses
as we plodded on and on at a monotonous, slow
trot, my eyes running and smarting, with pink spots
dancing before them. After a while, I suddenly

realized that I couldn't see a thing, and called wildly, "Al, where are you?"

"Right here, why?" came the answer from ahead.

I could hear his voice plainly enough, and the scuffling trot of his horse through the snow. But before my eyes there was only a sort of brown fog, and I told him this.

"You're just snowblind," he reassured me. But it was not much of a reassurance when he added, "I'm seeing a lot of spots myself."

"What do you do about it?"

"Oh, nothing much. It comes and goes, but it will go for good along toward dusk, which is pretty early this time of year."

Again, the consolation was only slight. Dusk seemed like a long time off and I wondered what would happen if, in the meantime, we both went blind.

"I'll tell you what," Al said, as if reading my thoughts, "there's a little bit of timber on top of this divide. Been several grass fires around here last summer, so there's bound to be charred wood somewhere. That'll fix us up."

I wondered how, and soon found out as he dismounted on the divide and told me to get off my horse, too. In the timber we were at least momentarily away from the unbearable glare, and my sight returned a little. I saw Al bending over a burned stump, picking around it until he dislodged a chunk of charcoal. He rubbed the charcoal in great semicircles under each of my eyes. Afterwards he gave me the charcoal and I did the same for him. That bit of make-up put the final touch to our outlandish appearance. Our faces, frozen, drooling, with icicles hanging from our noses and these great, black circles under our eyes, peered out grotesquely from under our hats, bent into weird shapes by being tied down by the dish towels.

But, despite the added horror of the charcoal, its effect on the eyes was miraculous. Immediately, my sight returned and, except for the running and smarting of my eyes in the wind, I had no further trouble seeing.

The boon of restored vision was a wonderful tonic. It filled me with new hope, which was just as well, for it was not long before I really needed all the vision and hope I could get, as we crossed the Rosebud.

How it ever happened that there was anything not frozen solid in that country at that time, I shall never know. Whether it was an air hole under the ice, or the result of spring water seeping to the surface, or one of the mysterious subterranean phenomena causing heated bubblings in the West, I cannot imagine. No clairvoyant, however clever, could have divined the presence of a bog at that time and place. But bog there certainly was; and into it Al certainly went.

First, there was an ominous, hollow sound under Tar Baby's feet and then, suddenly, a crash of thin ice. The next thing I knew, Tar Baby was thrashing about, up to his belly in cold ooze. The weight of Al on his back was making him sink slowly. Al tried to urge him back up onto the ice, but it was too thin and only broke under his hooves. Pulling one of his feet out only served to sink the others in deeper and, no matter which way he went, the situation seemed to get worse. Instinct urged me to ride up and grab hold of Al, but he waved me back, saying, "No use our both getting stuck here."

I was dumfounded at the suddenness with which this had happened, the total lack of warning, the improbability of the whole situation, and the extent of the bog, which did not show anywhere on the surface, so that it was impossible to tell from which direction Al could be approached with any degree of safety. I looked the situation over with horror, feeling that Al White was the only man in the world who could have located such a thing at such a time, and gotten stuck in it so completely and so suddenly. But I also remembered his wife's observations as to his Houdini-like ability for getting out of tight places, and I wondered whether she would be correct in this instance also. As I wondered, I doubted, for, inch by inch, man and beast were sinking. I made a hurried calculation that, in ten minutes, they would be out of sight; and that, if I went in there after them, in another ten minutes I would be out of sight, too. There would be no trace left of us, not even our Stetsons resting on the surface, unless we untied the dish towels at the last moment. We would simply disappear, complete with horses and equipment. Our old horses, from the ranch, would eventually return there, or hang up against a fence somewhere and be taken back by anyone curious enough to look up the brands on them. They would be without saddle or bridle. Their tracks back to the bog would have long since been covered up by the snow that had drifted, by then, over the refrozen scene of our demise.

What an awful end for poor Al, after his long string of misfortunes, I thought. And what an ignoble climax to the experiment which I tried to champion, back east, against discouragement on all sides. What would the staid and kindly trustees say when it appeared that my only accomplishments toward engaging in the cattle business were to put $10,000 on the barrel head and then disappear into a bog? I looked at Al again, and there he was, sinking majestically, like a proud captain on his ship, completely unruffled.

"Tell you what, Ned," he remarked calmly. "You've got a good rope horse there. I believe he can pull us out. See if you can throw me a loop."

"I'll try, but, you know, I'm not very good with a rope." Nevertheless, I unbuckled the coil of rope from my saddle. It had been coiled so long that it was like a circular block of ice. To unbend it was like trying to unbend a poker which had been coiled up red hot and then allowed to cool. To get a loop into it and make any kind of throw—even if you were a good roper—was practically out of the question. Furthermore, I could not get near enough with my horse to land a loop within Al's reach, as the rope would not fly out when thrown. It behaved more like a coil bedspring.

"Get off your horse and try," Al advised quietly.

I dismounted, but was not at all sure whether Sunday was broken to stand. There was no place to tie him, and I wasn't taking any chances on seeing him disappear into the distance, after the other two horses. So, I held the reins with one hand and wrestled with the frozen rope that way, gradually getting it more or less unwound into a long, stiff, wavy design. I put the loop end around Sunday's neck so as not to lose him, and, sliding cautiously over the snow on my stomach, inched toward Al, pushing the stiff rope ahead of me. The other end would just reach him. He had a tussle making it fast to his saddle horn, while I took the loop end off Sunday and remounted him. During all this time Al was sinking slowly into the bog, utterly unconcerned.

"Now," he instructed me, "take a couple of dallies around your saddle horn. Don't tie fast. And keep your fingers out of the way. Let's go!" He kicked furiously at the horse, frozen icicles of mud and angora flapping wildly on his chaps. I urged Sunday on for all I was worth.

The big black bowed his neck and strained every muscle. The little horse fought and floundered. Al hooted, hollered and gave the Rebel Yell of the Confederacy. I shifted my weight in the saddle to bear against the strain of the rope, and prayed silently. There were sucking sounds from the rear and we were making good progress in staggering lunges, "by sheer strength and awkwardness," so to speak, when my rope snapped. But Tar Baby already had his forefeet on solid gound. Al slid off and got around ahead of him, pulling on the reins to help him out. With a final, terrific lurch, the horse clambered to safety. We found a better place to cross, watered our horses and rode on.

Our second break came toward midafternoon. Al knew an old Cheyenne who lived with his children and grandchildren in a little hut somewhere along the way, and we were forced to call on them for help. There was a rude shed, into which we put all four of our horses, then went and knocked on the door of the hut. An old squaw opened it cautiously and, after taking one look at us, quickly shut it again. I could not blame her for perhaps thinking we were desperate characters. But she soon returned to the window together with several Indian faces, to give us the once-over. Al pulled the bandanna down off his face and gave them his quiet little smile. They recognized him, as some of this Walks Nice family had worked for the White Cattle Company, and they let us in.

Old Walks Nice was getting pretty feeble. He sat on a blanket near the stove: cross-legged, silent, observing and, obviously, the patriarch. He was an old-generation Indian and couldn't speak any English, but somehow, by gesture and grunt, he made you feel at home. He seemed to have dozens of children and grandchildren, slinking, slithering and scampering about silently on the dirt floor of the cabin. Apparently, we had interrupted them in an afternoon snack, as there was a big bowl of steaming something on the ground. Now they all resumed their places around it, making room for us and motioning us to sit down, too. I glanced sideways at Al for a cue to the etiquette of the occasion, as the prospects were not inviting. The steaming something gave off a sickening odor and so did all the Walks Nice family. But, after all, we were their guests, self-invited and very glad to be there, too. So courtesy was certainly in order.

Al said quickly, under his breath, "We've got to do it, or the old man's feelings will be hurt. Refusing food means an enemy."

I took a look at Grandpa Walks Nice. He wasn't missing a thing. Then there was a tug at my chaps and I looked down to see a place made for me beside a huge squaw. A large, rusty spoon was thrust into my numb hands. With some misgivings, I took my place beside the squaw, who was wrapped in what appeared to be a horse blanket. From this, a papoose stared at me wonderingly with its little beady, crossed eyes.

Conversation lagged, as the Indians spoke only a

few words of broken English, heavily interlarded
with Cheyenne and sign language.

I dipped my rusty spoon into the bowl cautiously, brought a modest sample of the potion toward
my mouth and looked over the top of it at Al. He
was already sipping his, so I followed suit. Actually,
it did not taste so bad, although the smell was most
discouraging. The pangs of hunger, I suppose,
somewhat tempered its taste. I looked around our
solemn circle of hosts, all sitting cross-legged on
the dirt floor, silent except for gurgling sounds as
they ate with us from the same bowl. I tried to smile
my appreciation and said, looking over at Grandpa
Walks Nice, "Skookum!" This, I had read somewhere, meant "Excellent!"—at least, in the language
of some eastern tribe.

Grandpa Walks Nice gave no sign of comprehen-
sion, but made a grunt as if someone had hit him in
the belly with a No. 2 iron. I thought that, perhaps,
I had not used the proper subjunctive.

Al turned politely toward the old brave and said,
"Haesta pow-wah!" thus, with Chesterfieldian man-
ners, both confirming my "thank you" to him and
conveying the proper word to me.

Walks Nice bowed his wrinkled head gravely,
thus assuring me that protocol had been complied
with.

I could not help wondering what this forbidding-
looking, steaming semiliquid was, and asked Al.

"Damned if I know."

Suddenly, Grandpa Walks Nice was standing over us, saying a few words in Cheyenne and making motions.

One of the youngsters with a smattering of English translated. "He say you take best food, special for him. Stir deep, puppy in bottom!"

Our dish turned out to be dog-meat stew, and the old Indian was offering us his pièce de résistance, an unborn puppy placed at the bottom. It was touching, but revolting. We made signs and mumblings, saying that we did not feel like eating very much (which was, by that time, indeed the truth). Having thus disposed of the amenities, we could arise with dignity, and hastened to do so, indicating that we would rather have a little coffee and let him enjoy his puppy.

We changed to our former horses, as the blacks were beginning to play out and we had to make time in order to gain the advantage of getting over the last wooded ridge before dark. At first, our new horses gave us some trouble by trying to turn back toward their erstwhile home, but finally they caught on and we managed to drive them ahead of us at a smart canter. The temperature went down with the sun and a biting wind came up against us. Cantering into this wind was close to unbearable, but we made the ridge by sundown. Once over it, we picked up the head of Prairie Dog Creek, a tributary of Tongue River.

It was only a question of the last eight or nine

miles now, but they were the most painful ones I
have ever experienced. The pangs of freezing blood
had moved from our extremities, which were by
then completely numb and senseless, further up
into our arms and legs. Our lung aches came back
with every breath, suggesting that the temperature
had again sunk to more than 40 below zero. How
much more, there was no way of telling, but weather reports next day claimed that a reading of 60
below was taken in the vicinity, and the state record
is somewhere in the seventies.

At last, we were at the ranch gate, then trotting
along in the lower pasture, only a mile from home.
When the lights of the ranch house winked at us,
our horses shook their manes, wrung their tails and
whinnied. The wrangling horse in the corral whinnied back. It meant "home" in a way I had never
known before. Those whinnies and the weakly
blinking lights meant more to me in one second
than all the blazing lights of Broadway and all its
tooting taxi horns had ever meant in all the previous years of my life. "Home!" How little, I realized,
some people knew what it really meant!

We put all four ponies in the barn, with plenty of
hay and grain as a reward, and went into the ranch
house.

Betty had waited supper for us. We staggered in
the front door (which is hardly ever used on a real
ranch) because it was nearer than the more official
kitchen door, thus coming into sudden view of the

dining room. There, with the children's help, she had just finished laying the table for all of us. "What've I just been telling you!" she exclaimed to Ted and Janie. "I *knew* it! I knew your daddy would be home tonight!" It was as if to say that she knew Al was the only daddy in the world who would pick that particular occasion for travel on horseback, and get away with it. On taking a second look at us, she let out a horror-stricken "Gawd!" and we wondered. For in the darkness, and our misery, we had forgotten how we looked in our get-up of charcoal and dish towels. But now, in the hall mirror, we were reminded of the awful truth.

We washed hurriedly in cold water, out of respect for our frostbite, but let our four-day beards stand, being too weak and numb for shaving. Our first luxury consisted of two double-size hot toddies, and for once Betty joined us, with a smaller one. It was a pleasant shock: both the toddies and her joining us, for she had never joined us before. Moreover, there was something pleasantly different about the quality of the whisky.

"Where did you get this good liquor, dear?" Al asked.

And then came another shock, at least for Al—Tom Bryan was back and had brought it from the family cellars in New York.

IX

Homesteader

I FELT that Al looked with jaundiced eye upon the coincidence of Tom's return to the ranch during our absence. There was, however, nothing to be proven, said or done about it, even though Tom seemed to have timed his reappearance to within a few hours of our departure.

Despite tension on that score, it did not take long for Tom to squirm back into our good graces. After his moodiness—which always attended recovery from one of his sprees—and Al's moodiness had worn off, we all had to confess that we were glad to see him back. Conversation gradually replaced glaring and the story of Tom's projected expedition to Paris unfolded.

It turned out that he had never reached Paris at all, or even progressed further east than New York. After his send-off from Sheridan by the police, judicial and sporting elements there, he had a long, dreary train ride to New York, where he arrived with most of his remaining $150 spent and in no shape to catch the *Aquitania*, which had sailed, anyway. He had availed himself of Dorothy Stett's financial arrangements, reserved a stateroom on the next ship to sail and, while waiting, had settled down to slake his thirst at a famous Prohibition-era speakeasy run by a family of four Irish brothers on East 52nd Street.[27] When his drinking cycle had progressed to the hopeless point, the four Irish brothers put him in a hospital for alcoholics, and there he remained just long enough to sober up to the point where he could appreciate the charms of a young lady patient. It was love at first sight, on both sides. The two made a mighty and successful effort to be discharged, then joined forces and took a trip to Florida, where thoughts of Dorothy Stett and the Paris jaunt were abandoned. At least, until cash ran short. The love trip then ended as abruptly as it had begun, back in New York, except that Tom was then again broke and friendless in the big city. And this time, Dorothy's bankers were not at all cooperative in financing the expedition further.

Tom had then found himself at the mercy of his family, and the embarrassment which he could cause these lace-curtain-Irish relatives was a well-established phenomenon. Grandfather Bryan had acted quickly and surely to curb it by having Tom taken into custody and incarcerated at a physical training institution up on the Hudson River and, while he was there, arranging to have him shipped back West.

The ranch family was united again and things

[27] Moriarty's where young blades hung out. The author recalls that his friend, Thomas Fortune Ryan frequented this gathering place.

went along pretty quietly for a while. Al and I
looked forward to the end of the winter, when our
cattle would be delivered and we could become active in our new venture. We often spoke of our
plans before Tom, who sat glumly listening to
them, saying nothing except by an occasional ex-
pression of the eyes, directed at me. I felt that he
was inwardly grousing about the whole situation
and put it down to the possibility that he might be
jealous of the fact that I, a comparatively poor man,
had cash to invest in a business, while his enor-
mously wealthy family would give him nothing. I
knew that he was jealous of Al, as he would often go
to extremes in deprecating him when we were alone
and I, therefore, decided that it must be double
jealousy when, in private, he began making guarded
warnings and advising me not to go into the cattle
business. I paid little attention to this, having already decided my course after due consideration,
and having already bought the cattle. Actually,
there was very little I could have done at that
time to change the situation, even had I wanted to.
So I just humored him along and turned my mind
to more constructive thoughts.

Foremost among these was the development of
my homestead claim and the building of my new
quarters, in which Al White offered further valuable help.

He generously revealed that, up in the hills, he
had an unused log cabin and a few miles of barbed-

wire fence, to which I was more than welcome and which he gave me forthwith, saying that they could be moved down to my land and that they would comply with the government requirements for a claim. I was thrilled at the idea of being given a house, as I had never known of anybody who had been given one thus, so I jumped on a horse and rode up to the place where he said it was, on Spring Creek and, sure enough, there was the cabin, set up on a little red-shale knoll in the pines. As Al had said, it wasn't much: just a deserted log cabin, barely sufficient to classify as a "habitable dwelling" when he had staked some homesteader to file a claim on Spring Creek, so that he could buy the land later, in the good, old-fashioned manner of cattlemen. I got off my horse, wrapped the reins loosely around a pine bough and went inside. Entrance was easy because the door and windows were out. The red shale roof had caved in at one end. The floor was completely rotten and useless, as I could observe from where I stood proudly, in the middle of it. Sunlight blazed through the hole in the roof, showing a patch of turquoise sky, and my spirits soared to unbelievable heights as I paced off the shaky floor, roughly measuring it. Four paces one way and seven the other: about 12 by 21 feet.

No, it wasn't much. But it meant everything in the world to me: the beginning of a home I could really call my own, fixing it up as I pleased and where I could do anything I wanted to without per-

Of this photo the author said, "My original homestead cabin (given me by Albert G. Brown, Sr.), which I moved from its former location on Spring Creek to a corner of my claim near the 4D Ranch, 1924. Today it is my kitchen."

mission from anyone, whether family, trustees or university authorities. I swelled with pride, walking about and inspecting it minutely inside and out, noticing particularly that the logs were good and sound which, after all, was the important thing. It would come apart easily and could probably be moved without too much trouble. I rode back to the ranch wondering just how this could best be done.

When I got there, a big man I had not seen before was hanging around the corrals, as if waiting for me. He stood well over six feet, was stockily built, with a barrel chest and a rolling gait, suggestive of a bear walking on his hind legs. He wore unbelievably old blue jeans, a battered, moderate-sized Stetson, a sheepskin coat, mule-hide mittens, and overshoes on his huge feet. He opened the corral gate for me politely, called me cheerily by my first name as if he had known me all my life, and smiled from ear to ear. He appeared to be so obviously relieved at our encounter that I could not help wondering how long he had waited to see me, and for what.

Fred was the most critical man I have ever met. He had the old-timer's habit of close observation, born of long, hard practical experience in the struggle for existence amid primitive surroundings. He did not merely look at a thing, he *saw* it. He also saw under it, over it, all around it and through it, practically at once. And, instinctively, you felt this the moment you set your eyes on his. For Fred's eyes were easily the most noticeable thing about him, after his dimensions, with which they were in rather sharp contrast, somewhat in the manner and proportion of an elephant's eye.

Riding up to the corral gate I had, somehow or other, felt this. Long before I even got near the gate, I could feel these eyes playing over me with the stark realism of anti-aircraft searchlights. Nor did they let up for an instant until they came to point-blank range with my own, when they seemed literally to burn with a sort of friendly inquisitiveness. I could see that, besides their comparatively small size, they were also distinguished in shape and color, being somewhat triangular and of an incredible blue.

His greeting had been simple and direct. "Glad to see you, son. Lauby's the name."

He shut the gate carefully behind me, making sure that the wooden tongue latch shot home, then shaking it critically and forecasting, "Someday, this whole goddam set of corrals is going to fall down flat."

After he had given the gate his entire attention for a few moments, he turned and focused on me again. He watched carefully as I dismounted, then removed one mitten and extended a great, muscular hand, looking me up and down as he did so. He walked slowly around the little buckskin I was riding, scrutinizing both horse and tack, occasionally commenting. "Throat latch is a little too tight, son." He slipped his fingers under the cinch, and

Fred Lauby, handyman, friend, uninvited roommate, and perpetual advisor to the author.

that seemed to suit him. "Funny, I could have swore he used to have another brand on him some-where—known him since he was foaled, over on Hanging Woman . . . Oh, yes. Here it is." He was scuffing the pony's shoulder with the back of his mitten, to make the brand stand out. "I heard you paid thirty-five dollars for him."

"That's right. What do you think?" I asked.

He shook his head. "Too much for around here. I wouldn't pay them fancy back-east prices out here if I was you. But then, you got to look at it both ways. The money don't mean so much to you and you got a good, quiet, dependable horse, like you need. He's plenty good enough for a winter horse, all right. And, of course, you can pack a gun on him. That's worth something."

I could see that he felt badly about the $35, though, so I ventured to reassure him that it was not really a drastic situation. "Oh, hell, Fred, I'm per-fectly satisfied."

"O.K." He nodded, indicating that the inspec-tion was at an end. "Water him and turn him loose, he's thirsty. So I guess you didn't cross the river, then?"

"No, I went the other way."

"Up Spring Creek?"

"Yes."

"I thought so."

"How did you know I went up Spring Creek?"

He laughed. "Well, I just figgered. It's a cinch

you didn't cross the river, or you would have watered your horse. Tom Bryan's been chopping out the water holes at the crossings twice a day. So when I saw that pony of yours sunk in the flanks, I figgered you must have been up in the hills where he couldn't get water."

"Why Spring Creek, though?"

"Well, seemed like there just wasn't much reason for you to go anywhere else. You wasn't packing a gun, so I knew you hadn't been hunting. But there again, I was kind of stumped for a while, because there's good water on Spring Creek, if you know where to find the spring. You just didn't go up far enough. Another half a mile and you'd have seen it, kind of stuck in under that red-shale bluff."

"Yes, I know where the spring is."

"Not far from that cabin where you were."

"Cabin? How'd you know I'd been up to any cabin?" I wondered why he hadn't, in the first place, asked me directly where I'd been, if he was so interested in the subject. But I learned later that such was not Fred's method of approach to any subject.

"Well, I know there's a cabin up there, because Al White grubstaked old man Tooley to file on that section years ago and then had the company buy it from him, and they never did nothing with the cabin, just left it there to rot, like they leave everything to rot around here." He nodded significantly at the surrounding corral poles, registering disgust, and then continued, "Next, I heard you had filed on a section yourself and he sold you the cabin for it. So I figured you might have just eased up there today, to look the snap over, since you was coming from that direction and there wasn't any other special reason."

"Al didn't sell it to me," I corrected. "He gave it to me."

"Gave it to you? . . . GAVE it to you!" he repeated, in astonishment. "Well, what the hell do you know about that? Them's good logs, boy. Several people wanted to buy them, or swipe them, or something, but Al would never turn them loose . . ." He trailed off into thought, and I got the feeling that Fred might have had his eye on those logs himself, and was disappointed.

"Sure, he gave it to me," I said proudly. "Why not?"

"Most people would say Al White is too poor to be giving anything away."

"Lots of people make presents when they haven't got much themselves, don't they? You know what the Bible says about being more blessed to give than to receive."

"Not around here, it ain't. Not when the banks have your ranch and cattle mortgaged up to the hilt and you still owe them money on top of that. Out here, that means you better be getting, not giving, Bible or no Bible. Any cattleman knows that, except perhaps Al White, and he don't know much of anything about cattle. No, son. There's not much giving in the cattle business, except when you have to give your cattle over to a bank, like he done. Any other kind of giving's bound to have some reason behind it." He squinted his eyes in the general direction of Spring Creek and cogitated awhile. Then he concluded, with a puzzled frown, "To give you my candid opinion, boy . . . Well, perhaps I shouldn't say it, but, to give you my candid opinion . . ."

I had not asked for his candid opinion, but I saw that there was no way of stopping it, so I waited expectantly while he floundered around, looking every instant wiser, more mysterious and more piercing of eye, until he finally blurted out, "It looks suspicious as hell to me!"

"Anyway, I'm not going to worry about it," I replied lightheartedly. "Why should I worry about being given a cabin? Looks to me as if Al must have had some reason of his own, and the logs weren't doing his family any good, up there. I don't care what his reason is, I'm damn glad to have it."

"Sure, who wouldn't be?" He was obviously burned up about this and fell into a short spell of "figgering." Presently he resumed his analysis. "Well, maybe it's like Tommy says, because Al's got you figgered out as some kind of southern ritzycrat. Says you're real kin to General Lee . . . You know, that General that lost the Civil War? . . . Is that right?"

"I suppose so, if you figure around far enough. But that doesn't prove anything."

"Whether it does or not, that's good enough for Al. The proof is, you got the cabin, ain't you?"

"Yes, but that's not the reason."

"Part of it, though. It's like Tommy says, Al figures you got a lot of high-toned folks back east there, with pots of money and handles on their names, and—"

"Nothing like the money Tommy's own family has," I interrupted. "Not even one per cent of it to tell you the honest truth."

"Maybe, son. But the way it looks to me is, Tommy's family is a kind of a scrub outfit, and Al don't like scrubs. Seems like Al's been looking things up, and Tommy wrote quite a lot to Betty from back there—I guess you know all about that—and they got it figgered out between them that your folks is mixed up with all kinds of generals and admirals and presidents and such. Or, maybe it's politicians, I forget which."

"So are a lot of people back east. That doesn't mean anything."

"Yes, I know. I was there as a kid. But I haven't been back since 'ninety-eight, the year my mother died, and I don't ever expect to go again. You know, there's something about this country that you can't beat. My education was kind of skimpy, so I don't know just how to explain it to you like I'd want to. But you'll find out, boy, you'll find out. I think you've got some kind of idea already, from what I've heard." He went into the barn, where he had tied his horse, and I strolled along after him, to be sociable. He approached the stall where he had tied his horse, having put a fair measure of Al White's oats in the grain box and pitched a few forkfuls of hay into the manger for good luck, although he apparently didn't think much of the hay. "Ho there, Fashion! Get over, boy." He put his hand on the horse's rump and entered the stall, calling over his shoulder, "Pretty poor hay Al put up this year. Mostly weeds. I have to feed Fashion twice as much of it as I did last year." Fashion, however, had a well-rounded appearance and was munching happily. The barn was cozily warm with the sun beating down upon it and pungent with the simple fragrance of horses, well-worn leather and alfalfa.

"Aren't you going to stay for dinner?" I asked. "It's about noon now."

"No. I've got some business down the river," he said, noncommittally, and forced Fashion back from the manger. "Sorry, because I'd like to talk to you some more. But you know where my cabin is, across the river, just opposite the island. Of course, the logs ain't quite as good as the ones you're getting from Al," he laughed, "but I'm going to patch it up, one of these days."

He took Fashion, bridled, out of the barn into the corral, carefully smoothed out the matted hair on his back, placed the saddle blankets and, with one smooth, effortless, lightning swing, clapped the

saddle well up on his withers. "So stop in, sometime," he continued. "You can ride over the ice
most anywhere, now. And bring that little buckskin. I'll pull his shoes for you, and trim his hoofs.
They sure need it. Now's a good time to rest his
feet."

"Thanks, Fred, I'll do that."

Although Fashion was gentle enough for Fred to
be packing a short-handled ax, a fence-mending
tool and an old nosebag partially filled with staples
on him, yet in mounting he took all the precautions
of a cowboy mounting a green bronco out on the
open range. Though a big man, weighing over two
hundred pounds and in his early fifties, he swung
into his old-fashioned saddle with a quick, sure,
fluid motion. The saddle was practically black from
years of exposure to the elements, with a high can-
tle, only a very slight swell and a spindly horn worn
to the metal from roping. Once in it, he gave the
impression of being thoroughly determined to stay
there. I noticed, in his profile against the sky, that
he had an uncommonly large nose, not unlike the
Duke of Wellington's, and that, except for the Iron
Duke's elegant trappings (excluding, of course, the
ax, nosebag and fence tool), there was a certain
fleeting similarity as to the businesslike manner in
which he sat a horse.

I was wondering, as the gate closed behind him,
what might have been the object of his waiting for
me at the corrals, when he called back over his

shoulder, "By the way, you going to move that cabin down to your claim?"

"Sure. As soon as I can figure out some way to get it done."

"That's easy. Now's the best time to do it, while there's still some snow. I know a couple of Indians who'll skid the logs down for you with their own teams. Nothing to it. No use bothering *this* outfit." He nodded toward the ranch house, and I felt glad not to have to call on Al White for any more favors. Then he unfolded the rest of his plans. "Of course, I'll have to go up there and mark them first, so we can put them up again in the same order. Then I'll show you the best place to build, just inside your line, halfway up the hill there, above where the old trapper's cabin was. I'll come over again tomorrow and we can run the line."

And so my building problems suddenly appeared solved, without my having to do anything about it. Fred waved the subject to a close and jogged off downriver to keep his business appointment, while I wondered vaguely how my financial arrangements with him would work out.

Next day he reappeared, this time in the role of surveyor. His equipment consisted of a few tall stakes with red rags on them, a pocket compass and a long telescope. Conspicuously absent were a transit and any kind of writing material. He just used his memory instead, and after taking one look at the legal description of the land, we were off.

We rode through the light snow, circling for benchmarks. We waved red rags, peeked through the telescope and set stakes for two or three hours. I didn't know what the procedure was all about, but had a feeling that everything would come out all right in the end. Somehow or other, he explained, there had been an error in the original survey, made with a magnetic compass which was deflected by unknown minerals in the hills, and this gave me an extra thirteen acres over the square mile. The fact confirmed my hope that all would be well. I was terribly proud at finding the first benchmark, and Fred explained the government readings on it. All these, I knew, were vital references to my land—it was "my" land already—and were recorded in Washington, which gave me a cozy feeling of playing footsie with Uncle Sam. I rubbed the little bronze disk bright with all the pride of a Mack Sennett cop in an old movie polishing his badge before going into action. I was going into action with Uncle Sam, and from him I would get my very own land, my little personal slice of original public domain, which had never had an owner before, except maybe Indians or prehistoric peoples.

My land was about six or seven miles around its irregular perimeter, and as there was no need for running the line all the way around just to figure out where I should build, we located only a few points on the boundary between my prospective building site and the Whites' house. When this was done, Fred looked over the intervening space carefully, assumed a grave air, shook his head and announced, "It looks suspicious as hell to me, son!"

"What looks suspicious?"

"Their telling you where to build. Why, unless you knew exactly what you was doing, you could be building your cabin on their land, and they'd claim it for themselves."

This seemed to me like an extremely remote hazard and nothing to worry about, inasmuch as I had originally suggested building on Al's land anyway. But I was thankful to Fred for wanting to protect my interests. There still seemed to be some three or four hundred yards between the two sites, with a good margin of safety between the boundary and my building site. I told Fred that I was satisfied, it would be enough.

"All right, then. I just wanted to show you where your land is, so nobody can put anything over on you, later. You see, part of what they consider their ranch here really belongs to you, if you want to fence it off." I didn't.

"Here's where the cabin goes," Fred indicated finally. "I'll have the Indians drop your logs here."

And so my future homesite was located for me. I never questioned Fred's judgment, or had a surveyor. Twenty-four years later, however (after Fred's death), a surveyor came through the country and I had him run the line past my cabin. The stake which Fred had set for the corner post of the fence was within three and a half inches of correct.

Winter slowly wore on to spring, and the logs of my cabin began to rise. Fred was now my self-elected architect and builder. He was, moreover, a very good one, and excellent at getting 100 cents' worth of everything out of each dollar I spent. I found out, to my horror, that he had paid the two Cheyennes who had skidded the logs down some five or six miles from the hills with their own teams $2.50 each, plus a sack of Bull Durham tobacco. He advised me daily against paying poor Ole, the stage driver, too much for hauling lumber from Sheridan, though he was already doing it for practically nothing, a few pieces at a time. He saddled Ole with the responsibility of accepting nothing but strictly first-grade lumber. There were to be no knotholes, rough spots, warped or split boards and, if any such found their way into our shipments, poor Ole had to haul them back again, free.

Each day, Fred commuted to the job from his own cabin across the river, taking meals at the Whites' under an arrangement I had made with them, and a small salary from me, as compensation. Transient Indians who stopped to camp at the ranch on their way to or from town were pressed into service chopping, digging or hauling shale for the roof, usually to be paid off with a piece of left-over meat, sugar, flour or tobacco, hardly ever in money.

The first thing we built was the outhouse. Fred

said that this was the proper way to start proving up on a homestead claim. He chose a little rise on the edge of a gully, back of the cabin, between it and the main road, where it stuck up like a sore thumb. He had various reasons why it should not be put down in the gully. "Stick her right up there where everybody can see her," he advised. "It does people good. There's getting to be too goddam much false modesty in this country since a few dude ranches moved in."

So up she went and I painted her Brewster green with a red roof (my father's yachting colors). Fred faced her to the east, so that on warm mornings he could leave the door open and enjoy the sun. He loved to read his *Pathfinder* there, and claimed that the roof was a favorite perch for meadow larks, whose sweet songs were relaxing to the digestive tract.

I helped in the cabin-raising too, learning the fundamentals of log construction, which has its own special problems. Occasionally, Al White would send Tom Bryan up to give us a hand with lifting the logs. We rigged pulleys and used ropehorses for power in getting the roof logs up. We hauled our water supply from the ranch house on a homemade stone boat carrying two barrels and drawn by a team. Finally, we got the roof on, the floor down, the windows in, a door hung and a roof-jack placed in one corner, to accommodate a stove pipe.

At last, my new home was turned over to me in

livable condition, wind- and waterproof, painted green around the windows, with a newly varnished front-and-only door, the floor oiled and a cheerful fire crackling in the stove. It certainly fulfilled the government stated requirements for a "habitable dwelling."

After a trip to town for furnishings, I moved in. No potentate was ever prouder of his palace than I was of my 12-by-21-foot cabin, complete with its small iron bed, potbellied stove, one table, four kitchen chairs, a tin washbasin, bucket and dipper, two oil lamps and my prize of prizes, a foot-powered player piano. Its physical drawbacks were completely overshadowed by the fact that it was a home, and despite them I decided to give a housewarming, with the Whites, Tom and Fred for guests. The housewarming got rather warmer than expected and started my home life off with a bang— literally, as I took a bottle of high-powered hootch away from Tom who, I thought, had had enough. He snatched it back and, for spite, threw it into the stove, where it exploded mightily. A shower of red-hot coals sprayed the room, sending a great belch of sparks up the chimney, as was later recalled by a passer-by. But not much harm was done, and Tom eventually quieted down.

Sometimes, on blustery evenings, when the Whites kindly urged me to sleep at the main house, I took great pride in letting them know, politely, that I was quite comfortable on the hill and that I enjoyed the walk up there. This was often much more true than any of them suspected, for the strained atmosphere created by Tom, Betty and Al in close formation around the open fire sometimes grated on my nerves. It was really a relief to grab my water bucket, fill it at the open well and start up the hill toward my own cozy, warm, snug little quarters.

I always got a thrill on opening the door, stepping inside and lighting a candle stuck in the neck of a bottle. There would be a lovely, faint homelike odor of coal gas, and a little shower of ruby coals as I shook down the stove grates. Then I would put on more coal, open the damper and light my two oil lamps, which burned with a remarkably soft, nearly white glow almost without odor, due to a special process of treating the fuel, taught me by Fred Lauby. After a little reading, or perhaps some music, I would get into bed with a feeling of homelike security, thankful for the big, fat stars spangling my neat windowpanes, and with a sense of the wondrous immensity beyond all understanding which they instilled, lulling me to sleep.

I felt that another milestone had been passed along the road toward my goal of creating some kind of useful, sensible life for myself. First, I had regained my health. Next, I had found a business venture which gave me an occupation. And now, at that point, I had established my own home. I was no longer floating about, just one more bewildered adolescent, but had a mooring imbedded in the soil of America.

Each morning I would wake up full of the joy of independence, shut off my alarm clock and lie there lazily waiting for the first breakfast bell to ring, knowing that it took me just five minutes to dress, five minutes to wash and five minutes to get down the hill. One morning, as I lay thus, I began to think: this is all very satisfactory, as far as it goes. But it doesn't go far enough. I am stranded here. I must move about more and see how other people in this country do things. I shall buy a car and add freedom of movement to my independence.

X

The Coyote in the Gladstone

THERE WAS, of course, lurking in my subconscious another reason for the automobile idea, as I had observed that most girls liked boys better when a car was involved. A car lent a false but effective halo. The finer the car the falser, but more effective the halo. I decided that my position would be greatly improved by a nice, new Cadillac.

Our local town of Sheridan did not then carry such splendor on tap, so the car had to be delivered from Denver and the local Cadillac agent planned to send a driver down there to bring it back. I had a little time on my hands before our cattle were to be delivered and felt like stretching my legs further afield, so decided to go along with the driver on the train and ride back in the new car. Tom had been on his good behavior for so long and was such good company that I invited him to come as my guest. Al granted him a three-day furlough from his chores, but nevertheless, bet me a dollar that I would not bring Tom back sober and on time.

Ole, the stage driver, picked us up and we headed for town. Some of my traps were set near the road and, as we drove along, we noticed that one of them held a coyote. I shot the coyote with Ole's .30-.30, took it out of the trap but, of course, could not skin it then and there. Fortunately, I was taking a cavernous old British Gladstone along, empty, to leave in Denver for repairs, and as this made an admirable container, I folded up the coyote and popped him into it, all ready for the taxidermist, next morning, where his fine, full winter coat would mount nicely as a mat.

We met the Cadillac man in Sheridan and all three of us boarded the afternoon train and settled down in the Denver Pullman, which coupled to another train at the junction point of Alliance, Nebraska, in the early morning hours. Considering Tom's recently excellent behavior pattern, I decided to risk a little drink before supper and had brought along some fairly good Prohibition whisky, camouflaged in a ginger ale bottle, which we poured surreptitiously into wax cups, cloak-and-dagger style, as required by the era. We drank, I thought, in moderate, gentlemanly fashion, after which I put away the bottle, which was, to the best of my knowledge, the only liquor in our party. After supper, the Cadillac man went sensibly to bed and, after talking awhile with Tom (who made several exits to the lavatory), I followed suit. It then became apparent that my knowledge about our liquor supply was incomplete, as Tom developed symptoms of having his own.

There were four nuns on the train, to whom he introduced himself as a stanch Catholic, thus start-

Edmund Randolph's Cadillac V-63, 1925.
The car of the coyote-in-court incident.

ing up a conversation. They were sweet and Christianlike in humoring him for a while and in trying gently to persuade him away from the evils of liquor, but the conductor soon had to come to their aid. He grabbed Tom by the shoulder brusquely and ordered him to bed. Tom let out a stream of profanity but, as I noticed through a crack in my curtains, nevertheless stumbled into his lower berth, which was across the aisle from mine and slightly forward. There were a few hysterical mumblings from timid ladies who rang bells to ask questions of the porter.

Toward morning I was awakened by unusual scuffling sounds in the aisle. Obviously, we were waiting over in Alliance. The car was still and quiet, except for a clinking of handcuffs in the silent night, as two muscular minions of the law were deftly taking charge of Tom, in response to an appeal wired ahead by the conductor. Backed up to the station platform was a police van with doors gaping, surrounded by a little crowd of the idle curious. The two officers were frisking Tom and whispering hoarsely. "Come on, tell us where you've got the booze!" one demanded. But Tom was noncommittal.

"He hasn't got anything on him," said the other, concluding his search of Tom's pockets. "But he's sure got it somewhere."

"Grab the bags," said the first one, softly bustling Tom toward the door, and they left with their prisoner, the second one with a bag in each hand.

Knowing that Tom had only one bag, I looked out the window with mounting interest. There he was, being eased, gently but firmly, into the Black Maria. He was slumped down in a most dejected attitude, peering forlornly out the door, dazed and disheveled, his hat knocked awry, his shirt open at the neck, with a necktie stuffed hurriedly into an overcoat pocket and shoes unlaced. The police were putting the two bags in after him and, under the platform lights, I could see distinctly that one of them was the old British Gladstone with its unusual and surprising contents.

At that point, I didn't particularly mind losing sight of Tom for a while, but I didn't want my beautiful, new coyote kicking around police stations and probably being turned over to the city scavenger. So, in slippers and with a great-coat over my pajamas, I rushed out onto the platform and hailed the police. "Hold on a moment! You've got the wrong suitcase," I pleaded.

"We got the evidence, if that's what you mean," said the officer in the van with Tom, hefting the bag to show its weight.

"That's *my* suitcase!" I answered.

"Your booze, too? Want to join our party yourself, do you?" the second officer laughed.

"Sure . . . let him come along!" Tom joined in raucously, swooning over on the officer beside him. "Good old Neddy!" And he belched audibly.

"Shut up, you!" the officer bawled.

"Who are you, anyway?" the other officer asked.

"I'm a friend of his. We're traveling together. You took my suitcase."

"It was under his bunk," said the officer, jerking his thumb at Tom and identifying the berth. "What's your number?"

I told him. There were some snickers up and down the platform. The little knot of idle curious had grown into a fair-sized gallery with a morbid interest in my plight. Tom was entertaining this element by making impolite, but guarded finger-noses at the police.

"We're just going by orders," said one of the officers, pulling a slip of paper from his belt and consulting it. "We took this bag that you say is yours, from under this drunk's berth."

I came down the steps toward the van, protesting. "I can't help it. I didn't put it there."

"Neither did we," said the officer, holding up his hand to stop me. "Why don't you put your baggage under your own berth, where it belongs?"

"I do have my other bag under there."

"Better watch out, sonny, or we might be investigating that other bag, too, and taking it along."

"I don't care. You can have it. But give me back this one."

The officer inside the van hefted the bag again. "Not on your life, sonny! Why are you so anxious about this particular bag?" He tapped it with his nightstick. "What you got in it?"

Tom's slurred and raucous voice interrupted, from the depths of the van. "I'll tell you bastards what he's got in it. He's got a goddam big coyote in it, that's what! . . . Good old Neddy!"

The inside officer pushed Tom down again and shook his nightstick at him. "Didn't I tell you to shut up? One more word out of you and I'll tap you to sleep with this billy."

A murmur ran through the gallery, which surged a little closer.

The outside officer spoke up again. "Well, buddy, if you don't tell us what you got in the bag, we'll have to let the judge decide."

Someone in the crowd jostled me and I heard a vague voice. "Go on, tell us! What you got in it?"

The outside officer had his hand on the door of the Black Maria and was about to close it. "You won't tell, then?" he asked, with an air of finality.

I pointed to Tom. "He's already told you. There's a coyote in the bag. Look and see."

"Coyote . . . coyote . . ." ran through the crowd, and somebody piped up, "Go on, open it. We want to see the coyote!"

The officers smiled at each other again and the outside officer called to his companion, "Come on, Tony, let's go!" When he had shut the door, he turned to me and advised, "You better get back on the train before you wake up. This is a hell of a place for nightmares."

"If you give me a chance to get dressed, I'll come

along with you. I'd kind of like to help my friend, here. He's lost his wallet."

"According to what he's been telling us, he won't need a wallet. He's one of those big millionaires from New York City, ain't he? . . . Sorry, son, you can't come with us. We're not running a free bus service. You can go to the Municipal Jail if you want to claim your property . . . especially, that coyote. Don't worry. The judge will give him back to you."

The police wagon sped off and I returned to my car, feeling sorry for Tom and slightly guilty at having brought any liquor along. I knew he hadn't a penny. Wiring his family for money wouldn't do any good, as they would probably rather see him in jail, and it might create unfavorable publicity for us both if the story got around. The thing to do, I could see, was to get him out quickly and without any fuss, whatever the cost. So I told the conductor I was leaving the train, and asked the Cadillac man to wait for us at the Brown Palace Hotel in Denver. Then I took a cab to the Municipal Jail.

By the time I got there it was about two o'clock in the morning and Tom had been locked away to sober up. I could not see him or the baggage, which had been confiscated and tagged as evidence. The arresting officers had gone off duty and the two who had come on knew nothing of my plight, or Tom's. They just knew that I couldn't hang around there, and referred me to the desk sergeant.

This official gave me a chill reception. "If you're a friend of that drunk we just locked up," he said, sharply, "I wouldn't boast about it too much. He's the orneriest cuss we've had in here for a long time. Won't give his right name. Says he's Jonathan Thomas Bryan the Third from New York City, grandson of the famous Wall Street big shot, but we got an idea that he comes from a ranch somewhere." Then he looked down at the police blotter in disgust and added, quoting from it, "'Occupation: Millionaire' . . . Said he had a coyote in a suitcase, too . . . No, mister, I can't help you. If you want to see him or claim some property, better come back here at nine o'clock. Maybe the judge will let him out if he's got all this money. He'll sure need it."

"He hasn't got any money at all, himself."

The desk sergeant nodded sagely. "I could tell the sonofabitch was lying."

"But he wasn't lying about his name. He's just on the outs with his family, that's all."

"I sympathize with his family. They should have drowned him when he was born."

"And he wasn't lying about the coyote in the suitcase, either."

The sergeant put down some papers he was fooling with and addressed me irritably. "Now listen, mister. I don't want to hear any more about that coyote in the suitcase. We're pretty full here tonight, but we got room for one more. If I was you, I'd run along to bed."

I felt that the audience was definitely concluded, but asked respectfully, "Sergeant . . . about the fine . . . What do you think the amount will be?"

He read from the record with official boredom. "Drunk and Disorderly, Disturbing the Peace, Possession of Liquor, Transportation of Liquor, Public Menace, Resisting Arrest . . ." and then he trailed off into something about pulling a safety cord on the train. "Well, I don't know exactly," he concluded. "But several hundred dollars."

My heart sank, as I had less than two hundred dollars on me and, at that hour, in a strange town, the chances of raising Tom's bail in time seemed slim. After some rest in a cheap hotel near the jail, I got on the telephone to Denver and tracked down an unfortunate Cadillac official at his home, who very obligingly agreed to wire me five hundred dollars as soon as the telegraph office opened. I got to court with the money in plenty of time.

Tom, battered and worn, was brought before the bench. His suitcase and mine were placed on a table nearby. It was obvious that my coyote had bloated a bit during the night, from the steam heat of both Pullman car and jail, as the old Gladstone was bulging ominously.

The trial proceeded. Tom answered soberly, establishing his identity and admitting his long list of misdeeds before a kindly old judge. Finally, the judge asked, "And are these your suitcases?"

Tom answered that one was, and indicated it.

This case, when opened, revealed an empty gin bottle and a dirty collar.

"And the other suitcase, who owns it?" the court pursued.

Feeling that this was my cue, I arose and said, "May it please Your Honor, I own the other suitcase."

"And who are you, young man?"

"A friend of the prisoner, Your Honor."

"Your name?"

I told him.

"Is there any liquor in this suitcase of yours?"

"No, Your Honor."

"What is in it?"

"A coyote, Your honor."

The judge became visibly annoyed, and admonished me, "Come, come, young man, this is no time for balderdash!" Then, addressing the policeman on duty, he ordered, "Officer, open the suitcase."

There was a tussle with the locks, which were jammed from the bulging, and another officer came to help. Then, suddenly, the lid flew up and out popped the coyote's head, glassy-eyed, with tongue protruding. An awful smell stole over the courtroom, while snickers came from several spectators.

"Very well," said the judge. "Close it!"

But that was not so easy. The two stalwart policemen, wrinkling their noses, struggled for some time before they got the coyote back in the case, while giggles filled the courtroom and even the judge himself could not hide a smile. "Young man," he addressed me, "I shall never question your veracity again." Then he turned to Tom. "One hundred and fifty dollars fine. Case dismissed."

By the time we got to Denver, it was too late to start driving back that day. We went first to thank the Cadillac official, then to the hotel to join our driver, who had the new car in the garage and all ready to leave early in the morning.

By next morning, however, Tom had disappeared without leaving us any clue to his whereabouts. After waiting a reasonable time to hear from him, I decided to leave without him. Knowing that he would wind up in jail sooner or later and would be obliged to call for help upon his only Denver acquaintance, the Cadillac official, I arranged with this long-suffering businessman to bail him out and ship him back to Sheridan by rail. Then I started off with the driver. What with the speed restrictions on a new car and the gravel roads of those days, it was a two-day drive up to Sheridan.

Things turned out about as I expected. There was a telegram waiting for me in Sheridan. Tom had been in and out of jail the same day in Denver, and had been put on the evening train for Sheridan. Thus, he had passed us in the night and arrived in Sheridan several hours ahead of us.

Not finding any trace of him at the inn, I could draw only one conclusion and called up the Police Department.

The chief's affable voice answered, "Sure, we got him back again, safe and sound, in his regular cell, No. 3. Looks like we'll be able to let him out sometime tomorrow. He's doing real good."

This time, as Tom was more or less at home, I let him plan his own salvation. My pin money and my patience were both running out. So I went back to the ranch alone and flipped Al a silver dollar.

XI

The V Bar C

AL WHITE had an old Oliver typewriter which
looked as though it might have survived the
Civil War. It was so worn to a frazzle, rattling loose
and caked with dust that, had he told me it came
from General Lee's headquarters, I would have believed him. For several days, he bent over this old
machine hours at a time and finally produced the
articles of agreement for our cattle partnership. It
made a beautiful document as he had set it down, full
of capital letters, asterisks and underlining.

"Why, I didn't know you were a lawyer, Al!"
I observed, in admiration.

"Oh, I had some training at the Military Institute," he explained modestly. "No use paying a
lawyer to draw up these simple contracts." He
tossed the matter off casually, as if it had been some
little thing an expert stenographer had snapped out
by second nature, whereas, actually, he had labored
over it the greater part of a week and appeared exhausted from his efforts.

Now, I had been told never to sign anything
without reading it and, if possible, having a lawyer
read it also. So I began reading, and feeling very
businesslike, while Al gazed out the window in a

faraway mood, visualizing thousands of straight-backed, stocky yearling steers, their chestnut hides (all of uniform color and markings, to attract top prices) bearing the V Bar C brand, being unloaded at the stockyards in Omaha or Chicago. Now and then he juggled his teeth around, ever so quietly, but he paid no attention to me whatever. With him it was a foregone conclusion that there would be no difference of opinion on an agreement between two gentlemen. He was perfectly at ease and his magnificent nonchalance inspired me with the utmost confidence.

I read on and on. It was several pages long. The new cattle company was dignified with an aura of intimated success which might well have been applied to the Standard Oil Company. Our lands and cattle, together with the offspring, increase in values and other sources of profit accruing thereunto, sounded most imposing. Even the brand we were to use, "V Bar C," sounded good and solid, with no complicated curlicues or impractical twists to it. This was, incidentally, an old and respected brand purchased by the Whites in some big cattle deal of long ago, now inactive from disuse but still registered in their name, from which Al had it legally transferred to our partnership. There were lines and lines of legal descriptions of the land they were to put up, and I was both intrigued and mystified reading about the northeast quarter of the southwest quarter, the north half of the southeast quarter, and all the rest of it. I was sorry to get to the end of the document, it was such pleasant reading. But there, finally, were the two dotted lines, all ready for our signatures, with more spaces and dotted lines for witnesses, and a place for the notary public. Al, at that point, was poring over the huge map on his desk and picking out some little splotches on it which he had painstakingly traced out in water colors for me.

"Here," he said, referring to the map when I had finished reading the partnership agreement, "here is the land we're putting up against your cash. It's all good cattle land, as I can show you if you want to ride up there with me sometime. It's worth more than that to us; we wouldn't sell it for ten dollars an acre. It's about the only good land we've still got that's free and clear of any mortgage."

This last argument was a clincher. They were putting up the only thing they had to put up. What more could I expect? It was somehow touching, as was Al's whole demeanor in handling the situation and in coping with my presence there at the ranch. His back was to the wall and he was looking right at me with not a trace of doubt in his big, sad brown eyes, offering a proposition that might help him a lot and certainly could do me no great harm, even if I lost my entire stake, which seemed hardly possible. The whole thing was my idea in the first place, and now it had boiled down to a question of disregarding the warnings of Tom Bryan—certainly no shining example of business acumen himself—and putting my faith in Al's honesty. I looked at his sad, anxious face again and could not doubt.

"Looks fine to me, Al. I'll sign it right now."

"Not yet." He waved the technicality aside as superfluous at the moment. "We'd better do it at the Land Office, where there's a notary and we'll have witnesses. My brother Herbert[28] has to sign for the company, too, and he has the company seal down at the other ranch."

Herbert, at the other ranch, and that side of the White family had not come much within my view at the time. But I looked at the document again and there was the place for Herbert to sign. I had been invited down to Herbert's once or twice and remembered him as a jolly, rotund, hard-working little man with a perpetual wad of tobacco in his cheek and a tiny, vivacious, pleasant little brunette wife who was the sister of Al's wife. Herbert was, I knew, wagon boss of the outfit in the old days and was now the active manager of their cattle. He had always been more in the saddle and less behind a desk than Al, being also different in that he had violently opposed education as a boy and, when locked up for punishment at school, had chopped his way to freedom with the fire ax, vowing never to

[28] Fictitious name given to Joseph T. Brown, Jr. of the Three Circle Ranch of the Brown Cattle Company. When he wanted to see his brother Albert, he came ten miles up the river.

return. Whereupon he sacrificed education for practical experience and never seemed to have regretted his decision.

After the signing ceremonies at the Land Office, I felt like a different person, relieved of the mental conflicts as to what I should do or should not do. I had signed the partnership agreement without a lawyer; had made the decision to take these people on for better or for worse and was definitely in the ranching business. I had crossed the Rubicon and burned my bridges. There was no turning back now, and I braced myself for my first practical experience in this new way of life.

It was not long in coming, for spring was already with us and we prepared to take delivery of the new partnership cattle. There were 350 cows, more or less, and nearly all had calves by their sides, or were about to calve. There were a few dry cows still within the breeding age and some so old that it would not pay to run them more than a year or so. Practically none were in the prime of youth. They were of the Durham breed and, although not of a very high grade, were still attractive from the standpoint of being big and rangy. Thus, our initial herd ran to somewhere between 500 and 650 head, counting the calves.

Delivery was to be made at a ranch on the Burlington Railroad, about forty miles distant. The bank was delivering through an officer of its livestock department, accompanied by a cattle foreman

and two or three hands. Al White was to receive for
our partnership with me as his assistant, in a sort of
figurehead capacity. Tom Bryan was to be our horse
wrangler. We were to hire one outside hand to
drive the wagon and cook for us. We would have to
forgo a standard roundup wagon, as the only one in
the country was needed elsewhere, but Al was to fix
up his old ranch wagon with hoops, a canvas cover
and a fly, and we would get along with a team of
two horses instead of four. We hired a young boy
named Sandy Miller,[29] from up on the head of
Hanging Woman Creek, as our cook and driver.
Thus we were to be four on the receiving end of the
deal, but there would only be Al, Tom and myself
to handle the 600-odd cows and calves.

Extra cowpunchers were practically impossible
to hire in the Tongue River country of the 1920s,
as the demand for their services waned with the
decline of the old-scale round-up outfits calling for
four-horse mess and bed wagons, large cavvies,
guard duty at night, horse wranglers and bronco
busters, nighthawks and cooks. These were jobs of
the recent past, to a great extent, although some
outfits still used them. But in the thinly populated
Tongue River district, although there were vast
tracts of Reservation and National Forest lands,

[29]Fictitious name given to Taliaferro Cox, a member of a
local family of Virginia extraction. At the time of *Hell
among the Yearlings* he worked for Albert Brown as a cowpuncher. Other members of this family are leading citizens
of Rock Springs, Wyoming.

there was no real open range left, in the old sense of
the term, and professional cowpunchers were hard
to hire, as most of our people had cattle themselves
and needed every hand they could get at that time
of year, usually recruiting them from among their
own families and friends. Women and girls were
not usually the established order, either at that time
or earlier—despite the popular but erroneous conception of the prevalence of "cowgirls"—but some
ranchers did have wives or daughters who helped
with the roundup from time to time. These invariably had their own tepees, set a little apart from the
men's. Otherwise, they behaved very much like the
men and were treated as such, custom requiring that
they never be waited on or given any preference.
Nor would they themselves have it any other way.
They were always welcome, were treated with respect and were always safe, whether married or single, plain or pretty, sixteen or sixty. There would
be, however, a slight toning down of profanity and
ribald stories in their presence. They were mostly
good horsewomen and knew cattle.

Al eased the strain by enlisting the help of his
young son Ted and daughter Janie. "I got to thinking about it," he explained, one morning after
breakfast, "the kids can help us. They're old
enough now."

"Janie and Ted? But how about their school?"

"They'll only have to miss two days, and they've
agreed to make it up, so Aggie Lester's going to let

them take Friday to Monday off. That gives them four days in a row, just about the time it'll take us to get back from the railroad. And we don't need them going over. I've arranged to meet them there."

That question settled, we turned to other details. Al's old ranch wagon was given the once-over by Fred Lauby, who pulled and greased the wheels, thumped authoritatively around underneath it awhile and reinforced some parts with wire. Al and I made a trip to town for supplies: horseshoes, canned goods, ropes, a canvas fly for the wagon, an extra tepee for the kids and the requisite parts of a roundup bed for me. We already had one tepee, which would do for Al and into which he kindly invited me, but I wanted my own bed for future use, anyway. The whole arrangement was somewhat makeshift, but it was the best we could do.

Al picked out the requisites for my roundup bed and, once back at the ranch, showed me how to build the bed according to standard usage, on a canvas bedsheet, or "tarp," about 17 feet long by 6 wide, folded and rolled in such a way as to be more or less weatherproof either rolled out, in use, or rolled up for transit.

We started on a beautiful, sunny morning, with Al expressing confidence that the good weather would hold out, whereupon (mindful of our ride to the Hawkes ranch) I immediately stopped at my cabin to pick up an extra sweater and some warmer gloves, even though I had already packed extra winter clothing in my roundup bed. As we pulled away, Sandy Miller, with all the enthusiasm of a carefree youngster, beamed with pride in his new importance as cook and teamster. The whole atmosphere was charged with spring and hope; our hearts were light and our stomachs full. Even Tom Bryan, for once, gave us no concern. He sang cheerily as he rode along beside the wagon, or trailed our little cavvy ahead of us, galloping away from time to time to open the gates. On the morning of the third day we got to the railroad, from which sounds of tooting, puffing and clashing couplings came floating through the clear air to us while we were yet several miles away.

"Where are we now?" I asked.

"Old man Grimby's place, not far from the Little Big Horn. . . . Where General Custer made his famous Last Stand. It's an ideal holding pasture for us, so close to the railroad."

I could see that Al thought the cattle wouldn't be able to stagger very far the first day. His mention of Custer had a foreboding ring to it. I wondered whether our cattle might be making their last stand here also.

The condition of the cows suggested this possibility. When we got up to them, most of the shipment had been unloaded and, I thought, in the nick of time before they keeled over. They stood quietly about the corrals, their heads hung dejectedly forward, their scrawny calves pulling halfheartedly at what seemed to be a milk shortage. With the bank men (who had brought their saddles along and whom we mounted on our spare horses) we pushed our tottering little herd into the pasture and onto water, where we left them for the night. After supper at the wagon, our guests turned in at Grimby's having agreed on an early-morning meeting for formal delivery of the stock.

Next day, the serious business of delivering a herd of cattle got under way, Al taking charge with the bank foreman, a great, red-faced, white-haired, smiling Irishman whom Al had mounted on the best horse in our cavvy: a big sorrel that, in his younger days, had been a top cutting horse for the old White Cattle Company. The Irishman and the sorrel made a fine sight, a mixture of brains, brawn and experience on the part of each, a man-and-beast team with perfect understanding of the business at hand—working the herd—and eager to go about it in that quiet, unassuming manner that is the hallmark of professional excellence in any walk of life.

Al himself was riding a quiet little cow pony belonging to one of the children. I was on my new acquisition, Tar Baby. We had brought Badheart, the unpredictable black, along with us and mounted one of the bank's bronc-twisting cowboys on him, to see if he was in a ridable mood, which he was. Nevertheless, Al didn't want Badheart around too close while they were working the herd, so he sent this cowboy off to a safe distance, with Tom Bryan,

to hold the cut. He sent me off in the opposite
direction to help hold the main herd, with the second bank cowboy and Sandy Miller. Then he, the
bank officer and the Irishman put their horses and
heads together on the sidelines, for some time.
They talked so long that I began to wonder whether
Al was telling them a Civil War story. Once in a
while they would look at the herd, long and hard,
then talk some more. After half an hour or so of
this, there was a slight turn for the better and I
could see some signs of action. There was much
thumbing of notebooks and wetting of small stub
pencils. The broad brims of Stetsons nodded "yes"
or wagged "no," or were cocked at various angles
suggesting intermediary stages of decision.

Then they began walking their horses into the
herd ever so gently, at a slow and stealthy pace,
stopping once in a while to study some particular
animal, then milling about again, eventually cutting
out a cow or calf, or both, and running them off
toward the cut, to be picked up by Tom and his
assistant. Occasionally there would be another conference on the sidelines, with more scribbling in
notebooks, scratching of heads and further longing
glances, now directed also at the cut.

Placed at the far side of the main herd and cau-
tioned against crowding it too close, I had been
hanging back and feeling terribly left out of this
whole deal, which I had not only conceived but
financed. My impatience mounted as Tar Baby fid-

geted under me, feeling like a jack-in-the-box with a very strong spring which I was just barely able to keep down. After all, I thought, what was all the mystery about? And I decided that it would be fitting and proper for me to inquire.

So, with the best of intentions but a woeful ignorance of protocol, I started toward the herd, meaning only to join the others and ask a few reasonable questions, while riding about in it as they were. But before I knew it, Tar Baby was on a dead run and I was having a struggle to pull him down. I looked up to see Al waving me back, frantically. The others were too astounded to say anything, but I knew right then that something was very wrong.

In no time at all, Tar Baby took me right into the middle of the herd. As we plowed through it, cows, bawling, scattered in every which direction and lost their calves. One or two bewildered, terror-stricken calves got between Tar Baby's feet and were bowled over. Some of the cows on the outer edge broke away and headed for the cut, their calves barely able to keep up.

I made a terrific effort and set Tar Baby back on his haunches. But by that time the damage had been done. The perfect tranquillity of our herd—which made it easy to work—was completely disrupted and the whole idea of maternal contentment (so carefully preserved through the hours) suddenly gave way to an atmosphere of bovine neurosis.

Embarrassed at this turn of events, I concentrated

upon getting out of the herd as fast as I had come in and staying as far away from it as possible. But my embarrassment was only then beginning, as I tried to make a hasty exit. Foolishly, I was wearing spurs—a practice which I gave up instantly and forever—and, in my haste to get going in the right direction, jabbed the pony smartly with them. My hat flew off as he jumped and started bucking. The situation was sadly enhanced by the fact that this particular horse, for some obtuse anatomical reason, always seemed to have gas on his stomach and, when excited, would expel it quite audibly. He was then thoroughly excited, and each jump sounded like a giant firecracker, adding to the panic of the herd.

The others seemed to take this trouble I had caused them with reassuring good humor (although I was ashamed to look them in the eye, even if I could have spared the time off from my equitation to do so). Far from shouting at me what I probably deserved to be told, they yelled "Yippee!" and "Ride 'em, cowboy!" in childish glee. Someone observed, "That little black sonofabitch must think it's the Fourth of July!" And I heard the smooth, twinkling tenor of the Irishman's voice singing out encouragement, "Stay with him, sonny, he'll quit when he runs out of gas!" By that time Tar Baby had shaken me loose in the saddle and I was forced to grab the saddle horn ignobly to keep from being thrown, and, undoubtedly, trampled by the herd.

When Tar Baby ran out of gas, I slunk back to beyond where I had started from, hanging my hat-less head, while the boys bunched the herd together again. One of them rode up to me with my battered hat, which I had completely forgotten and, in my misery, I could hardly muster a smile as he handed it to me. But he had a smile big enough for both of us as he remarked, "If we just had a flute, I believe we could teach that sonofabitch to play 'Yankee Doodle'!" I felt much better.

By noon they had finished working the herd and I was sent for to join in making our final arrange-ments with the bank. This time I was very careful to keep my horse down to a slow trot as I went over to join the others for what I felt would be another long and complicated session. But I was as surprised at the brevity of these arrangements as I had been by the languor preceding them. Smeared columns of figures were passed around between us; a rumpled contract emerged from the Irishman's hip pocket and was referred to briefly; some sort of legal re-lease was signed by us and witnessed by a cowboy who came galloping up at a signal from the bank officer and was told, simply, "Put it there, Gus." The cowboy then tore off again as if hounded by demons. Al and I turned over a bank draft and our business was done, all in less than ten minutes and without leaving our saddles. Then we shook hands all around. Someone raised the cry, "Let's go eat!" and the older men, happy as kids let out of school, joined the rest of us in whipping up and racing to our wagon nearby.

Later the bank officer, who had been practically silent most of the time, spoke up to me in a fatherly tone. "Never mind what happened this morning, kid. You've got guts, and that's what counts. Pretty nearly everybody around here knows about your deal, and they all wish you luck, just like I do. And don't worry too much about your cows. They're not half as bad as they look to you. Just ganted-up after shipping and a tough winter. Stay with them and you can't lose."

We must have made a sorry sight as we started on our four-day drive back to Tongue River with our straggling little herd, our skimpy outfit with its lone horse wrangler and not even a mess tent: a sad contrast to the erstwhile proud and openhanded White cattle dynasty. I felt that there was something slightly pathetic in the fact that Al White himself, until quite recently a shining figure in the ranching world, was now absent-minded, grim with worry and care, living in the past and known to be financed for a mere $10,000 by a New York greenhorn who hadn't enough sense to stay out of a herd.

Not long afterwards Ted and Janie showed up, by prearrangement with the schoolteacher and some friends at an intervening ranch, where they had put up overnight. They loped easily over the rolling range, a perfect picture of youthful exuberance escaped from the clutches of education. They rode admiringly around the herd and then fell in at the rear on either side of their father, giggling and bubbling over with joy.

Next day we found that we had lost a cow and Al sent Sandy back to find her, telling Tom to drive the wagon. Sandy was to catch up with us at the ranch of the Benson family, where we were to camp that night.

The Bensons invited us in for supper and we all got baths. Tom brightened up here, for the first time in days, and it was soon evident that an attractive young daughter in the family was his inspiration. Scrubbed up, shaved, in fresh blue jeans and with his boots polished, he launched an attack on this young lady with such gusto and apparent success that Al let him linger at the ranch house when we returned to the wagon and bed.

I pulled my bed in under the wagon sheet, as the sky had clouded over, and for some time lay awake, mulling over the events of the day, wondering whether Sandy had found the missing cow and where he was spending the night. A few drops of rain fell, so I got up and pulled Tom's bed in under the wagon fly, too. The sound of rain pattering on the canvas overhead was very soothing, as was the bawling of our cows and calves in the distance, suggesting that they were doing better and taking more interest in life. Al's tepee showed up as a glowing pyramid of soft candlelight with shadows crossing it occasionally, as he turned the pages of his treatise on Confederate strategy. I dozed off while watching him.

Suddenly I was awakened by the sloshing of hooves at a smart gallop passing my head close by. Al's tepee was still glowing. The galloping faded into the distance and came back again, accompanied by mumbling curses and the blowing of a winded pony. Tom was back in camp, probably somewhat the worse for wear, since he must have ridden right past without even seeing the beacon of Al's tepee. Then the liquor tinge to his voice was unmistakable as he spoke to his horse, "Hold still, you goddam little knothead . . . !"

There was a flapping of cinch leathers, the thud of a saddle in the soggy sagebrush and more frantic hoofbeats as he turned his pony loose.

"For God's sake, Bryan, shut up!" I pleaded. "The kids are trying to sleep."

He toned his voice down to a stage whisper, tiptoed over to where I lay and continued, "Pardon me, professor. I forgot we were in the nursery. And who are you, the Wizard of Oz?"

I could see that he was still in the primary, or harmless, stage of his jag, so ignored him.

He looked toward Al's tepee and sneered. "Anyway, I'm getting to bed before the General. Old Stonewall Jackson must be studying his battle reports. . . . By the way, how's the war going—or haven't you heard?" He made some disparaging remarks about Al's not going back to look for the lost

cow, and then his voice trailed off into gentler
channels as he wormed down between the covers
and sighed blissfully. "Oh, boy, did I have luck
with that little gal tonight!" Raising his voice to a
taunting resonance, for Al's benefit, he added,
"Fastest thing since Grant took Richmond!" then
belched twice and fell silent.

I could almost feel Al wincing. He couldn't have
helped hearing it all. But he just turned another
page with magnificent indifference.

It was daylight before any of us woke up. The
Benson cowpunchers were riding the flat where we
were camped, wrangling their horses and, incidentally, ours. I looked around me: drizzling rain. Tom
was snoring, apparently dressed. His boots were nowhere to be seen, so I supposed he had gone to bed
with them on. Our cook had not showed up. Silence
reigned in Al's tepee, but the children's showed
signs of life and giggles issued from it. I saddled the
stake horse which Al had tethered a short distance
off, and went to help the Benson boys wrangle. As I
rode by the children's tepee, they poked their heads
out and shouted a good morning.

"When do we eat?" Ted asked.

"Soon as I can get back to help your dad fix
breakfast. Sandy didn't come in last night, and Tom
is . . . er . . . sleeping."

"I reckon so," said Janie thoughtfully.

"Why, what do you know? Hear anything last
night?"

They looked at each other and laughed. "Not much," Ted answered shyly. "Only, Tom came awful close to galloping right through our tepee."

"Don't you worry about breakfast," Janie volunteered. "We can get it ready."

"You go ahead and start the fire, anyway. I'll get these boys to rope out our horses and bring them over."

They bounded out of the tepee and scurried away after firewood.

When I rode up to the Bensons' men, one of them asked laughingly, "Where's that head horse wrangler of yours this morning?"

"Still under the weather."

"Well, he made a pretty good job of drinking up all our snakebite whisky over in the bunkhouse last night."

When the boys learned that our cook was still missing, they insisted that we come over to the mess house for breakfast, and brought our horses to camp for us to ride back with them. We all thought this was a fine idea, except Tom, who couldn't be roused.

"Ain't no use tryin' to tail the sonofabitch up," one of our friends observed. "He couldn't eat, anyway. Better leave him lay."

So we abandoned Tom to his own resources, leaving him, however, with a fire started and a saddle horse staked nearby.

Now, minus the services of both Sandy and Tom,

our expedition was more or less stalled, so we sat around the bunkhouse for a couple of hours after breakfast, waiting for our patient to recover and Sandy to show up. Sandy didn't show up, but we found Tom grousing about the wagon when we returned. He was in one of his silent moods, spoiling for another drink, and not in the market for any help from the likes of us. He had eaten, saddled the horse we left for him, but evidently had decided against appearing at the Benson house again. Instead of following us, he had ridden over to the corrals and, finding our cavvy there, had roped out a team and brought them back. He had the team harnessed but not hitched to the wagon, and was sitting on a nail keg, hunched over the stove with his back to us as we rode up.

"Well, when do we pull out?" Tom asked peevishly, his back still turned to us.

"Right away," said Al. "Hook up."

Tom walked sulkily around the other side of the wagon to avoid us and started backing the team into place. I made a move to help him hook up the traces, but he would have none of that and spat out, "I can hook up a team by myself." He climbed up on the seat with a sour face and wouldn't speak to any of us. Thus, in a somewhat strained atmosphere and a slight drizzle of rain, we started off again.

As we pushed on, mile after weary mile, Tom took it upon himself to pull ahead with the wagon until he was practically out of sight, not once deigning to look back at us or even giving any indication that we belonged to the same outfit. Sandy caught up with us at about three o'clock, but he didn't have the cow. He had ridden all the way back to old man Grimby's that night looking for her, had spent the night there and found her on the way back, dead in a creek bottom.

"I'll have to dock your pay that much," Al told him.

Sandy looked completely bewildered by the announcement but rode off to point the lead without saying anything.

The rest of the day passed somewhat silently and we camped on Canyon Creek that night, only about ten miles from home.

Tom still didn't want to be around any of us, but just the same he sat down by the fire under the canvas fly as, in the rain, he didn't have much choice. Al sat across from him, on the opposite side of the little stove, also silent, endlessly rolling cigarettes and throwing them away after a few puffs. Alternately, he and Tom glared at each other and then returned their eyes to the stove, Al punctuating the silences with the clicking of his teeth. On the other side of the stove from me sat Sandy, glumly considering the lost cow and the prospects of his having to pay for her, which would take all his wages for the trip. I was flanked and faced by this strained silence, which was anything but golden, and certainly did not enhance the piquancy of our modest victuals. Even Ted and Janie were quiet, sitting by themselves on a bedroll, probably considering their return to school after only one more day of freedom. After a while Tom got up without a word, put on his yellow slicker and went out to sit on the wagon tongue, in the rain.

After supper this happy gathering broke up early. Ted and Janie scuttled down the creek bank with a big water bucket, washed the dishes cheerfully and brought in some more wood, their mere activity somewhat dispelling the gloom. Then they ducked into their tepee. Al retired to his and struck up the candle. Sandy and I rolled out our beds under the fly. But Tom, disdaining our presence, crawled in under the wagon, as far away from us as he could get without being in the rain. Again silence reigned in camp, except for long, regular breathing sounds and a light snoring which emanated from the apparently sleeping Tom.

Presently Sandy spoke up, annoyed. "You know," he said, "I may be a dumb sonofabitch, but I just can't figure out why I've got to pay for that cow. I didn't kill her."

"I know you didn't, Sandy."

"And if anybody around here thinks—" he started off, in righteous indignation.

"Nobody does," I interrupted him.

At this point Tom stopped his snoring and joined in testily. "The hell nobody does! Old General Jigglejaws, over there, had it all studied out.

Maybe the cow wasn't dead when you found her. Maybe she dropped out to have a calf. Maybe she'll show up sometime next fall, after her calf's weaned and has someone else's brand on it . . . maybe not. The Crows might have butchered her by then. You know how it is on the Reservation."

"Yes, I know," Sandy answered sadly. "Still, you can't figure that way without proving something. Hell, I never rustled anything in my life."

"Old General Whistlebreeches figures a lot of things differently from anybody else. Just stick around awhile and you'll find that out. He's coo-coo, I tell you. This whole goddam outfit's coo-coo. Everybody knows that."

I wondered whether Tom included himself as part of the outfit, and remarked, "Of course, their hiring you doesn't do much to change that reputation, either."

"They don't have to hire me unless they want to," Tom said.

"And you don't have to work for them unless you want to. Why don't you work for some other outfit, if you think this one's nuts? . . . Why do you hang around at all? You wouldn't be missed, lots of the time, like tonight, or last night. What's the attraction? Do you just love cattle, or is it something else?"

"Mind your own damn business," he snapped.

"You mind yours and we'll get along all right with ours."

"You won't have any business to mind if you let the old General run it for you. He doesn't know whether he's afoot or ahorseback half the time. Look what he did to his own business, and look how he's starting on yours right now, losing a cow the first night out. Maybe she's got a calf, too, running around slick. He wouldn't know, or care. With all the fancy rustlers on the Reservation, you've got a fat chance of getting your calf back. You can imagine how long it'll stay slick after it's old enough to brand: just about as long as it takes to heat an iron. But what does a cow and calf mean to the General? Nothing! He just docks the cook's salary and keeps right on studying the Civil War."

Then Sandy roared at Tom, "You think I can't tell whether a dead cow's just calved, or was going to? What the hell're you trying to say, anyway?"

For a moment I thought he was getting ready for battle and I tried to ease the situation by remarking, "Sandy says the cow's dead, and that's good enough for me. He didn't say anything about her having a calf. He could have told whether she'd dropped out to have a calf, couldn't he? There's no calf involved, and no rustling."

Tom ignored the logic and resumed his attack on Al from a slightly different angle. "I don't give a damn if you lose a cow, or calf, or both," he said, bored. "Just like the General." He seemed to doze off again, and I hoped the subject was closed, but after a while he flared up once more. "If he thought the cow wasn't dead, why didn't he go back and see for himself? I'll tell you why. He's just too goddam lazy to ride a few extra miles to see about a cow he didn't have to pay for himself. He'd rather just read about the Battle of Bull Run and dock the cook's salary instead."

The conversation was getting a little loud, and I wondered whether Al could overhear it. I eased up on my elbow to get a look at his tepee. It was lighted, and if he overheard us, this certainly gave him no concern as he was still turning over the pages with sublime detachment, as recorded by the flickering shadows.

"Say, fellers," Sandy piped up politely, "I didn't mean to start an argument. I wasn't griping. I was just asking. I'm not getting paid much, and if I get docked for the cow, I won't be making anything out of this whole trip. You know how it is. So I was just asking. But I guess it'll turn out all right, so let's forget it."

"I'll see that it turns out all right, Sandy," I told him.

He rolled over and soon dropped off to sleep, apparently relieved at the idea that his pay was safe and that he wasn't being suspected of rustling.

I lay there, listening to the rain pattering on the canvas, pondering my general situation and wondering how in hell people got the idea that all was moonlight and serenading in the cattle business, until I went to sleep myself.

Back at the ranch the next day, Sandy got his check, and there was no deduction for the cow.

XII

The Cheyenne Range

AT OUR BRANDING with the partnership V Bar C brand, both Tom (who had by then reverted to his old self) and old Fred Lauby approached me with the greatest consternation. They could see nothing but ruin ahead for me. Their grounds were that I, as a partner of the bankrupt White Cattle Company, assumed all its debts, which were enormous; that, since I had put up all the cash, the brand should have been registered in my name; that the Whites could claim returns from these cattle equally with me; that they might mortgage the cattle for a personal loan, or be helpless if creditors decided to attach them.

I was at that time about halfway between being annoyed at and being touched by their persistent and uninvited comments on my personal affairs. It was obvious, however, that they were trying to help me and that these conditions did exist. I could not deny facts and was able to answer only that I didn't think any of these possibilities likely to materialize.

Whereupon, they cited my total ignorance of the ranching business; stated instances where just such things had occurred in other cattle deals; reminded me of the part which pure mismanagement had

played in bankrupting the Whites; mentioned the
dangers from rustling, especially on the Reservation, and expounded upon the sometimes terrible
winter losses which, from time to time, were inevitable unless ample provision could be made against
them.

They then lectured me, alternately, upon the utter inability of the White Cattle Company, in its
current state, to provide for any protection against
these dangers. The company had a chronic shortage
of winter hay, which that year was more acute than
ever. Fred had been out sizing up the haystacks,
taking measurements and making forecasts as to the
prospects. It seemed that the whole hay output on
both the White ranches would average only a scant
half-ton to the head when divided among all the
cattle, whereas it should be three times as much for
safety, but not less than a ton in any case. It seemed,
moreover, that there was no hope of their increasing
the hay crop, as there was no money for labor, for
new machinery, which was sorely needed, or even
for patching up their old reapers, stackers and hay-
racks. Fred added that the irrigation system was in a
deplorable state, probably past repairing as a result
of neglect, and that all weather indications, as he
had observed them over a period of thirty years,
pointed to a drought that summer.

There were, of course, also other pitfalls to the
cattle business, and upon a few of these Tom and
Fred touched lightly, but just enough to send cold

shivers down my spine. They wound up their dissertations with a joint assurance that the one thousand acres which the Whites had put up as capital to balance my cash, valuing it at $10 per acre, was completely worthless, dry hill land, composed of rocky crags without access to water and, therefore, unmarketable by itself. Also, probably, mortgaged.

In short, the whole picture could not have looked blacker, I thought, and laughed a hollow laugh. My only comforting thought was that these two men were not world-beaters themselves and probably were in no position to lecture me upon how to be a successful rancher. Furthermore, they both had axes to grind with Al White. Tom, the Don Juan, had his jealousy complex; and Fred, I felt sure, was thwarted in some plan he had laid to get the cabin which Al had given to me. And so their testimony was probably misleading to a certain extent and, in any case, showed only one side of a story, the other side of which I would have to get from Al. But there was a certain disturbing element about what they told me, because much of it was a question of fact which could easily be proved or disproved, concerning which there would be no point in their lying to me. Al, I hoped against hope, would be able to refute some of this lugubrious testimony. Even if he couldn't refute it all and had to leave some of the picture looking fairly hopeless, there was still the chance that the guardian angel who looked after Al in hopeless situations might still be around.

In the meantime, my die being cast, I could do nothing about it but put up a front, disagreeing with their theory that I had walked into a trap, even though I could not deny my legal responsibility for untold thousands in back debts of the bankrupt cattle company. I sought to bolster my front with the thought that, insofar as losing my investment was concerned, except for the good laugh which my family would have on me, I need not be too worried. But I did secretly wince at the prospect of having the income from my trust fund attached and being put in a ridiculous position with my former guardians, who had taken a dim view of my actions, anyway.

I decided upon a course, to start out with, of keeping quiet about my fears. I would put my faith in Al and in the advice of the bank's livestock official, delivered with the cattle; I would trust to luck in as cheerful a manner as I could muster up; I would set to work with a will, learning everything possible about cattle, horses and ranching in general, so that gradually I could check up on the facts with which Tom and Fred assailed me and, surely, find some way to cope with them. These things decided in my own mind, I was able to relax a bit.

After branding and resting our cattle, we trailed them up to the Whites' Cheyenne leases, where we were welcomed with great jollity by Herbert White and his crew of neighbors, who were all working from the community roundup wagon. This was a standard roundup wagon, but it was not moved very much, as wagons were in former days. Rather, it was a sort of semipermanent line camp, being moved only between the Indian leases on one side of Tongue River, the National Forest leases on the other, and the home ranch.

The wagon itself was a four-horse affair with the regular accommodations for cooking and serving meals built into a large boxlike structure in the rear end, containing drawers and compartments for utensils and supplies. The back of the box was hinged at the bottom and let down to form the cook's worktable. In transit, this was buckled up and the cookstove carried behind it on two special supports projecting from underneath, while the stovepipe was carried (bolted together in sections) on a long pole passed through it and strapped to the side of the wagon.

Connected to the wagon by a canvas fly overhead, at the rear, was the mess tent, measuring possibly 15 by 18 feet. The canvas also went forward over the wagon, supported on hoops, to protect our food supplies and other contents. A big oaken barrel of drinking water was fastened to the left side of the wagon and kept filled from a nearby spring, while from the right side there protruded a stout iron arm with a hook at the end, from which hung a freshly killed quarter of beef. Near the entrance to the tent were a basin and buckets of water, with a couple of towels fluttering from the guy ropes at that corner.

The tent was cozy and warm inside, with a mixed aroma of food and sagebrush. The stove was snapping cheerfully and leaking a little pungent blue smoke. Behind it was the cook's corner, in which, by custom, no one but the cook himself was ever supposed to set foot. There, where he kept his roundup bed and personal belongings, he was blocked off by the stove, the woodpile, an array of buckets and pans for dishwashing, and the mess table. At mealtimes, the food and eating paraphernalia were set out on this table, past which eaters filed in orderly procession. There was little else in the mess tent except bedrolls, strapped up, ranged around the edges for use as seats in the daytime, whenever anybody had time to sit down.

Other bedrolls were lying around the wagon, under the fly at the sides, with some, and a tepee or two, out in the open. A short distance away was the rope corral into which the horses were run to be caught for use, twice a day, and the bed wagon, used for hauling the roundup beds, tents, tepees and other impedimenta of an outfit on the move.

As we came within sight of the wagon with our cattle, riders were sent out to relieve us and invite us into camp. There we found ourselves in a sort of cozy supper club in the mess tent, with everybody knowing everybody else, not necessarily because they had been introduced, but because they were all there for a common purpose understood by each, and everybody was a neighbor or friend of every-

body else. Whether they had been introduced or
not seemed to make no difference. Actually, I was
the most strange, the least known, least accomplished and most out-of-place individual there.
And yet, when I walked through the tent flap, it
occurred to me that I had never enjoyed such a
feeling of warm, totally unsophisticated welcome,
of friendliness and of "belonging." It seemed to
surge over me, emanating from a dozen or so people, most of whom I had never seen or even heard
of before, and none of whom said anything special,
either to or about me. They just looked up and
smiled, or looked up and didn't smile . . . or, perhaps, didn't even look up. But regardless of what
they did, or didn't do, they just made you feel at
home.

Except for our little Janie, the assemblage was
practically straight male. However, I was surprised
to find two very beautiful young women present,
both about the same age, which was somewhere on
the borderline between the teens and twenties.
One, whom they called Laura,[30] was a flip, flashing
blonde. Her partner, Babs,[31] was a somewhat quiet-

[30] Fictitious names given to two beautiful teen-age daughters of Carol St. John of Virginia. St. John was a partner of
Charles Taintor, owner of the Flying V ranch, some five
miles up the river from 4D. The St. Johns lived at the FL
ranch of the Brown Cattle Company, still a part of the
Brown holdings. The old Flying V has changed hands and
names; now it is known as the Diamond Cross.

[31] On Babs see above.

er brunette. But both were so bubbling over with
life, so completely enmeshed in the work at hand
and so obviously a part of it that their presence
seemed to flow naturally into the background of
men without creating the slightest disturbance sex-
wise. I tried not to stare, but I had never seen anything like this. They were treated exactly like the
men and exchanged verbal fisticuffs with them in
their own lingo, though not a profane word was
expressed or even hinted at. Among the general assemblage there was, apparently, no thought of their
being anything but good fellows. But, to my un-
trained mind, it was impossible to overlook the fact
that they appeared to be physically perfect young
women, so far as I could judge from their tight-fit-
ting blue jeans and the attractive strain placed upon
their blue cotton work shirts.

I learned that Laura and Babs had a tepee not far
from where I had intended to roll out my bed, and I
strained my ears that night to see if I could hear
what they were talking about, and whether they
might have any male heart-interest around camp.
But my efforts were completely fruitless and only
led me to smiling at myself as I dropped off to
sleep.

In the morning our routine started: the incredibly aggravating roll-out call at four o'clock; the
clean, sweet smells of dawn, unsullied by a single
atom of carbon monoxide; the gastronomic mon-
strosity but sheer joy that was breakfast; the sport of

trying to rope one's pony from the whirling cavvy in the rope corral (and finally, after several unsuccessful throws, having some cowpuncher, only half watching, drop a successful noose for you as if he had done it by accident); the saddling and polite, quiet waiting for the last man to mount; the gay, sympathetic understanding when someone had a difficult horse. . . . It was all in such good taste, so practical and so right, without anybody having been taught out of books how to do it, that I wondered why people generally, in all other walks of life, couldn't behave the same way. Finally, Herbert White, his profile quietly indicating both a modest knowledge of authority and the usual contour of his tobacco plug, would lead off toward the highest divide, his riders clustering about him at a canter, everyone seeming fresh and happy in the blaze of dawn, but still businesslike and listening attentively for Herbert's orders. He sent the riders off, two by two, down this creek or that, in search of cattle to be driven to a predetermined point. Every rider readily complied with his instructions.

Weeks passed thus, in the course of which I found that Laura and Babs, despite their boyish veneer in camp, were perfectly normal girls a few miles away from camp, but would put up with no nonsense in any way holding up the business of gathering and working cattle as long as they were, technically, on the roundup. Fortunately, the roundup did not last all summer.

That summer, fall and winter I stuck around pretty close to both the White ranches—Herbert's and Al's—taking part in their seasonal operations and mixing into any activity where I thought there was any chance of learning to do something connected with ranching. I stayed with the spring roundup until it was over, learning about "rastling" calves, branding and castrating, in all of which operations we were helped by Babs and Laura. They continually amazed me by their calm efficiency and utter matter-of-factness, no matter what the job was: riding circle, holding a herd, branding or keeping tally. They roped and saddled their own ponies, hardly ever missing a throw or catching the wrong horse. They knew how to build and tend a fire for the branding irons; just how hot to let an iron get; the correct irons for the men to use on different animals; all the different brands and earmarks, and how to apply them. If need be, to spell someone off, either of them could grab an iron and slap a brand on as quickly, neatly and painlessly as almost any hand on the wagon, seeming perfectly at home in the yellow, acrid smoke of the operation and knowing just how long to leave the iron on to kill the roots of the hair and produce the faintly pink mark which shows that the animal has been effectively, but not cruelly, branded. They could size up a herd for numbers, or an animal for weight, with surprising accuracy and could count cattle under any conditions, whether still or on the move.

There was a very simple and effective method of tallying the calf situation where a bunch of mixed bull and heifer calves would all be earmarked with a crop and the bull calves castrated. The bookkeeping on such occasions was based on the principle of saving all the ear-tips and testicles. Half the latter showed the total number of bull calves; the balance were heifers. The testicles were carefully saved for culinary delicacies and known as "mountain oysters," to be consumed by all of us straight-faced, and without any attempt at witticisms so long as the girls were present.

When the spring roundup was over and the wagon pulled in, I transferred my energies to the haying: pitching, stacking, buckraking and generally learning all I could about hay, including the amounts which would be available for winter feeding at the different ranches, and thinking how far away winter seemed as we sweltered through long days with the mercury only a few degrees on either side of the 100-mark, although nights were usually cool enough to call for light blankets.

During the early summer Al made a deal for some purebred Hereford bulls to sire our next year's calf crop, as our present calf crop ran to only 60 per cent, which was not too bad under the adverse circumstances, but needed improving, as to both numbers and quality. Somehow, with his old Oliver typewriter, he got in touch with Ringling Bros. Circus interests, who owned a very fine bull ranch in Montana, and, as a result, the V Bar C Durham cows could thereafter look forward to larger and much more aristocratic families.

After haying came the fall, or beef, roundup, in which the herds were gathered again, brought down to winter ranges near hay supplies and such beef steers worked out as were ready for shipping to market. There were no V Bar C steers worth shipping that first year, so we decided to forgo trying to get any return from our investment at that time, pull in our belts, pray for an easy winter and hope to make up for it in added weight next season. But I went on the fall roundup anyway, to gain experience and see how others fared with their fall beef shipments.

When the community steers were shaped up into a beef herd, we trailed them to the railroad, a four-day drive over much the same country as I had seen on the quest for our cows and calves, only under different conditions. The range grass, instead of being in its greenish, growing stage, was now cured and it waved like a silver sea in the crisp and chill November breezes. Gone were the timid prairie flowers' flecks of color, replaced now by autumn's blazing wild plum thickets, from which coveys of sage hens and prairie chickens rose and flapped away at our approach.

At the end of our long trail over the range, there again were the symbols of civilization: the gleaming rails, the metallic clashing of couplings, the loco-

motive—always, however, called "The Power"—
spewing great cottonlike mushrooms of vapor into
the frosty sky and marking the end of our drive.

XIII

In Business

THAT YEAR I decided to go East for Christmas and the cold midwinter weeks, when activity in the cattle world was at its lowest ebb, consisting of the methodical feeding of hay as conditions required. But when Fred got wind of this plan he shook his head in dismay, and from that moment until my actual departure the happy anticipations I had entertained about seeing my family and eastern friends again were systematically dulled by predictions of impending calamity if I should leave the ranch.

Fred explained, in his terrifying paternal vein, "You see, son, the Hard Winter of nineteen-nineteen started off just like this." He pointed to some tall cottonwoods with a few leaves still clinging to their bare limbs. "Leaves stayed on the trees all winter, that year. First we had a dry summer, just like this year. Then we had an early freeze. Now you take this year. The ice harvest was away too early. Of course, that don't say the big snow's coming, like in 'nineteen. That year we didn't see a green living thing from the end of November till the end of April. It was sure a fright, I'll tell you. Cattle bawling around here all winter with nothing to eat, coming right up to the house—I seen them on the front porch—looking for food. Starving to death every day, tipping over by the hundreds. God, it was awful! Got so you hated to look out the window, for fear of staring them in the face. You'd even dream of the poor critters, just standing there at the window, looking in at you and bawling."

"But you say you don't think the big snow is coming again this year?" I asked hopefully.

"I wouldn't say for sure, son. But it might. All I can say is, if she starts in snowing within the next two weeks . . . watch out, boy! These things is likely to happen about every seven years or so, and the time's getting mighty close." He seemed to be figuring up the intervals between disasters of the past and added thoughtfully, "Sometimes six years, sometimes eight or nine."

I was hoping that it might be one of the latter cycles this time and that, with all my other worries, at least, I would be spared the humiliation of winter disaster and a financial crash in my very first year of business. But even this sandy foundation of hope was being slowly washed away by the continual trickle of words coming from Fred.

We were sitting in the cabin, bathed in a warm glow from the potbellied stove, watching gray clouds gather over the hills beyond the river. The cozy warmth of the stove buoyed up my struggling hopes, which had a natural tendency to rise, anyway, but gathering clouds and Fred's chill trickle of conversation had the effect of pulling them all down again. I sought an ally in my player piano, sitting down to it and loading its breech with the most cheerful music rolls I could find.

"Yessir, them sure looks like blizzard clouds to me," Fred would get across, in a soft-pedal interval.

The piano would offer, "Just around the corner there's a bluebird on high, sitting on a rainbow in the sky . . ." or "Look for the Silver Lining . . . whene'er a cloud appears in the blue . . ."

"Goddam that pianner! Can't you choke the son-ofabitch down a little? Hell, a man can't hardly talk in here. I was saying, if you let Al run your business while you're back east, you might as well kiss it good-bye. Now if it was me, I'd tell the whole outfit to kiss my . . ."

The words and music rolled majestically by: "Somehow, I'd rather be kissed . . . to the strains of Chopin or Liszt . . ."

Of course, snow did come within the next two weeks, it then being nearly the middle of December. I couldn't see anything terribly alarming about that, or about the fact that we had to feed out a little hay. Nevertheless, Fred remained perturbed and continued his almost daily inspections of the feeding pastures, trotting through them slowly, disdainful of both the quality and amount of our winter hay supply, but letting Fashion munch upon it freely. In the conversations which followed, I could see that he was looking ahead, not only at the cattle situation in which I was becoming involved, but also at my future in general and of his own possible connection with it. One morning, as I was riding the pastures myself, he joined me and, with a great big crescent of a smile stretching from ear to ear, laughed, "Come on, boy! If you've got a little time, follow me. I'll show you something you ought to see that's worth looking at."

He took me across the river and up Dead Man Creek three or four miles to a little clearing in the timber, where someone had started to build a cabin and then abandoned the project. Dismounting, he took his fence-mending tool from the nosebag tied to his saddle horn and tapped several of the logs smartly, pronouncing, "Sound as a dollar. Every one of them."

"They look like fine logs, all right. Well, what about them?"

"Naturally, it ain't none of my business what your plans is going to turn out to be in the future. But I figgered you're going to be here for some time now, what with being in the cattle business and all. Perhaps after a while you might get married and want a bigger cabin, or something. And just in case you *did* want to build on . . . why, here are the logs, already cut, peeled and seasoned. Just the right size, too. And they can be bought cheap. Thought I'd mention it to you before you leave for New York."

I felt that by some fate of the gods I was being

sold a house, but it looked like an interesting proposition, so I suggested measuring it off.

Fred already knew the dimensions. "These logs is cut eighteen and twenty-four feet," he announced. "That gives you a room about seventeen by twenty-three on the inside. Just a handy size. Imagine how it would look added on to one end of your cabin, T-shaped, with a big open fireplace in the middle of that side wall. Why, you'd have the finest log cabin in the country! You could use the old part for a kitchen, sleep in here and have lots of space left over for that pianner."

There was some sense to what he said. But I shook my head.

"You don't want them, then?"

"Not just now."

"All right." There was a trace of disappointment in his voice. "I kind of thought you'd want them." He mounted Fashion and turned back down the creek.

As we neared home, he elucidated apologetically, "I had a reason for bringing up the deal now. I figgered, if you wanted the logs at all, now is the time to buy them, as I could skid them across the river for you while you're back East, before the ice goes out."

I thought he might have cooled off a little on the price by that time—perhaps even a hundred dollars or so—and therefore asked outright, "How much?"

"Eighteen."

"Eighteen what?"

"Eighteen dollars."

"Per log? . . . Let's see . . . That would come to something pretty high, considering how short some of them are, between the windows."

"No," he explained. "Eighteen dollars for the outfit."

It made no sense to buy a house for eighteen dollars or, at least, the major materials for it, even F.O.B. Dead Man Creek. So I asked, "How do you figure that?"

"I know old Henderson, who owns them logs. Made him an offer of fifty cents a log for them, and he took it. She's nine logs high, and four sides. That makes thirty-six logs at four bits. Eighteen dollars."

"How about the ridge log?"

"I told him you wouldn't pay for that at all, because it has a bow in it and we couldn't use it. He's making good on it by throwing in the other two roof logs."

I shuddered to think what opinion Henderson must have had about me. "I didn't notice any bow in the ridge log."

"Well, as a matter of fact, it's so slight you can't notice it unless you sight along from one end." He winked at me and continued slyly, "Just between you and me, I think we can turn the bow up and shave an inch or two off the top with a drawknife, and it'll make a hell of a good log."

I secretly congratulated myself on having drawn

Fred as my minister of finance and never doubted
his motives again. Of course, I bought the logs. A
few days later I made out a check for $18 and
marked it, "Full payment for house," hoping that
someone in Wall Street would be thoroughly mystified. I sent the check by Fred, wondering if he
would get a brokerage commission out of it, but did
not meet Henderson. I was ashamed to.

This practically free acquisition of the Henderson logs appeared to Fred as something of a *coup
d'etat*, giving him a neck-and-neck position with Al
in the matter of providing me with low-cost housing.
He was very proud of having made the deal, as I
could feel from his remark, "Won't old Al be surprised when he hears that you've got another cabin
now, bigger than the one he gave you? . . . Better
logs, too!" he added, mentally pinning a rose on
himself.

But Al, when I mentioned it to him, didn't seem
so very surprised. He merely looked up from his
book and, without seeking to take any credit, remarked casually, "I told Fred some time ago that
you ought to have those logs up there. When are
you going to build?"

"Soon as I can get back out here, in the spring."

Al put down his history book and looked up at
me with his sad little smile. "That reminds me.
When you do, I've got a lot of good galvanized iron
pipe in the hayloft over the barn. You might as well
have it. Then you could hook up with our artesian

well and have water up there in your 'new' cabin."

"Thanks a lot, that sounds like a big help."

He was not only giving me a thousand or so feet of pipe, but also his water and the use of his pump to force it up the hill. This would put him another jump ahead of Fred. I was certainly doing well on both my housing and utilities projects.

"You see, long ago," Al explained, "before we went broke, I planned to put a reservoir up on that hill above your cabin, to supply a stock-watering trough below. In fact, I even started digging it, so you'll have that much work done, to begin with."

I climbed up into the hayloft to look for the pipe. It struck me that a hayloft was a strange place to have pipe, anyway. But I kicked around under the hay and soon found it, good inch-and-a-quarter pipe. Then I remembered the nasty loan association which had put the Whites out of business and was waiting, vulture-like, to close in on their ranches, and I was glad they hadn't found the pipe. Al was not only generous to let me have it, but also not so dumb, for once the pipe was laid four feet underground, they would certainly never find it.

When Fred heard about the pipe and my plans for a water system, he elaborated upon them and it became immediately apparent that he had again elected himself chief surveyor and engineer for the project. He reappeared one morning with his surveying telescope, sticks and rags. "You see," he began, without waiting to be commissioned for the job, "we've got to figger on the pipe running under the new house, so we'll have to lay that part of the line before we build. Then we've got to figger how far the bottom of the reservoir will be above the cabin, to make sure it's enough to give you good pressure without going further up the hill. And we want to make damn sure that the reservoir's on your own land, too."

Already, he was fretting about whether or not I was going to be edged out of something by the Whites, even after Al had given me the pipe. It seemed to be a regular mania with him as he set his stakes, waved his rags, peeked through his telescope and shouted instructions through a little stubby megaphone he had made by cutting down an old-fashioned phonograph horn.

After the survey, we staked and measured off a general plan, showing roughly the layout for house, reservoir and pipe lines. Not until the last detail of this plan was decided upon would Fred hear of my packing to go East. "I want all these things settled before you leave," he announced, with executive efficiency, "so there won't have to be any arguments or writing back and forth, afterwards." He was moving right in on the job; there was no doubt about it.

The last suggestion he had to offer was launched just as I was leaving for town. Like most of the others, it was casually eased into the general trend of conversation. We had been talking about his hiring Cheyennes to do the digging for trenches and the reservoir. "You know," he said, "while all this digging is going on, you know what I'd do if I was you?"

"What?" I felt that, whatever it was, it would not cost very much, so there was no harm in asking.

"I'd dig me a little root cellar first, and then build the new addition over it, so's you wouldn't have to go outdoors in wintertime to get to it."

"What in hell do I want with a root cellar? I'm not going to be putting up any vegetables."

Fred shook his head doubtfully. "You never can tell, boy." He paused a moment and then added, "You can put all kinds of things in a root cellar. It could be fixed up real nice inside, with rock, at the same time the stonemason builds the fireplace, and have a concrete ceiling and an iron trap door you could lock when you go away, in case you'd want to put valuables or something down there and not have to worry about them. Fireproof, too. Now's the time to figger on it. Not after you get the house built."

I could see that he was right on the economic angle and decided that he might be right on the principle also. A hidden trap door in the floor could be covered by a rug and furniture. Its very invisibility would alone be the greatest guarantee of safety. "All right, Fred," I decided, "let's figure on it," without really being able to imagine one single thing for which I could use it.

As I finally pulled out, Fred sidled over to the

car and smiled wisely. "Say, if you could send a
charred oak keg back from town on the mail stage,
it might be a good idea. I could start some pretty
fair moonshine aging for you, for next year."

I stared at him inquiringly and he proceeded
with the details. "Haven't you heard the news?
Haven't you noticed anything extra special down
there at the ranch lately, especially during the ice
harvest? All those hot toddies Al was asettin' up.
Where do you think he got the booze from, all of a
sudden? You know, Al can't buy booze."

It was true, Al couldn't afford much whisky and
there had been a lot of it around during the icing.

"Might have been Tom's booze," I suggested.

"Tom's . . . Hell! You'll never see that sonofabitch turning loose any of *his* booze, especially for
Al White!"

This also, I could see, was true. "Where did it
come from, then?"

"You know Sammy Doyle, in town, don't you?"

"Yes."

"Well, Sammy's lost his source of supply . . . the
big still up near Hardin. It got pinched, so now he's
going to make his own. Brought a couple of partners up here from Kentucky, awhile back. Real
good moonshiners. They was looking for a nice,
quiet place to run the still this winter, further back
from the main roads than that Hardin outfit was,
and they run into Al in town, so they jumped him
about letting them come out here."

"What happened?"

"They said the old General didn't talk over no deal with them, because they couldn't understand what he was saying, as he had his teeth out. Seems like he went to town to have them overhauled, and they wasn't ready when he run into Sammy and these moonshiners, so he couldn't talk very good. But the nearest they could figure out was that he didn't give a damn if there was a still on the ranch or not, so long as he didn't know where it was and could get a little good drinking-whisky once in a while."

"Maybe they ought to try him again with his teeth in."

"No, it's best to leave things lay just like they are. Everything's fine now, and the still's working, and the General don't know where it is . . . at least, he pretends not to. And there's some pretty good moonshine coming out of it. So I thought you might like to have me lay in a little while you're back East, and a charred oak keg would be just the thing, if you can send one out from town."

So I promised to send two charred oak kegs out from town by the mail stage. Fred's specifications were a five-gallon and a ten, for some obscure technical reason. By that time I was beginning to understand the root cellar project.

"Don't tell that blab-mouthed Ole what he's hauling for us. Have the kegs boxed up. We don't want this news to get around, or the first thing you know, the government men will be out here, and that won't be too good when it comes to proving up on your homestead claim."

"What in hell has it got to do with my proving up? . . . Say, where *is* this still, anyway?"

"Oh, it's just over the hill, here," he mumbled hurriedly, looking a trifle embarrassed and then getting off the subject. "I seen them setting her up. Watched the whole thing through my glass, from across the river. They're up in a coulee where they can't be seen too easy and where there's going to be lots of snow until pretty late in the spring. That's what them Kentucky moonshiners wants, lots of snow for their distilled water. Seems like that makes the best whisky." He was waxing interested in the details of distillation.

"Are they on my place?"

"Well . . ." He scratched his head and frowned. "They *might* be awful close to the line, but they don't know it. They think they're on the Whites' land, and they may be. I haven't run the line on them yet, but I'm going to, and I'll let you know. It's best not to go poking around there too much now. Let them get settled down for the winter without no worries, so they can put their minds on their work."

I left for the East with a vague suspicion that I might be in the moonshine business too.

XIV

Spring on Tongue River

BEING OF AGE when I got back to New York, I no longer had to cringe before the trustees, beg them for my income nor ask their advice or permission before doing anything. It was a grand, free feeling to be able to stride down Wall Street and drop in to see them casually, just because I liked them.

They were, of course, curious to know what had become of my schemes. These I laid before them as brightly and cheerfully as possible (omitting, of course, any mention of my prospects as a moonshiner.) I stressed a happy outlook in general and skipped lightly over the dire predictions of Tom Bryan and Fred Lauby,[32] mentioning Tom's name freely, however, as I thought it sounded well in

---

[32] The author's self-appointed caretaker, Ted D'Auby, who moved in with him ostensibly to assist in the building of his cabin, and didn't move out until his death, twenty-three years later. Ted D'Auby was found by Albert G. Brown in January of 1947, frozen in a sitting position on his bed, presumably the victim of a heart attack. Some consternation resulted from trying to remove Ted's huge physique from the cabin. Since he was frozen, the removal party found it necessary to take an axe and tap his extremities together. This action mightily upset one lady who kept screeching "Don't whittle on poor old Ted, Don't whittle on poor old Ted." No one would have appreciated the sight more than Ted D'Auby.

Wall Street and would impress them. I even let them think that, perhaps, someday, this great financial name might be linked with my own in the founding of a really great cattle enterprise. But, just as I thought I was making a good impression, one of my elderly friends took the wind out of my sails by remarking casually that he had seen Tom's tycoon grandfather shortly before and remembered that the old gentleman had mentioned having a namesake grandson out West somewhere who was a great nuisance and family disgrace and had been relegated to more or less the status of a remittance man.

Abandoning that tack, I strove to come about on the winds of fortune by referring glibly to the great cattle companies founded by conservative British and Scotch capital, involving millions of acres in the Northwest, hundreds of thousands of cattle and enormous dividends paid out during the very first years of their operations. This did not go so well, either.

One of the dear, elderly gentlemen of the trust company pressed the tips of his long, pale, conservatively manicured fingers together and asked one profound, searching question: "How many of these great cattle companies still exist in your area?"

Of course, the answer was, none, which had not occurred to me until then. But when this and other hard, cold facts began to dawn on me as a result of our talk, I marveled at the great extent to which my former outlook on the cattle ranching business had changed in the short space of a year, despite what I had considered my sound and conservative thinking. How was this so? Could Al have deliberately concealed well-known facts, to deceive me? It seemed incredible, and as I sloshed along through the slushy streets to the subway station, I thought of him, probably at that very moment sitting comfortably by his fireside, reading history and rolling cigarettes, with not a trace of guile about him. I knew it was impossible.

When I got back to my college club, there was, nevertheless, a letter with more dark forebodings—this time about shipments of salt and barbed wire I had ordered. I went upstairs to my grim little room, sat on the bed and pondered.

There was no escaping the fact that I was in a quandary, and I had to admit it, at least to myself. Perhaps I had overestimated the glories of the cattle-baron era, as described to me by Al White during his flights of ideology about the Scottish-British boom days, his tales about the fading fascinations of the once-famous Cheyenne Club—that organization unique in the annals of America, where the sons of noble lords from across the seas mixed freely with hard-bitten men of the range under the mellowing influence of easy riches—and his fond but somewhat unfounded theory that this way of life would come back again. Of course, I was forced to conclude that it wouldn't come back any more than the old days of the South would come back. That was just one

more of old Al's pipe dreams and, if I were going
to be practical in my operations out there, I must
disregard it.

Gradually I began to see some rhyme and reason
to the dark forebodings of Tom and Fred; to their
incessant talk about winter and hay; to the lesson of
the dry cows I wanted shipped, but which were being squeezed through the winter, anyway. Some little items of barbed wire and salt that had been
charged to me began to take on a different meaning,
as did Fred's measuring of haystacks and all the
other hints which he and Tom had thrown my way.
Each was a straw in the wind, and although nothing
serious had come of them, they were indications, on
a small scale, pointing right down the old flowery
path to ruin. I decided that the dry cow question
should at least have been referred to me and that, if
I ignored this deliberate concealment of information, others more important might follow later. I
decided also that the barbed wire and salt incident
would have to be looked into. If the Whites were
using V Bar C cash and credit for other cattle, that
called for a showdown.

Out in Montana that spring things looked entirely different. After the first few hundred lungfuls of
tangy air had dispelled the last traces of Pullmanitis
and I had had a good night's sleep at the town inn,
followed by a hearty breakfast, the world seemed to
smile again. I stepped out on the porch to survey it.

There it was, sure enough, seeming, in its spring finery, bigger and better and happier than ever. The modest lawns about the inn and the railroad station across the street were emerald green. Birds twittered gaily in the tops of the tall cottonwood trees. Even the clanging and banging of the switch engine was inoffensive, while the great cottonlike puffs which it shot into the dazzling blue sky were positively beautiful. Several thousand sheep which had just been unloaded came surging down the street, bound for some pasture on the edge of town, and filled the air with their plaintive baas. The warm spring sunshine and the clean range smell from sagebrush circling the town made one's blood tingle with reassurance that there was nothing whatever wrong with the western scene. It just shouldn't be viewed through a dreary little city window two thousand miles away.

I had put in an order with the operator on the party telephone line to get a call through to the White ranch and, while she was fighting gamely for it, I strolled uptown to get my beautiful new car out of storage. There was a certain satisfaction in checking it over and contemplating how much better a ride it would give me out to Tongue River than I had had on my first trip there, with Ole in the doomed mail stage. Everything was accounted for: tools, chains, rope, shovel, extra gasoline cans. It purred contentedly on the way back to the inn, where the operator was holding a call from Betty.

"Yawl better hurry on out here!" Her voice vibrated welcome. "We got fried chicken and cawn pones for supper. Abbit says to tell you the cattle been doing just fine and we're sure glad to have you back . . ."

I called the post office to see what report they might have had from Ole on the road conditions. There had been a heavy rain and Big Spring Creek was flooding. But it was going down fast and they thought I could get across by early afternoon. There were no bridges over the creeks in those days and one often had to sit at the fords for some time, waiting for flash floods to subside. I started out carefully, traveling mostly in second gear, sometimes in low, and presently reaching the Big Spring Creek crossing.

There was Ole, standing beside his stage on the other side, scratching the back of his little bulletlike head under its battered old Stetson and contemplating the swirling waters.

He waved a wild welcome and shouted, "I tank she's safe enough now, boy. Anyvay, I make a try . . . Here! . . . Ve drink to luck!" And he tossed a pint of moonshine across the creek.

I caught it, took a small swallow of the vile stuff, choked and tossed it back.

Ole drained the bottle down by about a quarter, smacked his lips and exclaimed, "Vunderful visky!" Whereupon he took to his cab and soon had the little truck shivering violently under full throttle.

"Here I come!" he yelled from the window. "If I get stuck, you pull me out." And he charged the stream with a will, disappearing from view behind a great splash, but presently emerging on the other side with his engine still running. "Nodding to it!" he grinned. "Now you try!"

My new Cadillac proved itself.

When I was on the other side, he threw the pint bottle back to me. But this time, I kept it, for his own good, and called back, "Ole, I've got a terrible cramp in my arm. I'll keep this safe for you." He started to blow up, but I was soon grinding on my way again.

I got to the ranch in plenty of time for supper, feeling, as I approached it (even in spite of its obviously run-down condition), a certain sense of homecoming which amazed me. Ted and Janie White ran out into the yard when they saw the car approaching, shouting a childlike welcome and bursting with the news that Tom Bryan had gone to Paris, France again and was going to send them some postcards of the Eiffel Tower.

Al was openly delighted that Tom had gone to Paris and said he didn't mind doing without electricity for a while. For, of course, the electric light plant was not working.

Betty bypassed the subject of Tom and went about fixing up some mint juleps.

The old fireplace was still going, as Al liked to use it right up to the brink of summer. We gathered

around it with our mint juleps and I asked how the
winter had passed. Al twirled a cigarette thoughtfully and looked pitifully at his toes, as if ashamed
of something.

Betty filled in his silence. "Well, we had an easy
winter, all but a couple of weeks. Cattle did just
fine. We didn't lose more than one or two head that
fell through the ice. Didn't even feed out all the
hay. I got a chance to go avisitin' down in Mississippi, so I took it—being my first trip away from here
in six years—and I missed out on the cold snap. But
Abbit can tell you all about that." She looked at Al
significantly.

My fears for the cattle were relieved, but I could
see that something was troubling Al, who twisted
his toe about and smiled his sad little smile without
saying anything.

"Go on, Abbit, tell him," she prodded.

"What happened?" I asked.

"Nothing much," Al evaded. "Just a little trouble
with the plumbing. We'll get it fixed up soon." He
smiled sweetly at his wife.

"What yawl mean, nothing much?" She shook
her mint julep at him. "Like to've had no home left
when I got back . . . that's all!"

"Betty, how you do run off at the head about an
old boiler! It wasn't any good, anyway. I was planning on getting a new one next year, when our shipping money comes in. Might just as well get it this
year. Reckon I'll *have* to."

"Listen at him! You might think we were Rocke-
fellers. He's just ashamed to tell the straight of it.
Go on, tell him what happened, Abbit!"

Poor Al was so visibly uncomfortable that I said,
"Never mind," and looked around the room casually, "It can't be too serious. Everything here seems
to be the same as usual."

"Yawl just don't look in the right places. Take a
look at the steam radiators. All cracked. Froze up
and busted. Go down in the cellar and take a look
at the furnace. Same thing."

Al was gazing out the window with a faraway
gleam in his eyes, gently puffing a Durham cigarette. It was obvious that he had detached himself
again from the present, in preparation for his wife's
"running off at the head" in more detail, which was
immediately forthcoming.

"Well, sir, I might have known better than to
leave two men alone heah with a couple of kids. I
never knew it to fail: every time two men's left together, they either get to fighting with each other or
they get to raisin' sand together. Couldn't have
picked two worse ones than Tommy and Abbit.
First I heard of anything was a letter from my sister
saying Ted and Janie were down at their ranch for a
while, as there was a cold snap on and it was closer
to school. But I smelled something wrong and came
home right now. Well, sir, when I got heah, it was
still sure cold. I saw Sandy afeeding the cattle down
in the meadow, but no sign of Tommy. Must be he's

dead drunk in the bunkhouse, I thought. But no, sir, he wasn't in there. So I looked in his bedroom in the house. No Tommy. Well, I thought, Abbit's shot him at last! . . . No fire in the kitchen stove, and the house was real cold. So I shouts out, 'Who's heah?' No answer . . . Just a kind of spooky sound coming from the living room, like bones crunching. Then I thought, maybe it's the other way round: maybe Tommy's shot Abbit and disappeared. I thought of that old dead sheepherder they used to tell about finding in the deserted cabin, with a bob-cat gnawing on his bones . . . GAWD!"

Al returned to the present long enough to remark casually, "Now, Betty, you know I don't go around shooting people, and nobody's out to shoot me. That was all decided the time Cliff Stanley went wild. You just got shooting scrapes on the brain." So saying, he resumed his contemplations and was soon riding over the purple sage again, trailing a huge beef shipment with no mortgage on it, and headed for the railroad—preferably his own rail-road, which he still believed was going to be built.

Betty added a little bourbon to his glass, as if to prepare him for further strain, and charged on with her narrative, pale-blue eyes flashing and the eve-ning sun glinting in her auburn hair. "I grabbed the old kitchen shotgun and came asailing through the dining room into the living room right now. And heah was Abbit in that old rocking chair yonder, drawn up real close to the fiah, just areading and

arocking and astamping his feet. He had on his angora chaps and his dad's old buffalo hide coat and a
fuh hat. He'd piled the fiah all up with coal and
splattered some around every which way, even under the rocking chair, so he was acrunching it as he
rocked, reading a History of the Confederate War.
. . . Mad? I just snatched that old book away from
him and he hasn't seen it since!"

Al winced at her lack of respect for the tome and
consoled himself by remarking quietly, "You'll
never find the other two volumes." He had hidden
them somewhere for safety.

I had hoped, for Al's sake, that this was the end
of the story. But such was not to be the case.

Betty continued: "When I got back, there wasn't
any heat and there wasn't any light, as Tom had quit
and gone to Paris-France, and I don't blame him."

"Considering pictures I've seen of Dorothy Stett,
I don't blame him, either," Al interposed wryly.

"Never mind about Dorothy Stett. If you'd just
learn to run that electric plant without practically
executin' yourself every time, maybe we'd have a
little more light around here."

I tried to make peace. "As far as the light plant's
concerned, I'll be glad to go down and get it started, Betty." I made a move from my chair.

But she motioned me back into it. "Never mind
right now. We got lots of daylight left. I just want to
tell you how helpless two men can be when you got
the right two men. Well, sir, here they was, Sandy

and Abbit. The house all frozen up: no water running, no light, no heat. They were packing water in
buckets from the well and eating out of cans. Sandy
was sleeping in the bunkhouse and he had the stove
going over there, but Abbit just had the open fiah
heah. He'd sent to town for a couple of oil stoves,
but he couldn't get them going. So I says to him,
'Abbit, how come this house is so cold with these
two new stoves heah?' And Abbit says, 'I reckon
they're just no good, they won't light. I've tried and
tried.' So I looks in the fuel tanks of the two stoves,
and they're both plumb empty. Not a speck of oil
in either one!'"

Al gave her an imploring look over his shoulder
as if to say, "Let's not go over all *that* again!"

But Betty persisted. "So I says to him, 'Abbit,
you fill those stoves up right now and put one in
the bedroom if you expect me to sleep there. It's
mighty cold in that bedroom!' Then Abbit packs
one of the stoves into the bedroom and goes out to
the engine house for some coal oil. Instead of coal
oil, he comes back with a can full of high-test gasoline for the Coleman lamp, puts that in when I
wasn't looking and lights the stove. . . . Well sir,
what I mean, that stove went to crackling and pop-
ping right now, and spitting out blue flames all
over. Al's gloves were soaked with it, so they went
up in blue flames too, just as he was saying, "There,
it won't be so cold now, dear.' Next thing I knew,
he'd pulled off his gloves and thrown them on my

bed, so that started ablazing, too. I ran for the mopstick and was abeating around with it and trying to beat him away from the stove, which sure was offering to explode while he was still a-peeking under it and poking at it. But Abbit, he says, 'It isn't going to explode at all,' and he picks it up with a couple of towels, calm as can be, and carries it out, flaming and spluttering sparks all through the house, and sets it down in the yard and goes to peeking under it again, and poking it. So I yells at him to come on in and help me beat out the fiah. Well, sir, he hadn't gotten more than ten feet away from it when that stove blew up and what I mean, it blew up! Abbit, he just looks back over his shoulder at it and trudges right on in the house. By the time he got in here, I had the fiah out."

Al relaxed somewhat and gave his wife a weak smile, as if to say, "Well done, but thank God, *that's* over!"

In the intermission I again seized the opportunity to wrestle with the mechanical problems of the engine room, and, making some remark about the sinking sun, repaired to that dismal cavern to learn what had baffled Sandy, now that Tom Bryan had transferred his light-giving talents from there to Paris. Actually, the trouble was nothing more serious than a piece of barbed wire which had been inexpertly introduced into the ignition system and was grounded, so I soon had the old ranch house glowing again, and, when I presently came up from

the Slough of Despair, the whole situation seemed
infinitely brighter.

The spring roundup dispelled what few fears remained from my winter's accumulation. Of all the
neighboring outfits joined with us in the community pool which ran the wagon, not one could produce cows and calves any better than ours, nearly
all of which answered the roll call (excepting only
the negligible winter loss already mentioned). The
cows had fattened up noticeably even to my un-
practiced eye. Nearly every one had a large, husky,
big-boned calf by her side, speaking up for Al
White's foresight in buying the Ringling bulls: a
little deal he put over quietly, almost when I wasn't
even looking. To my great surprise, some of the old
cows, which I had given up as barren, had excellent
calves with them, and even the others were very
much the better for having been held. The market
was rising continually, spring rains had been good
and grass for the year was practically assured. In
fact, it was quite obvious that every animal we
owned was paying its way, and more. There was no
doubt about it, the company was going to make
money its very first year.

These simple truths dawned on me in the saddle,
as I rode along with the cowpunchers—often beside
a silent and dreamy Al—or wrestled in the dust
with roped calves, to down and hold them for
branding, castrating and vaccinating. They were

truths which just sort of slipped up beside me and suddenly said, "Hello!" Nobody had to point them out in a classroom. Nobody even mentioned them, least of all, Al White. He had a quiet way of taking everything for granted, but taking credit for nothing. Even when I tried to compliment him on his good judgment in holding the dry cows, he would have none of it, simply shrugging his shoulders and saying, "It was easy to see, the way things turned out after you went back East, last winter."

I jumped him about the shipment of salt over which Fred and Tom had made such a fuss. "We fed some of it out. The rest is all there, in the shed, ready for next winter. It seemed a cheap buy at the time," he explained. And when I got around to looking up the prices of salt, I found out that he was right. As to the barbed wire which Fred Lauby had seen shipped in, Al explained that he hadn't ordered very much. "Just enough," he added roguishly, "to prove up on your homestead. You know, one boundary of your claim is the same as one side of a pasture where we winter the V Bar C's and it ought to be fenced, for the good of both. I figured we could use the fence there and charge it to the company, so it'll come off taxes. We won't make the fence line too solid; just good enough to get by until after you prove up your claim. Then we can rip it up and sell it, after it's done time for you and the V Bar C outfit. The White Cattle Company needs some fence up on the Reservation. I was talking to Fred Lauby about it, while you were in New York. Thought of using this same fence. The White Company would pay the V Bar C just about what it cost in the first place."

So, that was all there was to the villainy against which Fred and Tom had warned me! How could I have doubted poor old Al? I felt somewhat small about it as I watched him jogging along beside me on his fat pony, rolling Durham as he went, completely innocent (and, fortunately, ignorant) of the charges brought against him.

"You know," he continued, "I never cared too much for fences. The country was much better off when we hadn't any. But there's one good thing about a fence: it has two sides. And in this particular case, that comes in mighty handy for you."

I had not been on the roundup wagon very long before my last fear was gone, dispelled not only by the facts as they turned up, but also by a certain quiet dignity in the personality of Al himself. Surely this was not the stuff of which dark and crooked schemes were concocted. I felt that, no matter what my quandary at that time might have been, or how many of the old-fashioned faults it may have included, it still did not have that sickening factor common to most of the great cattle failures; the sinister, avaricious master mind overtly plotting against the unwary investor. That just wasn't in Al. And I felt that no matter how black and hopeless other factors might appear, I could stomach them.

Being now as completely happy about my prospects as I had been miserable about them only a few weeks before, in New York, I began to ask myself the question: what in heck kind of business is this, anyway? One moment, all signs, calculated according to the very best formulas, point to disaster. At another moment—not unreasonably distant—all signs, based *not* on formulas (however reliable) but on indisputable facts, personally observed from the saddle, point the other way while, in the meantime, all pertinent factors involved remain substantially the same. What sense, I thought, does this make?

A roundup wagon is a very busy community with, it always seems, many long hours of work and a very few short hours of rest and no hours, of any length, in which to worry about the outcome. One gets so physically tired that, by evening, there is no potential left over with which to carry on the process of worrying. If one tries to worry, it is just a fizzle. Nature draws blood from the brain, which does not need it, to aching muscles, which do. The result is oblivion, and happily so.

A pleasant fog seemed to settle over my being. It was so pleasant that I felt it couldn't be real. Something within me said that it had a catch; that it wasn't real; that I was simply so tired I couldn't think. Perhaps, I reasoned, it was a sort of fake Nirvana, an attempt at escape into the life of a lotus-eater, which was bad because, someday, the supply of lotus flowers would run out. But when I looked

about me, there seemed to be lotus flowers everywhere, as far as the eye could reach.

The lotus flowers never ran out, either on that
roundup wagon or any other I ever knew. Lotus
flowers are, after all, nothing more than being use-
fully occupied during the day and healthily tired at
night, plus the factors of good food, good sleep and
good company, no matter how primitive the latter
might be.

One day Ted and Janie White rode up to the
wagon, bringing us mail and messages. They were
delighted to have received, several weeks before, the
promised postcards of the Eiffel Tower from Tom
Bryan, which they brought along and exhibited
gleefully all around camp. They said that Aggie
Lester, the schoolmarm, had received one too and
also some other postcards of Paris, but that she had
refused to tack up the other ones in the schoolhouse. They couldn't imagine why, but she had acted very flustered about them and had torn them
up. Tom wrote that he was having a wonderful
time in Paris, hoped the light plant was working all
right and would soon be back. But he wasn't, yet.

In my mail there was some further, explanatory
news from Paris, in the form of a newspaper clip-
ping from New York, stating in true newspaper par-
lance how the "wealthy scion of one of New York's
most notable families, the grandson and heir of Jonathan Thomas Bryan . . ." etc., had been forcibly
removed from a French liner in Cherbourg harbor

as she was about to sail, by a squad of gendarmes on telegraphic complaint from the Paris police. He had been held awhile in the local jail at Cherbourg. But he had been unable to straighten the matter out and, after the ship had waited a few hours for this distinguished passenger, she had been obliged to sail without him, taking with her, however, his close friend and traveling companion, a certain Mrs. Stett. A short but piquant reference was made to Dorothy Stett's pending divorce action, in which the "scion" had also figured, and this was followed by the concluding statement that Tom, having proved most uncooperative toward the Cherbourg police, was remanded to Paris for more questioning.

The trouble seemed to be that Tom, in writing certain checks, had lost track of his bank balance and then consoled his creditors by promising that the unlimited family resources in New York would automatically take care of the situation. Some over-cautious Frenchman, however, had upset the apple-cart by being so indelicate as to cable New York, just to make sure. Jonathan Thomas Bryan had blown his top and made it very clear to the French-man that no help was coming from *him*.

Tom, of course, eventually wriggled out, as he always did, and came back to the United States. But the incident caused a prolonged delay in his return to the ranch.

About a week later—our work on the roundup temporarily over—Al and I cut our little string of ponies from the cavvy and headed for home. We wound down creeks and gullies single file, he leading, followed by our six loose horses (two carrying our beds), and I bringing up the rear. For many miles we were silent, but as we neared the ranch he spoke up. "You know, I've got a feeling that Tom's back again. And if he is, I'm going to fire him."

He was right about Tom's being back. In fact, Tom had been there for several days.

XV

Roan and Rumpus

WHETHER TOM was actually fired on that occasion, or not, I never really knew. Nor did it make much difference, as he had been fired several times before and never took it seriously. Being fired meant to Tom simply that his wages would stop for a while and that he would go to work for someone else, or just go off on a round of visits until the labor situation at the Whites' ranch became sufficiently acute for him to be recalled.

Sometimes, also, when feelings got tense, Tom would "quit," which amounted to substantially the same situation. It was often difficult to tell—when one found Tom performing odd jobs elsewhere— whether he had been "fired" or had "quit." For in neither case did he remove his belongings from the ranch and his mail continued to pile up on the chimney shelf. Usually he kept a pony or two feeding on the ranch pastures and sometimes he even dropped in for a meal, himself, preferably if Al was away. In a pinch, he would help with the chores. And eventually he would be back at the old job, sometimes because of intercessions from Betty and other times because poor Al would simply be worn down by the problem of finding someone to do the chores for such wages as he could afford to pay. Sandy Miller—our erstwhile cook and teamster when we took delivery of the cattle—was holding Tom's job at that moment, but the situation was bound to be only temporary.

Tom told me only that he was "going to be free for a while" and could help me with building on the extension to my cabin, if I wanted to hire him. The trouble here was that I didn't know where I could feed him, except down at the Whites' ranch, on some kind of paying agreement, such as I had made for Fred Lauby. But just what Tom's status might be at the ranch, and whether he would be allowed at the table, were questions to be discussed with Al White. So I held Tom off for a while—which was simple, as he was headed downriver anyway, to visit Babs and Laura—and took up the matter with Al at the first opportunity, mentioning that I was hiring old Fred again, and ringing in Tom as an afterthought.

"Sure, Tom can get his meals down here if he's working for you. There just isn't any other place for him to eat," Al said pleasantly. "I'd like to see you get that cabin finished and the water system built, as it'll do all of us good. So we'll feed Tom, and you don't have to pay any more, either."

I thanked him for this noble little gesture and wondered anew how it was that I had ever even doubted his kindly intentions toward me.

Then he continued: "You know, Tom doesn't

really bother me, except when he gets drunk and ornery. Otherwise, he's a good worker. He might be just what you want up there, for a while. There's one thing about Tom: he's good with a team, and you'll need at least two, with slips, to dig that trench. You can use ours any time, and I think there's at least one old slip out behind the corrals, somewhere."

I laid in a supply of tools and, in due time, the digging began, being performed in exemplary democratic manner by Messrs. Jonathan Thomas Bryan III, Willis Medicine Bull, Ben Lame Bear, John Wolf Tooth[33] and myself. Fred would help us once in a while with advice, direction finding or prodding a rock loose with the crowbar. But for the most part he stuck pretty close to the white-collar class, acting as our foreman, architect, engineer and general adviser, which latter we were often glad to have.

The Indians pitched their tepees at the foot of the hill by the Whites' irrigation ditch and lived there, at a comfortable distance from us. They had a wagon with them and an old squaw who cooked dreadful-looking things on an open fire and waddled back and forth from the ditch with buckets of water.

Tom, Fred and I slept in the cabin, Tom in his roundup bed, which he spread out on the floor with some hay under it, and Fred in a little iron army

[33]The Indians who worked for the author were all Cheyennes from the Lame Deer Reservation.

bed, which he had brought over from his cabin across the river. We ate our meals down at the ranch house and everything ran along smoothly.

After a few days of excavating, we were ready for the stonemason from town, to build the cellar and fireplace. I drove in for Sven, a great, bulky Swede, and brought him back with his equally bulky apparata: huge stone hammers, long chisels and bits, a keg of blasting powder. The cabin was then really crowded as we huddled together in the evenings. During the days we trudged about the neighboring hills, locating likely blocks of sandstone, which Sven blasted out and chopped up into handy building sizes, and which we later hauled with Al's team and wagon.

I knew that Sven liked his little sköl occasionally. He had been good company and a fine worker. When his job was done, I felt genuinely sorry to have him leave us and decided upon risking a little drink to wish him well. Up to that time I had studiously avoided having any liquor around, because of Tom. But as the occasion now seemed justified, I asked Fred whether we could get some good moonshine from the boys he had told me would be operating the still on or near my homestead.

It turned out that Fred had already filled one of the charred oak kegs during the winter and had hidden it in a draw about five minutes' walk from the cabin. We slipped out with a flashlight and he showed me where it was. "I've been rolling her around once or twice a week, to make her age," he explained proudly, spotting the keg with his light. He had brought an empty quart bottle along and we siphoned it full with a piece of rubber tubing. In the cabin lamplight, our sample glowed a dismal yellow. But this lack of color Fred promptly remedied by burning some sugar in an old spoon and whipping the black, gooey mess into the liquor, using a large bowl and an eggbeater. We then filtered out the carbon particles by pouring our concoction back into the bottle through absorbent cotton. "This batch is on approval," he explained. "I told them we wouldn't pay them anything for it until we had a chance to try it out."

It was, of course, a mistake to produce the whisky with Tom Bryan around. He got away with most of the quart and, when it was gone, wanted more. By morning he was really concentrating on the problem of getting it. He invented various bizarre reasons for wanting to ride in to town with Sven and me, but I told him that, unless he stayed and worked on the place with Fred, he might as well quit the job for good. And I left him there in a huff.

I spent the night in town and drove back early next morning. Fred met me at the cabin door, shaking his head ominously. There was no sign of Tom.

"We lost our workingman," he announced.

"What happened?"

"Oh, he was just spoiling for a drink and I wouldn't get him one, so he took off for town."

"How?"

"Saddled up that little bay Johnnie Shane loaned you. Said he was the fastest horse around here. Last I saw of him, he was cutting across country, headed for town on a high lope and just whipping the bay on both flanks with the loose end of his throw-rope. I had the telescope on him till he was out of sight over the hills."

The little bay was Johnnie Shane's top horse, loaned to me for the roundup, and I was very grateful for the loan. I was particularly anxious to return the horse in good shape and had been putting it off from day to day while working on the cabin. I couldn't bear the thought of Tom's whipping him all the way to town (a distance of about forty miles, even the shortest way), perhaps foundering him or breaking a leg, because of his craving for whisky.

"When did he leave?"

"Not long after you did. Probably stopped off at old man Williams' for the night. I hope so, anyway. It'll be pretty tough on the pony if he didn't. Ought to be in town by now, probably sitting right in Sammy Doyle's."

I got into the car again and headed back to town, planning how I would lay for Tom at Sammy Doyle's. On the way in, I scanned the country carefully, thinking I might be lucky enough to head him off before he got to town, and catch him at some gate, where I would take the horse away from him, unsaddle, turn him loose and set Tom afoot. . . .

Perhaps even whip him down the road a little way
with the throwrope. But he had beaten me to town.

He must have ridden pretty fast, for when I
caught up with him at the saloon, the little bay was
all in and badly lathered up. Tom had not fed or
watered him, and had him tied up in a cold, windy
alley back of Sammy's place. The poor animal
stood there faithfully suffering, ready for a good
spell of pneumonia, while Tom himself was drinking in the cellar. He had not even loosened the
cinch. The noose of the throw-rope was unbuckled
from the coil and the hondo knot—a wicked whip—
dangled at about stirrup level.

For this cruelty, I gave Tom a good piece of my
mind and told him that I was taking the pony, so he
could shift for himself afoot. I went back out to the
narrow alley, mounted the bay and turned him
around, only to find Tom blocking the way with
outstretched arms, in a blue haze of verbal abuse. I
warned him to stand aside and let me pass, but
without effect. So I unbuckled the rope strap and
took down another two or three coils, planning to
whip some sense into him. Seeing this, he suddenly
made a lightning snatch at the bridle. But the bay
reared up with a snort and Tom just missed. Then I
threatened to ride him down unless he stood aside,
but also without effect.

I could feel that, even after his long jaunt, the
horse still had a good bit of steam in him, so I let
him go full tilt right at Tom, who tried to dodge,

but was not quick enough. We hit him a glancing blow, knocking him up against the wall, where he banged his head and spluttered with rage. Pulling the pony down to a slow walk so as not to tax his strength further, I started him up the main street, through the whole length of town to a livery stable at the other end, where I could get him properly looked after. Tom followed along, raving, but at a respectful distance from my throw-rope and, of course, attracting a gallery. The one-man police force, having had much experience with Tom, fell in with the gallery and tagged along also.

When I came out of the livery barn Tom, who had been laying for me back of the door, launched his attack, swinging wildly but not too effectively and grazing me on the neck from behind. So I turned and tangled with him. It was obvious that not much more than an elementary knowledge of sparring was required to catch him off balance as he spun, practically unaided, face down into the manure. There I straddled him, rubbing his face well into it while lecturing him on horse stealing and cruelty to animals, until he pronounced himself cured. When I let him up, he started immediately for the nearest blind pig, covered with manure and blood. But the police force sauntered after him and persuaded him to rest up a bit in the friendly jail, where he was put into his regular cell, No. 3, with the door left open, although he was not allowed out of the building, on pain of being locked up.

I told the liveryman that I would be back for the horse in a few days, or send someone; that they were to grain him and turn him out in their little pasture on the edge of town, but not, under any circumstances, to let Tom have him. And, as an added precaution, I took the saddle and bridle along with me.

On my drive back to the cabin I decided not to have anything more to do with Tom. But I was soon to revise this decision, as it was impossible to stay mad at him very long.

XVI

Room for a Charred Keg

Without tom, my Indians were harder to handle. He had a way with them and was good at sign language, which he had a natural faculty for picking up and liked to use. I had come to depend upon Tom for communicating with my little crew, for old Fred Lauby had the Westerner's disdain for Indians and shunned any traffic with them.

My original crew of three Indians increased alarmingly, as word spread on the Reservation that there were good pickings up at my homestead. Before I even knew it, I had a dozen, then two dozen, camped around. They came in wagons, on horseback and afoot. They brought their squaws and papooses, flea-bitten horses and cur dogs. They hung out their wash and ghastly-looking pieces of raw meat in painfully conspicuous places between my cabin and the Whites' house. They beat softly on tom-toms at night to summon the proper spirits when someone was sick or something went wrong.

Sometimes the Indians just seemed to be visiting or vacationing. They did not all provide me with workers. But enough workers showed up—some for a day or a week, others only a few hours—that I soon had to send to town for more shovels and picks. There were Willis Medicine Bull, Charlie Sharpnose, Frank Little Sun, Bob Standing Elk and Eagle Fighting Bear. There were several other kinds of "Bears": Lame, Playing and even Weasel Bear. I had a time keeping them all straight. "Bear" was always a popular factor in Indian names of that country, as it still is (according to a late report from there mentioning a certain Bear-oh-stop-it). There were the birds: Sand Crane, Young Bird, Swallow and Blackbird. I divided them mentally into several animal categories. Then there were the "free lances" like Tom Little Old Man or Pious Red Neck,[34] whose names would not fall into any particular group and just had to be remembered. My pay-book for the summer of 1926 lists thirty-four of these noble redskins. With each I ran an account, not only in dollars but in goods. Entries have an odd ring today, such as: "August 13. Paid off with $3.90, 1 caddy Durham, 64 pounds of potatoes at 2 cents and one share in Tom Salverson's cow."

Three Indians had a share apiece in this cow, which shares were traded back and forth between them and with other Indians. Sometimes the shares would be subdivided, like shares "split" on the Stock Exchange or (what was still more maddening) reunited.

Despite these labor handicaps, the logs went up and up; the trench got longer and longer, the hole for the reservoir on the hill deeper and deeper. Af–

[34]The comment in footnote 33 applies here.

ter a while we could only see the heads and shoulders of the Indians, digging away; then, only the tops of their hats, with an occasional feather bobbing about. Finally, the only indication of their presence in the hole was the sight of earth being spasmodically thrown out of it by their shovels. When they got down to this level, where they could not be seen, interest in their work lagged. They squatted down on their heels, rolled cigarettes and let go their shovels to talk sign language. It was cool and pleasant down in the big, deep hole, especially during the heat of day; a comfortable place to work, so they were not too anxious to finish it.

At last the great day arrived when water spurted from a tap in the old part of the cabin, which I had decided to use as a kitchen. The new part was finished and, I thought, it was surely a masterpiece of architecture, from its beautiful red-shale roof to the silent, clammy depths of its little vault. The roof was not only beautiful, but practical, taking advantage of whatever moisture there might be, to ward off the sun's cruel rays in summer; acting as an insulator to retain heat in winter; guarding against sparks from the chimney and never needing repairs or painting. It was of the country and looked right against the sky, as did the red-shale hills themselves. There was nothing fussy or "store-bought" about it.

Down in the vault, our two kegs of moonshine also looked natural. There the contents could age properly, in the right temperature, and one did not have to hike up a draw half a mile away in order to swish it around or pour off a sample. Fred had figured out that detail sensibly. I don't think I ever locked the vault, or left him without a key to it, and nothing ever disappeared from it or elsewhere on my property.

Obviously, there were certain purchases to be made in town for the new addition, so we sat down with pencil and paper to "figger." Fred started the figgering by suggesting that he might move some things over from his own homestead, across the river. But the way he put it was, that it would save me quite a little money in future if we used some of his furniture for the time being, as furniture was high just then and he thought there would be a break in the market. He suggested taking his wagon when the river was low and hauling these things over: just a bed, somewhat better than the one he had been using, which was uncomfortable; a favorite swivel chair, which would be most useful for us, and a few little personal belongings which, if I didn't mind, he would throw into a suitcase. This would tide him over for the several weeks' work remaining, for he had thought up all kinds of additional projects: a garage, a coalbin, a tool shed, a brick flue for the range, drains, a cesspool and fences for keeping livestock from bashing in our windows or falling into the reservoir.

Needless to say, when he finally arrived with the

wagon, it was loaded down to the gunwales. But, with all our new space in the cabin, that didn't matter much. What if the poor fellow *did* bring over an extra trunk, an enormous Webster's dictionary, some well-thumbed picture books, stacks of back numbers of the *Pathfinder*, the other part of his phonograph horn (a useless truncated cone of metal left over when he made his megaphone), several kegs of horseshoes and a few blacksmithing tools? "We'll be needing them all," he had explained, adding that he would have put more in the wagon except that the riverbank was slippery and he was afraid that the team might not have pulled it.

First on our shopping list came the coal range. Then all the utensils of cooking, eating and executing household chores—full lines of each—followed by furnishings and miscellaneous requirements right down to a hydrometer for testing the moonshine. Our food list mentioned cases of this and that, great bags of sugar, salt and other staples. I didn't see how Fred could think of it all, but when we actually got into the stores in town, he thought of a great deal more.

We wasted no time getting to town and back on our shopping trip, for Fred was violently opposed to urban life and couldn't bear the thought of putting up with it for more than one night. "This city life gives me a pain," he complained. "Dressing up with a necktie and walking around on that hard pavement. It sure ruins your feet."

The night before the great event, he dusted off a little black medical-looking grip which he had acquired by mail order. Into this he put a change of linen, his toilet articles (including his pair of ancient English razors), a flashlight, extra matches in a little bottle, a copy of the *Pathfinder* and, on top, his necktie. Then he locked the bag carefully and put it under his bed. "There!" he sighed in relief. "Now we're all set for an early start! . . . Got gas in the car? . . . Tires all pumped up?" He was as nervous as a bride planning her wedding trip.

On the way in to town, he sat erect with his little black bag between his feet (where he knew it was safe), one hand firmly gripping the side door and one eye on the speedometer. He looked more than ever like the Duke of Wellington in his town hat, a little piece of foppery which, until the moment of our departure, he had concealed from me. It was a rather broad-brimmed Stetson, but conservatively under cowpuncher dimensions, and suggested someone in authority on a big outfit. He wore a heavy Oxford-gray suit in an old-fashioned weave and high gusset shoes which, with the necktie (when he put it on at the edge of town) set him quite apart from other men. During the entire trip, he kept his eye on the speedometer. When it registered 30, he would begin to fidget. At 35, he would lean over toward me and warn in a low confidential voice intended to conceal his nervousness, "There's kind of a bad curve up ahead, boy," or, "Watch out for this next creek crossing, it's a sonofabitch!" Twice he asked, pointedly, "Say, son, is that speedometer working right?"

As I drove up to the inn, he would have none of it, and waved me on. "I hate these high society places where they think they can get away with charging $2.50 for a room just because it's got a bath! And in the morning, they don't even open the dining room till seven o'clock. A man goddam near dies of hunger before breakfast. And it's too far from the stores. I always stay uptown at a sensible rooming house." And he directed me there. It was called the Perfect, and had a sign painted over the entrance, "Rooms and Bath. Reasonable Rates."

All of which was very true. "Bath" was correct; it had only one. Rates were certainly reasonable, as announced on another sign tacked up over the register at the head of a long, straight, narrow stairway: "All Rooms 75¢. No arguments. Pay in advance." At that price, there seemed little reason for "arguments." It was certainly a perfect place for Fred, as he was on friendly terms with the landlady—the daughter of an old-time cowpuncher, who knew a thing or two about cattle herself—and could gather from her all sorts of news over which they chuckled knowingly, but which meant absolutely nothing to me. For a moment I suspected that, in his younger days, he might even have garnered there a little hurried romance.

On our shopping expedition, Fred just naturally

seemed to assume the role of chief purchasing agent
for me. Everybody knew him in the stores, especially the older employees, many of whom had worked
on ranches or with cattle themselves. And, as he
seemed to know everything about what we needed
to buy, I was quite content to let him play this role.
At that time I had charge accounts in only one or
two stores. But everywhere we went our credit was
good: hardware, clothing and feed stores, food markets, plumbing shops or ranch supply houses.
Fred's method with all was the same: short, sweet
and definite. He would stride through the door, his
huge bulk in a peculiar, aggressive, rolling gait, nod
pleasantly to the first clerk and, the little elephant
eyes twinkling merrily, blurt out, "The boy wants a
few sacks of oats . . . How many do you want, son,
about ten?" And then, without giving me time to
answer, he would address the clerk again. "Yes,
ten'll do. Send them out on the Birney stage."
There would follow a short identification for the
bookkeeper and he would stride out again, suggesting, "Come on, let's clear out of here, it's getting
late!" By evening we had completed all purchases
and were ready for an early-morning start home.

There was always something restful and satisfactory about leaving the little town, jouncing off the
end of the pavement into the rolling range country.
Each trip along the narrow, winding earth road was
like a little adventure in itself, of greater or less
difficulty, according to the weather. One stopped

when meeting friends, to exchange a few pleasant words and the ever-popular road information. One slowed up or waved, even for strangers. And one never, under any circumstances, passed a car stopped by the roadside without pausing to inquire as to the trouble and offer help, be it friend or foe. In winter one carried a rifle and would sometimes be rewarded with a sporting shot at a coyote or bobcat. In bad weather, a tow rope, ax, shovel and plenty of matches were standard equipment.

We got home in time to unload before supper at the ranch, where Fred was the center of attraction with his detailed account of the journey. He was careful to make the point that we had accomplished as much shopping in one trip to town as any bunch of women, gabbing about in the stores, could have accomplished in ten.

Our visits to the ranch house for meals now discontinued, and we took great pride in having the Whites come to *us* once in a while for a little return hospitality. Fred, having been a roundup cook, handled the food question with great dexterity. But our food, unlike the traditional fare of the roundup wagon, lacked that pork-and-beans, meat-potatoes-coffee monotony, or the rubber-pancake-soggy-soda-biscuit combination touch. It was good, solid roundup wagon fare enhanced by the advantages of having plenty of fresh milk from the Whites' cows, lots of butter and eggs, water that did not have to be drawn from some muddy creek, ice from the ranch icehouse, plus fresh fruit and any other delicacies we wanted from town, via the mail stage. Fred did his own baking, and the excellence of his bread, pies, cakes and muffins surprised me.

In the evening, Fred loved to sink into his special easy chair, the one he had brought over from his cabin. It was an old-fashioned, swivel rocking chair mounted on casters which he kept meticulously lubricated. It was adjustable for height, like a piano stool, and for rocking tension by a spring device and worm gear arrangement underneath. In short, a lazy man's dream chair. For this masterpiece he had traded an old watch and two No. 7 Victor coyote traps, several years before. He was so happy in it that he called it his Paradise chair. In it he could slide swiftly from window to window, merely by giving a few shuffling kicks, and its maneuverability was a great aid to him when he was following some passer-by through his telescope.

After the porch had been built, he liked to move his Paradise chair onto it in the cool of the evenings and avail himself of special rests for his telescope which he had provided by driving nails here and there. He had nails for looking upriver, downriver, across the river or toward the ranch house, and they were in two sets: a higher set for standing positions and a lower one for observations from the Paradise chair. I often sat out on the porch with him, drowsily watching the evening sunlight fade on the colorful bluffs across the river, thinking more about the future of my little herd than about what Fred would be saying as he droned away. In this period, I began to have a very definite feeling that he was settling down for good.

"You know, son, this is the finest location in the world for a cabin," he observed one evening. "I've always thought that, for years and years. See how we can look down on the alfalfa fields and watch the haying. . . . Keep tabs on them feeding out the hay in winter, too. You can see everything that's going on from up here—practical things that does you some good, I mean, like that haying down there, or watching for deer signs across the river in winter, if we should want a little venison once in a while. We can even watch what everybody's up to down at the ranch. Why, hell, I can look right into the living room with this glass and see what poker hands they've got. Yes, sir, it's the finest spot in the world. Always wished I could live up here, ever since I was a little shaver."

I took this as a rather direct hint toward getting a steady job with me, but made no comment.

"You know," he continued, "when I was a young pistol, about thirty-five years ago or more, there was a cabin almost right where we are now, that I always admired for location. It was just a few yards down the hill, there, where you can see that little flat place with the rocks still kicking around. But Al, he needed firewood a few years ago and pulled the old cabin down, as it was mostly rotten anyway."

"Who lived in it?"

"An old trapper named Lanford. One of the last wolfers in this country, like Charlie Gorrie, who showed you that coyote lure, couple of years ago—remember?"

"I'll never forget the stinking stuff." I felt like retching at the thought of it. Even then the smell came vividly to my nose. Yes, I remembered.

Fred chuckled to himself. "Yes, I heard all about that. . . . Well, this old Lanford was the same kind, but a hell of a gambler, and crookeder than a ram's horn. He used to lay for the cowpunchers and freighters coming by here, or anybody he could get into a poker game, and fill them with whisky and then beat them out of everything they had. . . . Well, one night, there was a bunch of them here in a poker game. It was in the winter—way below zero, too—and snowing pretty hard. They'd hired me as a dumb kid, to chop wood for them and pack water from the river, so their game wouldn't be interrupted. I was lying on the floor, dumb-like, and they thought I was asleep, but I could look under the table and see old Lanford pulling aces out of his boot tops, the crooked sonofabitch. By early morning he'd cleaned them all out and was taking their I.O.U.'s, too. I wanted to say something about it, but knew I couldn't prove anything if he got ornery. Besides, he was drunker than hell and had an awful temper anyway, and he had a forty-five on him. So I decided to mind my own business. After a while, he said he had to go outside. So out he went, and I always thought it was to put some more aces in his boot. The others couldn't stay awake any longer, so they all folded up and went to bed, and so did I."

"Then the old boy didn't get a chance to use any more of his aces?"

"No, sir. He sure fooled himself that time."

"Came back and found them all passed out?"

"No, sir. He just never came back at all. When we woke up, about six or seven, he wasn't in the cabin, and his bed hadn't been slept in. So, after breakfast, we all went out in different directions, hunting him. There wasn't anything to go by, as it had kept snowing hard all night and his tracks was covered up, and it was still blowing a blizzard all the time we was hunting him. We never could figure out why he'd gone so far . . . whether he felt sick and lost his direction, or what. But he'd gone about five hundred yards from the cabin and fallen face down and died right there. I saw this little mound in the snow and there was his body, frozen just as hard as a rock. Must have been a heart attack. Served him right, after stealing from all those innocent fellers. So, then I told them about him pulling the aces out of his boot."

"Handy information, but kind of late for them to call him to account," I suggested. "What did they do about it?"

"Well, they took a vote and called all bets off

and divided up their own money again and burned up all the I.O.U.'s. Just emptied his pockets right out. They took another vote to forgive him for robbing them and to hope he'd go to heaven, anyway. Then they drank a toast to the old sonofabitch with his own whisky. Then they took another vote."

"Sounds like Election Day. What did they vote for next?"

"Well, you see, none of them knew how to pray, so the best they could do was vote. They was just trying to say something nice about the old bastard and help him get into heaven. But I'll bet he's still trying to make the grade, right now. . . . Anyway, they voted not to talk about it any more, but to remember it as a lesson to them all, so it would help them to mend their own ways. To this day, not one of them ever did talk about it that I know of, and after that happened, they was always the squarest-shooting bunch of men that ever blessed this cow country. Even I forgot to talk about it till now, though I wasn't included in the voting. But sitting up here on this hill and looking down at where that old cabin was, I just couldn't help remembering."

He focused his telescope on the ranch house, steadying it on one of the nails and adding, as an afterthought, "They did cut me in, though, when they divvied up on his whisky and we all gave him a farewell toast."

"What's going on down there?" I asked.

"Oh, nothing much. They're just lighting the

lamps. It's a cinch Tom hasn't come back to roost yet, or the light plant would be working. But he will, though. He will. I've never seen it to fail."

Somehow, I kept thinking of old Lanford, and pursued the subject. "What did you do when you found his body . . . I mean, after getting your money back, and all the voting and the toasts?"

"The body? . . ." He focused a little closer. "Oh, we had a hell of a time with it," he added disgustedly. "First they put it in a haystack, so the coyotes couldn't work on it, figgerin' on burying it later. Had to keep him cool, you know. Then somebody said we could get in trouble that way. First place, we couldn't just bury him without legal doin's or an undertaker, or finding out whether he had any folks around. They couldn't have dug a grave anyway. The ground was frozen four feet down, harder than flint. And besides, if we'd done away with the body, it might look as if one of us had killed him. So, they figgered they'd have to get him to town one way or another.

"Well, did they?"

"Yes, but it was one hell of a proposition. The old bastard was just about as ornery dead as alive. He was froze up hard—and all kind of sprawled out—so he wouldn't fit any way we tried him on a pack saddle. We tried to knock his arms and legs together with an ax, but it seemed like we'd just whack an arm or a leg off, and that'd look bad for all of us. So we took him in the cabin by the stove and turned him around slowly, to let him thaw out a little. After a while, when he got pretty well limbered up, we took him outside again and draped him over the hitching rail, so he froze up in a kind of a U-shape and we could get him on a pack horse. Even at that, we had a hell of a time loading him. The first pony bucked him off and spoiled his shape. You know how horses are about strapping anything dead on them. So we molded him again and let him freeze up real tight next time, and tried him out on another horse. Finally, we got him loaded all right and lashed down solid, and two of the boys rode on in to town with him. They got well paid for it, too. Turned out that he had a lot of money in a bank there—most of it stolen, I guess . . ." He paused a moment, as if half regretting the last remark, and then concluded, "Anyway, he's dead now, so perhaps we'd better leave him lay."

Eventually, our bathroom came into being, although its odd dimensions (6 feet by 21) made it look more like a bowling alley. But Fred reasoned—and, I have always thought, correctly—that one could not mess around with architectural considerations in a log cabin, and that the proper space for a bathroom was wherever it happened to fit in. "Goddammit, boy, a log cabin's got to look natural, like it's been built, and not bought out of a catalogue."

So we sacrificed custom to convenience and, in this bowling alley of a space lined up a tub, an icebox, a depository for empty luggage and an oat bin, the latter providing a practical method of graining our saddle horses through the window in winter, without having to go outside. It also yielded an occasional field mouse, thus feeding Fred's tom-cat as well, besides providing him with a favorite sleeping place safe from the dangers of our hot-water barrel, the cover of which he had a habit of prying off, so that we were always afraid of boiling him some night.

This oat bin served its function in the bathroom for many years, with the single exception of one occasion when, after a considerable absence, I returned to find it full of coal, and my bathtub brimful of oats. This was the first of the few occasions on which I had to lay down the law to Fred. "Fred," I reasoned, "this won't work. So far as your convenience is concerned, I'm willing to go along with your ideas to a reasonable extent. If you want to keep on taking your bath in the kitchen, that's all right with me. But I'm taking mine in the bathtub, and I don't want it full of oats.

"It's the best place for the oats," he argued. "The mice can't get in. And it saves running outside for coal all the time in the winter."

"Oats in the oat bin, coal in the coal shed, water in the bathtub is what makes more sense to me, and that's the way it's going to be."

He just couldn't see my logic and came back at me with every argument in his arsenal, from a theory about freezing pipes to an article he had read in the *Pathfinder* about accidents in bathtubs, concluding, "I tell you, they're dangerous as hell, bathtubs!"

"I can't help it, Fred. That's just one of the risks you'll have to take around here."

He took it, but grudgingly, with the remark, "You and your goddam city ideas! I suppose you'll be moving the outhouse in here next."

He anticipated the event correctly, but never lived to suffer from it. He also got around to using the bathtub, on the sly, mitigating its dangers by hanging a rope from the ceiling overhead, by which he could ease himself in and out. Our differences were thus reconciled and life at the cabin went along, on the whole, very smoothly.

XVII

The Soiled Dove

FOR A LONG TIME all had been quiet down at the ranch house, until one day Betty White came panting up the hill to my cabin in a great dither. Al was downriver at the family's other ranch, where he had gone for a directors' meeting of the Company.

"Tom's back in the country!" she called out while still hardly within earshot, repeating it again after a few steps. "Tommy's heah . . . I mean, he's theah, down yonder at the post office, but he's coming this way. Be on the mail stage today. They telephoned up from the directors' meeting!"

"I figgered it was about time," said Fred. "But what's that to get all lathered up about?"

"Guess what!" she panted on, disregarding him, her eyes starting from their sockets and her red tresses, slightly disheveled, burning against a turquoise sky. Then she blurted it out, unable to wait any longer: "He's married . . . *married!*" This climax over, she seemed to relax, with a tendency toward swooning against the saddle rack.

I led her inside, sat her down and got her a glass of water with a little whisky and sugar in it. Giving her time for a few gulps, I asked, "And is his wife coming with him?"

"Gawd, no!" she gasped in the middle of a gulp, nearly spouting it out.

"Who is the . . . er . . . lucky lady?"

"That's what I wanted to know, but I was so surprised, I forgot to ask the first time. So I called them back at the directors' meeting, but the men didn't want to say what they thought over the party line, so they put Granny White on the wire. You know how sweet and kind little old Granny is, even though she's lived with cattle outfits ever since she married Abbit's father."

"Well . . .?" I suggested curiously.

"Granny called her a 'soiled dove' and you know, for Granny, that's pretty strong. So I made a few other calls up and down the river, but by that time everybody else was on the line, so I got all the details. They say that Tommy married a straight-out fancy girl from a house somewhere down in Wyoming. Her father's a coal miner and she has a brother that works for this house, getting customers . . ." She paused for breath a moment, during which Fred added indelicately, "That's what you call a pimp in those circles."

Betty took a deep breath and continued her narrative without interruption until it was exhausted. "Well, whatever you call it, this brother and the father and the girl got Tommy drunk and they got him to take out a marriage license and they bribed some justice of the peace to get them married in the middle of the night and they nearly didn't get the job done because Tommy was so drunk they had to haul him to the county seat with a load of hay in the back of a pickup truck and when they got him there he couldn't talk enough to get married, so they propped him up under a corral pump somewhere and pumped water on his head until he could say, 'I do,' and what I mean is, that's just exactly *all* he *could* say, and when he woke up he was *married*." She divested herself of this information in a steady, relentless stream, somewhat like that of the narrator in Mark Twain's *Jumping Frog* story, but with more excitement.

I couldn't help thinking what terrific repercussions this news would have in New York when it reached the watchdogs of the Bryan millions. When she had settled down a little, I ventured to ask, "Well, what's going to happen now?"

"That's just what *I* came up here to ask *you* about. Abbit, he called back from the directors' meeting in his slow, easy way—you know Abbit and how he means every word he says—and we had a long talk, and I'm half scared." She finished off the rest of her drink.

"What about? What did he say?"

"He said they'd all been listening in on the telephone line and he had a lot more information about the girl, and then he went on with a lot more details which don't look too good to me, and then he said he wouldn't have Tom on the ranch. But Tom's headed up here right now."

It seemed that the question of Tom Bryan and his soiled dove had just about broken up the directors' meeting. "Is the meeting over now?" I asked, as a conversational filler, sparring for time to consider what had best be done, as I had a growing feeling that Betty hoped I would harbor Tom and, after my scrap with him, I wasn't particularly anxious to do so. In fact, I didn't want to at all.

"No, the meeting's still going on. Looks like it might go on for hours yet. They've got some awfully important business to decide, but so far they've spent most of their time listening in on the telephone and trying to decide what to do about Tommy. He's been over there at the ranch, drunk, and trying to get in the poolroom to break up the meeting. Said he needed a horse real bad and was going to rope one out of the corral, but Abbit told the boys not to let him have one while he was drunk, so now he's shouting outside the poolroom door and abusing Abbit and trying to get into the meeting. But Abbit, he doesn't give a hoot about that—you know Abbit—and it seems like the rest of them's too busy listening on the telephone and hearing all about the girl to pay much attention to Tommy, or the business meeting either. It's real important business, too, Ab says."

I wondered what "real important business" the White Cattle Company could be up to, as Betty brought up the point again.

Fred had his telescope resting on one of the sight-ing nails and was scanning the country downriver. "No sign of the stage yet," he announced. "Maybe Tom won't wait for it, either. If he ever gets his leg over one of those horses down there, it's a dead cinch he won't."

"What's his big hurry in getting back?" I asked Betty. "He was anxious enough to get away from the ranch, the last I heard of him."

"He isn't especially anxious to get back to *our* ranch. As I make it out, he's just got to keep moving somewhere. You see, this girl and her folks are really raising sand with him. They got him to write out a check when he was drunk, for some money that he never really owed them, and they kept threatening him to make him pay more, so he skipped out of that place down in Wyoming and went up to Billings and then stopped payment on the check. Now they've got lawyers and are laying for him, so he couldn't get back here through town as he'd have to cross the Wyoming line again and they'd serve papers on him. That's why he had to come around the other way, through the hills. Gawd knows where he's headed for now!"

I had a feeling that this was my cue to step in and offer Tom a haven. But I had had so much trouble with him in one way and another that I had not yet quite cooled down on the subject and wasn't a bit anxious to rise to the occasion. "Betty," I said finally, when I could get a word in edgewise, "I don't see that there's anything much we can do about it right now. We'll just have to wait till he gets here and see what the situation is. Then maybe I can help him out somehow."

"The situation will be pretty bad if Abbit finds him here," she predicted glumly. "Abbit's plumb fed up with Tommy this time, and no fooling. I can tell just by the way he talks over the telephone—extra quiet-like, and aclacking his teeth. He just can't seem to see the sweet side of Tommy at all."

There was a guffaw from the porch and Fred's voice boomed sarcastically, "Neither can I, to give you my candid opinion, which you didn't ask for. But, then, I'm not a woman."

She shot him a withering glance through the open door, where she could see him on the porch, peering through his telescope and changing its position from nail to nail, sweeping the country downriver. But her scorn was wasted upon Fred, who remained transfixed to the eyepiece, searching his quarry, and she turned her attention to me again. "And, oh, I forgot to tell you, that's not all. Abbit called back again from the directors' meeting to say that the sheriff's after Tom in Montana, too, for something he did up in Billings."

"Somebody else he *didn't* owe money to?"

"I don't know what it is, but Abbit says they've got a warrant out for him unless he pays up."

"A real fugitive from justice, eh?" said Fred, coming in and hanging up his telescope. "Well, I don't see any sign of him or the mail stage either.

But one thing's certain: he'll be coming up the river pretty soon, one way or another. Probably on the stage, 'cause old Ole will hide him under the mail sacks, and a county sheriff has no right to stop the U.S. mail. He can't go anywhere else without a horse."

"Of course, if he had a car, he might make a run for it," Betty suggested hopefully, looking at me. "Tom's a good driver."

I shuddered to think of Tom behind the wheel.

"No chance, Mrs. White."

"Why, Mr. Fred?" She and Lauby always addressed each other with prefixes.

"Because he'd only smash it up and probably kill himself. Besides, a man would be a fool to get mixed up with the law helping a fugitive from justice and probably having his car confiscated."

Fred had proved himself a diplomat by answering Betty's implications for me and getting me off the hook about lending Tommy my car, for which I felt very grateful. "Yes," I agreed, "a car might be the death of him."

"A horse, then. Why can't you lend him a horse?" Betty pursued eagerly. "I'll bet that's just what he's coming up here for, since they wouldn't give him one down at the other ranch."

Fred answered again. "I don't think he'd be coming around *here* for another horse. Not after what happened last time."

"You just don't want to help him, that's all."

"Mrs. White, you don't seem to realize that helping a fugitive from justice is ticklish business, and we'd all be in serious trouble."

"Stop calling him a fugitive from justice!" She stamped her foot at Fred. "He's no fugitive from anything."

Fred chuckled at her show of temper and asked casually, "Why is he in such a big hurry to get going, then? What I'd like to know is: if he's not a fugitive, what is he?"

"Well, anyway, he's not a criminal. He's just having woman trouble and needs a little time to get it straightened out. He hasn't hurt anyone. He's just trying to defend himself against a bunch of crooks and blackmailers. And as for whatever it was he did up in Billings, Tom'll make good on his paper. He always does. And what do you expect, anyway, when a man's family quits him?"

"What's his family got to do with it?" Fred asked. "They're the ones that get him out of these scrapes, aren't they?"

"Yes, and they darned well ought to. If they'd looked after him right in the first place, he wouldn't be getting into them all the time. They only write a few checks for him once in a while, and it serves them right, I say. What money they pay out for Tom don't mean *that*"—and she snapped her fingers—"to them. Why, they've got more millions than almost anybody else in the world."

"It's a wonder, then, that they don't give him

enough money to have a few horses of his own, so he won't have to run around swiping other people's when he needs one real bad in a hurry, to get away from a sheriff or something."

"Tommy can always ride any of our horses he wants to. Why don't yawl go out and wrangle? There's a stake horse down in the corral."

"Mrs. White, what's the matter with your chore boy, Sandy? Can't he wrangle?"

"Why, Mr. Fred, you know what would happen if I sent him out? Abbit's put him on a special irrigating job, and if he comes home and finds Sandy out wrangling for Tommy, there's bound to be another one of these very . . . er . . . awkward situations we have down there once in a while. And I don't want any more trouble on the ranch, so I'm not going to do anything that might start some, that is, if I can help it. We've had enough shooting and fighting down there since Tommy came to us."

"There's no time for wrangling, anyway, if Tom's in such a big hurry to get away. So that puts an end to the horse question," Fred concluded.

"There are some horses in the corral right now," she pursued.

Fred trained his telescope on the corrals and announced unenthusiastically, "Nothing he could ride. Only the stake horse, and that little lame mare, and Badheart."

"Badheart's my horse. Tom can ride Badheart. Hasn't bucked for a long time now."

"Nobody's tried to get on him since he bucked Al into the watering trough, and that was a good five weeks ago. God knows what he's like by now. Most likely he hasn't changed his ways one whit."

"Well, Badheart always was a little bit peculiar."

"A *little* peculiar, did you say, Mrs. White? Why, that horse is plumb loco! That's why the boys don't want him on the roundup. They don't mind a bronc bucking, that's to be expected. But when a full-grown horse like Badheart, eight or ten years old and supposed to be broke, will let Tom Bryan get up on him with a jug of moonshine one day— and so drunk he can't hit the ground with his hat in three throws—and then the next day blows up for no reason at all, and then the *next* day is gentle as a lamb—*that's* a dangerous horse, Mrs. White, and nobody ought to get on him. He's crazy, I tell you, plumb crazy!"

"Oh, pshaw, Mr. Fred! You just imagine that. Tom can ride him."

"Well, Tom's crazy too, I think. They're both nuts, him and the horse, and that's why they get along together. In all my years of experience on the range, I never saw a horse like that, and nobody else did, either."

"It does seem queer, the way he favors drunks," Betty conceded.

"*Favor* them? He *loves* them. And I've seen him throw a dead sober cowpuncher higher than a kite."

"We'll go down now and get him before Al or

the sheriff shows up, and have him all ready when Tom comes along," I said, grabbing my hat and nodding to Fred, who rose, smiling and shaking his head dubiously as he lumbered out on the porch and unbuckled the throw-rope from his saddle on the rack. "There's just one thing, though, Betty. God knows where Tommy has his saddle, and I can't lend him mine. I need it."

"That's plumb all right. I don't expect you to lend him anything. If his saddle's not down there, use mine—the silver-mounted one, with the bridle and martingale to match. I'm not one speck afraid of losing anything."

The three of us started down the hill; Betty headed for the ranch house, Fred and I for the corrals. She promised to ring the dinner bell if there was any special news, and we were to come over to the house if we heard it.

Tom's tack was nowhere around the corrals, so we used Betty's, which made Badheart look as handsome as any picture horse on a calendar. We wondered if he was in a mood to be ridden, so I led him into that haven of comparative safety, the small, round corral, to see if I could get on him. But as soon as I put my foot in the stirrup, he threw a hump in his back and whirled away from me. I took up on the near rein, pulling his head well around toward me, while he stood snorting, showing white in his eye and quivering in the withers as I got set to try again.

"It's no use!" Fred called out. "Stay off him, son. He's having a bad spell. No use getting busted up if you don't have to. We're doing enough for Tom as it is, without going to the hospital for him. Lead that sonofabitch up the hill and let Tom top him off if he wants to. He'll smell like a jug of whisky and old Badheart likes that. Didn't I tell you the horse is plumb loco?" He coiled up his throw-rope and added disgustedly, "Ought to be shot before he kills somebody."

At this point the dinner bell rang violently, so we left Badheart in the round corral and rushed over to the house to see what late news Betty had from the directors' meeting.

She met us in the yard, shouting, "Hurry, hurry! Abbit's just left the directors' meeting on a trot, so he ought to be here in an hour or so. The sheriff's fixing a flat tire five miles the other side of Birney, but he's heading this way, sure as Gawd made little apples. Tommy's hiding in the mail stage outside the post office and Ole's fixing to get started soon as they finish sorting the mail!"

"Who do you reckon's going to get here first?" Fred asked.

"Gawd knows! But you'd better be hiding Badheart somewhere, right quick, in case Abbit does. He wouldn't think much of this idea. He'd rather see Tom get caught. . . . By the way, how's that horse acting?"

"Oh, he's in pretty fair shape," Fred said. "But he

needs someone with a little liquor to get on him. Tom ought to be just the man."

"Having a bad spell? Gawd! I hope Tommy doesn't sober up on him and get hurt!"

"Don't worry about that, Mrs. White. He'll be safe." Fred turned to me. "Come on, son. Let's get going!"

We led Badheart up the hill without any trouble. I drove the car out of the garage, but there wasn't any chance of getting the horse to go in. He balked, kicked, reared, plunged, and not even a hatful of oats proved of the slightest avail.

"No use trying to force him," Fred warned. "It won't do any good. And even if we could get him in there, he might go wild later and cut himself on the tools. We've got to put him somewhere else."

I drove the car back in again and suggested, "Why don't you just stake him out behind the shed, where Al can't see him when he comes in?"

Fred shook his head. "This is no stake horse."

"Hold him, then. It won't be very long before Tom gets here."

"You think I'm going to make a jackass out of myself, holding the crazy sonofabitch all rigged up in *her* fancy silver-mounted outfit, behind a barn in full view of the road and have everybody going by laughing at me?"

It sounded as if he expected a great concourse of people to be going by, all of a sudden. "Who's going by, except Tom and Ole?"

"If you're so goddam sure, why don't you hold him?"

"All right, I will." So I took the reins and spoke softly to the horse, scratching him a little on the neck to quiet him down. I felt that Badheart was really wondering what this was all about. "As a matter of fact, why should either one of us stand here at all, when there's a perfectly good gully over there, not a hundred yards from the cabin?" There was, indeed, a steep little washout hard by which would easily hide a man and horse from sight of anyone not riding practically right to its edge, which no one was likely to do.

"Get on down in there with him, then. That might be a good idea."

"The only bad part about it is that I can't see what's going on around here, or who's slipping up on us. I'd feel a lot sillier getting caught holding a horse down in a hole than up by the shed, where I might have just ridden in."

"Don't worry about anybody slipping up on us. I'll see to that. And besides, it's a lot better for me to be in the cabin alone when Tom shows up. This whole thing's complicated enough as it is, without having you and Tom doing any more fighting around in the cabin, like I heard you did in town."

I could see that he was for keeping Tom Bryan and me separated, and acting as arbiter between us. "All right," I said, "have it your own way," and led the horse down into the gully.

Fred returned to his lookout post on the porch and got his glass into focus. First he reported Al coming through the lower meadow on a high lope. "His horse is sure lathered up. . . . Now he's going into the house. . . . I guess she'll keep him in there and give him his Civil War book, so he won't notice anything going on outside. The battle smoke from that old-fashioned black powder gets too thick to see through five minutes after he starts reading!" He sighted the mail stage at a distance and kept his glass glued on it until it deposited Tom at the ranch gate. "Tom's just crawling out from under the mail sacks now."

Tom's spare, wiry form emerged from the truck and weaved about uncertainly as he rubbed various sore spots on his anatomy. Then he headed downhill toward the ranch house. But Fred, calling through the old sawed-off phonograph horn, caught his attention and waved him over toward the cabin. They had a short conference, during which Tom, now hatless and somewhat threadbare, seemed to be shaking his head in disagreement. Then Fred headed for my gully alone, consternation written across his face.

"Well?" I inquired.

He squatted on his heels beside me, nervously fingering his phonograph horn. "Bad news, boy," he said, gloomily.

"What's the matter?"

"He's drunk, all right. But he's not near drunk

enough to get on Badheart. I don't know what to advise you. I don't want to be responsible for any accidents around here, especially on your place, with things like they are between you and him."

"Badheart's quieted down a lot," I said hopefully. And indeed, the big black was standing peacefully at the bottom of the gully, just where I had dropped the lines, with his head meekly lowered a little. "You know how he is after he's been saddled awhile."

Fred glanced grudgingly at the handsome animal, with some disdain but no comment. Then he turned to me and asked, "What next? It's up to you."

"Take Tom inside and give him a few shots. When you think he's ripe for Badheart, bring him out here. I'm sure it'll be all right."

"He won't come inside, after what happened between you and him in town. Says he has to be invited by you and no one else."

"Well, goddam him, invite him! Tell him I told you to, only he hasn't got an engraved card about it because I have to stay out here holding his horse."

Fred went back to the conference, returning in a few minutes.

"What news?" I asked, as he approached.

"Well, son, he wants to talk to you, but he won't tell me what it's about. Says it's private business."

"I'll be right there. Here, hold this horse." I put the reins in Fred's hand.

"Now, boy . . ." He nudged me in the ribs. "No scrapping. Take it easy. Tom's in bad shape."

I could see that he was in bad shape long before I got to him. He was having the nervous shakes and looked at the ground just in front of me as I approached. Then, pathetically, he put out his hand. "Gee, Duke," he faltered, "I'm sorry about all the lousy mess between us."

The new name by which he then began calling me was, and still is, unexplained. It seemed to prevail mostly when he had the jitters.

"What of it?" I said, shaking his hand.

"Gee, Duke," he repeated hopelessly, "I guess I haven't got a friend left but you. I never expected to find you waiting here for me . . . with a horse! I thought you'd never let me have another horse."

"I wouldn't. Didn't Fred tell you what horse?"

"Maybe, but I didn't catch it. What difference, anyway? You've got a *horse* for me, haven't you? That's the main thing."

He was so foggy that there was no point pursuing the horse question, so I quickly changed the subject by asking, "How about a snort?"

This suggestion elicited intense enthusiasm, and we went into the cabin slapping each other on the back, he repeating, "Good old Duke!"

He stretched out on my bed in the cabin while I went down the ladder into the vault to bring up a copious sample of moonshine whisky from my best charred oak keg. When I emerged from the depths and saw him there—gaunt, ill-fed, tattered, penni-less, practically friendless, and pursued like a hunt-ed animal—I wondered what sense it made. He was just a maverick, belonging to anyone who could put a brand on him. What brand it was, no one cared. He didn't either, any more.

After several stout rounds, the tale of his mar-riage came out. He finished it up by explaining, ". . . So I told this guy Tony off. I asked him, 'Now, for the last time, will you please get your daughter away from me? I don't want her. I wouldn't touch her with a ten-foot pole.' And Tony says, 'If that's what you think about my little girl, what did you marry her for?' So I said, 'Who mar-ried her? You dirty, lying—' And then he swung at me." Tom rubbed his jaw where there were traces of battle, and continued, "Well, when I came to, there it was, marriage license and everything, in-cluding a check they said I gave her as a wedding present. Five hundred dollars. I still don't know how they did it."

"Is that the check you had the . . . er. . . . trou-ble with? Betty said she'd heard something about a check."

He looked down at the scuffed toes of his boots, embarrassed. "No, that's another one, up in Bill-ings. I got up there on a cattle train, soon as I could stagger over to the freight yards and catch one. I always heard they have some pretty good lawyers up there. I tried two or three, but none of them would bother with me, and they all wanted money in advance. I wired the family, but they didn't even answer. . . . Well, I had to eat and get out of town somehow, so I cashed a check at the hotel, but they telephoned the bank about it and found out I was overdrawn and started making a big fuss about the few measly dollars, when they know they're going to get it back, anyway. By that time I was heading down the Yellowstone, so I guess it did look kind of bad for me."

"Afoot?" I asked.

"No, by train. Bought a ticket this time and was lucky enough to catch a local headed east. Got off at Miles City and ran into a traveling salesman headed for Ashland in a little old Ford, but he didn't know the way and wanted company, so I went along with him. But by that time the hotel had set the sheriff after me. I borrowed a horse and saddle from an old dry farmer down there who knows the Whites and said if I worked here I could ride him as far as Birney and turn him loose in the pasture behind the post office. So when I got there, I went over to the Whites' downriver ranch to clean up. And what do you think I found?" He took a large gulp of moonshine which, I thought, should be the finishing touch to put him in just the right condition for getting on Badheart without any trouble, and added, "A big cattle meeting. All the outfit was there, in the poolroom, even Granny White. They're cooking up some scheme, I tell you, and you'd better find out what it is. I tried to bust in there and get some information. Didn't have much luck, but I heard rumors that the outfit was sold out to their old Uncle Ebenezer down in Louisiana somewhere, who's an ex-Mississippi River steamboat gambler, and I'll bet he's got your cattle mortgaged right now."

This somewhat imaginative speech confirmed my diagnosis of Tom's approach to perfection as a jockey for Badheart. I would have liked to have heard more, but time was slipping by and old Fred would be fuming in the gully. So I got up and said, "Well, if you really need a horse, we've got Badheart all saddled up for you, out here in the gully."

"Good old Badheart!" said Tom affectionately. "I wish they wouldn't call him that stupid name."

The big black took a whiff of Tom and gave him a welcoming nuzzle. Tom stepped right up on him, swinging easily into the saddle without any trouble, and rode out of the gully shouting back at us, "So long! And thanks for everything. I've got to be going now."

"Where to?" I called after him, feeling a sudden pang of remorse at letting him ride off aimlessly into the hills when, only a few moments before, he had been trying to give me what he considered useful information about my cattle prospects.

He drew up and, pathetically at a loss to answer, scratched his hatless head. "Oh, I don't know exactly, but I guess I'll find some place."

I knew just how he felt. "Look," I called out, "why don't you stay awhile? Maybe tomorrow we could figure out a better plan."

"By tomorrow I could be in the clink!" he answered gaily.

"If it's the sheriff you're running away from, it's no use. He'll catch up with you sooner or later, and it'll be all the worse. Hang around awhile and maybe we can patch things up."

He laughed. "Haven't got a *sou-marquis* to patch anything up *with*."

"If it's just a question of cash, I can—"

"Look!" Fred's booming voice interrupted us. "What's this coming up the road?"

"That's the sheriff now," said Tom, dismayed. "That's his car, all right."

I had been hedging, hoping in the future to keep clear of Tom and his troubles, knowing that fixing up one of his situations only paved the way for another. Also, there was never any telling as to what substantial sums might be required to smooth over his misdeeds. He looked so miserably unhappy that I had avoided asking him details about the check. Now, however, it began to dawn on me that, whatever the situation, it had better be cleared up immediately. For if Tom now streaked for the hills under the very nose of the sheriff, with Betty's horse and my connivance, the inescapable day of reckoning would involve us all.

"It's too late for a getaway now, Tom," I said. "If

that's the sheriff, he's already seen you—*and* us. He'll be up here asking questions as soon as he gets finished down at the house."

Tom dismounted and peered down at the ranch house, looking more hunted than ever. "I guess you're right," he agreed dismally.

"Come on inside and take it easy," I suggested. "We'll get this fixed up somehow."

"Gee, Duke, I really feel lousy about it," he apologized, in an almost touching tone, and sounded as though he really meant it.

We unsaddled the horse and turned him loose, stowing Betty's tack out of sight in the garage. Then we went back to the cabin. Fred stood guard on the porch, with his telescope. Presently, he announced, "Here he comes out of the house now. Yep, that's the sheriff, all right, I can see his badge. Pretty nice-looking sort of a feller, too. . . . I suppose he'll be coming up here next. . . . No, he's not getting back into his car. . . . Looks like he's going to have a look out around the corrals first."

Tom registered each news flash with a slight twitch as he paced the floor in silence.

The time for some kind of action had definitely arrived. It would be inhuman to let the sheriff come up and take Tom from my cabin in irons, on top of all his woman trouble. I took a wad of bills and a blank check from my desk drawer and headed down the hill to intercept the sheriff at the corrals. He was poking around the barn, a big, rotund, jolly man with a ready smile. He was coatless and had a bright metal badge affixed to his belt. "Anything I can help you with, sheriff?" I asked.

"Oh, hello, son!" he said pleasantly. "Well . . . I don't know whether you can or not. You live in that cabin up on the hill?"

"Yes."

"Seen anything of a bad boy around there? . . . Not *too* bad," he added apologetically, as if to spare my feelings. "I hear he's a hell of a nice kid when he's sober, but just can't help himself when he's drunk and does these things. But they say he always fixes them up afterwards, when he gets a chance."

"He's ready to fix this up right now, but he's pretty sick and can't see anybody."

"Well, now, the poor feller doesn't have to see me if he doesn't want to. I've been kind of hoping I wouldn't have to catch up with him until he had a chance to get out of this little trouble. We've got a lot of mutual friends up and down the river and they all speak right highly of him, except when he's drunk. Even the police in town put in a good word for him on the telephone, so I don't feel like I'm chasing a criminal. I'm a family man myself, and I know how these young fellers fly off the handle once in a while, without meaning no real harm. So I don't have to actually catch up with him, as long as he'll make good on his paper. Such a small amount anyway, it's hardly worth making a fuss about."

This was the first cheerful remark I'd heard all

day and it helped me screw up my courage to ask, "How much?"

He mentioned a modest sum, well within the bankroll I had in my jeans, and I paid it off. He gave me a receipt for the money, Tom's bad check and a big smile. "That's the way I like to see things fixed up," he said. "Tell the boy to hurry up and get well and stay sober. . . . Say," he added as an afterthought, "is he the boy from that millionaire outfit back east that got married the other day, by accident?"

"Yes, that's Tom Bryan."

"Well, he's getting pretty famous, isn't he? Now I see why he's not feeling so good. He's sure got a lot of sympathizers up and down the river, especially among the cowboys. They say that woman's got a hell of a temper. . . . Well, I guess I'll be going back to Forsyth now."

"Won't you stop by the cabin for supper?"

"No, thanks, son. I ought to get this report in tonight. Some other time, maybe, when I'm not on official business."

A feeling of relief came over me, both because the matter had been finally resolved and because the amount was not crippling. Tom reimbursed me for it within a reasonable time.

The atmosphere at the cabin took on a much lighter vein after my return with the news.

"Guess I've got some good friends left, after all," Tom said, more cheerfully. "You two and Betty."

XVIII

Cattle Train to Omaha

THE LEGAL repercussions of Tom's matrimonial blunder, and their attendant publicity, both east and west, were terrific. Many and violent were the statements issued to New York newspapers by his old tycoon grandfather, already goaded to superheated fury by another member of his brood who had cornered the market on a certain Wall Street stock of which the old pirate was short. On the western front, Tom's bride was spluttering, threatening, suing and pursuing through a battery of lawyers that made it very hard for Tom to go anywhere. At the White ranch, he was *persona non grata*.

Much of this storm he rode out in my cabin, thus coming to be a fairly steady visitor. I always felt that he sought to repay me by gathering data which he considered to my advantage and helping Fred with the continual detective work they pursued in order to keep me from falling into the traps they imagined set for me.

One day they both came to me, saying that they had followed up Tom's suspicions about the directors' meeting and had uncovered facts of the utmost importance to my success as a cattle rancher. It was indeed true, they revealed in dark, foreboding tones, that Uncle Ebenezer,[35] was transferring his activities from the Mississippi River to the Tongue. He was, they explained, a sharper of the first water. "Take my advice," Fred repeated several times, "remember, *he'll bear watching!*"

Actually, Uncle Ebenezer was no news to me. I had seen him, on and off, about both the White ranches, where he visited in summer. I couldn't see anything unusual about his coming back to the country for another visit. I knew him slightly as a middle-class southern small-businessman, aged about sixty-five, with a penchant for figures and a reputation as the family's financial genius. Exactly why he should be so classified, or in what form his financial brilliance manifested itself down in the swamps of the South, was not quite clear to me. I understood that he had some modest interests down there: landowning, storekeeping or such. I knew nothing of his youth, which seemed rather remote. He could have been a river gambler for all I knew, or anything else. To me, he was just a thin, tired, drab and somewhat seedy little old man who occa-

[35]Uncle Ebenezer is the fictitious name given to William B. Powell who came from Mississippi. He was the father of the two sisters, Anna May and Willie B., who married Albert and Joseph Brown, respectively. After that hard winter of 1919, Powell refinanced and took over as the President of the Brown Cattle Company, leading it back to solvency, while wisely retaining the now highly valuable mineral rights.

sionally had the very normal urge to flee the summer heat of his native swampland and visit his relatives on their nice, cool Montana ranches, bankrupt though they might be. The idea that, at his age, he should start out to be a cowboy, or run any kind of cattle outfit, was to me just a little farfetched. I suggested to Tom and Fred that the old boy was only coming North again on one of his usual vacations.

Their theory, however, was vastly different: Uncle Ebenezer was coming to Montana for good, and he was coming to fleece me. For this purpose, he had sold out his interests in the South, borrowed some capital and persuaded friends to invest with him. Thus financed, he had gained control of the practically defunct White Cattle Company by buying up from its creditors, for a few cents on the dollar, all its obligations, exchanging them for stock at crash prices and then buying up whatever other stock he could get after having established the low market for it. For this business and to elect Uncle Ebenezer president, the stockholders' and directors' meetings had been called. As a result, Uncle Ebenezer was now boss of the White Cattle Company, and therefore, of its interest in the cattle which I had bought and paid for in our little subsidiary partnership on a 50-50 basis, although for this interest they had paid practically nothing. Many were the blood-curdling rumors of Uncle Ebenezer's heartless business ethics, and it was only to be expected that they would now be turned against me. "That's why

we're warning you: *he'll bear watching*," Fred repeated. They were both terribly concerned over my
predicament, especially since I was so new in the
country.

I might have been new in the country, but actually I was doing much better than either of them. My
cattle venture was then in its third year, making
money and going strong, despite all their previous
forebodings of disaster. I hinted at this fact casually,
but not suggesting a comparison between any of our
various achievements.

"Sure, it's making money," Tom agreed. "That's
why they're trying to get it away from you. You
ought to be able to figure that one out."

"And it's going to make a lot more money," Fred
chimed in, "what with cattle prices going up every
day, and all those fine calves you branded this year,
from the new bulls, and last year's steer crop from
them ready to ship this fall, and the break in the
winters we've had for three years running. . . .
Sure, it's going to make you more money. Old Uncle Ebenezer's got that figgered out and he wants his
share of it, or more than his share if he can get it.
Just you watch and see. And, as I tell you, boy, *he'll
bear watching*."

This state of watchful waiting on my part contin-
ued all summer, spurred on by Fred and Tom.
There was nothing I could really do about Uncle
Ebenezer's being president of the White Cattle
Company instead of Al White, whom he had suc-

ceeded, but I found myself much more conscious of the old boy's words and actions from then on. I began to notice him more in detail. I saw that his years and a lot of bitter experience had armed him with knowledge of every business trick and I was satisfied, after a while, that he was not above taking a mean advantage wherever possible. Probably he considered me fair game. I never liked the old fellow, and later had some sharp exchanges with him, but I must admit that the courage with which he, at that age, started off to learn the cattle business was admirable. His success at learning it subsequently turned out to be phenomenal. He had a noble resignation to hardship for the purpose of regaining the confidence of banks and government lending agencies. His refinancing of Indian leases and other vital operations did, indeed, border on a form of genius. And the iron rules of sound management which he enforced were certainly the main reason for his company's eventual recovery.

It was possible to be alert and still continue on my usual friendly basis with all the White family, especially with Al. I felt that, with regard to Al personally, no matter what dark schemes might be afoot under the rule of Uncle Ebenezer, he would not be in accord with any of them. I developed a growing conviction that Al didn't even like Uncle Ebenezer but had to put up with him as part of the family and their only hope of getting out of the red.

At the time, however, all was practically smooth

as velvet. On this pleasant basis the summer rolled
by and we all had a good time. Money was a little
more plentiful with the Whites, so that their southern hospitality and natural bent for entertainment
were given a freer rein. Parties and dances at their
ranch houses came back into fashion, these happy
assemblages being swelled by young boys and girls
invited from dude ranches far and near, who never
seemed to miss their supercomforts while enjoying
the rigorous entertainment of Tongue River. Barri-
ers of age, rank and wealth dissolved in the heat and
fun of unforced hospitality. Children of great families from the East, taken out of their strait jackets,
mixed freely with local cowpunchers and other cattle people, each respecting the other's viewpoint or
way of life. Some even stayed to marry and start
ranches of their own.

There was much visiting on horseback from
ranch to ranch, with tall, cool drinks at the end of
the trail. Our supplies of whisky were aging nicely
by that time and our private moonshiners up that
draw somewhere, between Al's property and mine
were outdoing themselves to please us.

Meanwhile, our cattle were peacefully fattening
on the range and a good store of winter hay for
them was ripening in the meadows, while beef
prices continued to rise, slowly but surely. We had
a good fall roundup and cut out a very respectable
little beef herd for shipment to market.

Al White said he was going along with the beef

shipment himself this time and suggested that I had better go with him, to learn how all a cattleman's efforts on the range are finally converted to cash in the bank (provided, of course, that things go right!). So I decided to make the trip to Omaha with him.

For the spluttering subsidiary of a bankrupt cattle company, I must say that we trailed a pretty fair little herd of V Bar C steers to the railroad that fall. Of course, we had lots of company, being in a group with all the other Tongue River outfits who were also shipping. But on the four-day drive—beef herds must travel very slowly, so as not to lose weight—from the Tongue River country across the Cheyenne and Crow Reservations to the Burlington Railroad yards at Wyola, Montana, I never saw any better steers than ours. They reflected the breeding of the Ringling bulls and the forethought of Al in straining our credit to buy them. . . . Quiet little Al, who, in his black angora chaps, rode silently along in the drag, taking credit for nothing, lost in thought as he rolled an occasional cigarette, giving us all gooseflesh as he knotted his reins together and dropped them over the saddle horn during the rolling, or took one foot from the stirrup to pop a large kitchen match on the shank of his spur.

Just to watch Al do these things was torture. His sublime disregard of personal safety could have come only from above, and the guardian angel who apparently held his horse's bridle during these ticklish moments never left his side. He gave us one horrible thriller by forgetting even to knot the reins, simply dropping them, so that they fell on either side of his horse's neck and trailed along the ground. He was unconcerned that the horse stepped on them from time to time. Then, when the cigarette was rolled and lighted, he had calmly leaned over and picked up the reins again, after several futile gropings for them, while the rest of us looked on with bated breath.

We trailed our combined herd slowly and, toward the end of the fourth day, reached Benteen. There was our old friend, the Power, waiting for us with its usual hissing welcome.

I was keen on the idea of going to Omaha with the beef, not only because it was a good chance to learn more about my business but also because, as a child, I had always wanted to ride on a freight train. The golden opportunity had arrived. Al gave me a few vague pointers on the etiquette of travel by freight. The gist of this was to travel light and not expect too much in the way of comfort. By "light" he didn't mean with a light suitcase. He meant without any suitcase. A suitcase is an impediment to running and one sometimes has to run after, away from or between freight trains—occasionally, over the top of them. Moreover, it is customary to be prepared to do so at all hours of the day or night, in pelting rain or driving snow, and without asking questions. For the habits of freight trains, judged from the standpoint of a person trying to get somewhere on one, are very, very strange. There are times when you feel sure that nobody knows why or when they stop, start, appear or disappear.

Then there is the mystery of the vanishing caboose. I have always suspected that some train crews deliberately hide the caboose because they don't want cattlemen riding in it, regardless of the fact that you represent revenue to their railroad and are entitled to be on the train that carries your cattle. The owner of cattle, or his agent, has a right to watch over his shipment of livestock, to see that the laws against cruelty to animals are enforced and to guard against any conditions which might tend to shrink their weight unduly. Nevertheless, the train crew (usually four) seem to play a game of hiding the caboose, in which they are all in cahoots. The engineer and fireman in the cab talk back and forth with the conductor and brakeman in the caboose by means of cord pulling and whistle tooting, so you are never sure what they are saying about you. But there is often the feeling that it is something nasty.

In short, they don't like your trying to run their train. But they must pay some attention to your requests to feed and water at certain times because, if they don't, and a loss should occur, you have a wonderful chance in a lawsuit. You, therefore, are the most undesirable kind of shipper. A shipper for whom they move a carload of coal, for instance, does not sit with it to see that it is properly treated and doesn't lose weight. But a range man is distressingly different. He is just a plain nuisance. So, the sooner they can get him to sign a release and hide the caboose away from him the better.

In briefing me upon the golden opportunity to fulfill my childhood dreams of freight travel, Al did not go into all these explanatory details at once, but left developments to unfold as they might. I followed his lead, taking along nothing but a little war sack containing a fresh pair of blue jeans, a change of linen and some toilet articles, all of which was to come in handy after we reached Omaha. He had explained that I might find the trip somewhat uncomfortable, due to cattle trains having given up their old custom of providing a special coach at the end to accommodate cattlemen. (This, I later decided, was part of the plot to keep us off freight trains.) But, he said, it was not a long trip to Omaha, and our discomforts would soon be over once we arrived there.

About the discomforts, he could not have spoken more truly, for they were beyond anything I had ever imagined on rails. In the hard-riding caboose there was no place to sit, except on the storage chests along the walls. These had thin mats on them, but no sign of a spring. There was no way of getting anything to eat, nor was there any bathroom. One depended upon grabbing a bite when the train stopped at a town, and upon supplying himself with sandwiches against the many times when it didn't. One's bathroom was the great outdoors. There were, of course, no sleeping accommodations. One stretched out on a mat and used his war sack for a pillow (another good reason for not taking a suitcase). The hard-riding qualities of the caboose, plus the fact that it jiggled not only up and down but sideways, and also jerked back and forth at the end of the long, loose-jointed train, all made real sleep impossible and even an occasional rest period precarious. For with only one inch of play in each coupling, a 100-car train will add up to about twelve feet of slack as the area over which the caboose can be snapped back and forth like a whiplash.

Often, this terrific jolting makes you wonder about your cattle: whether some of them are being thrown flat and trampled, unable to get up again. But usually there is not too much trouble if the cars have been properly loaded: the right number of animals in each car, so that they can move around comfortably and still brace each other, just snug, but not jammed. The results of a severe jolting can be checked up on by looking down the roof hatch of each car. If there is a bad situation, the train can be stopped at the next loading pen to correct it. This hatch inspection with the train in motion is a nerve tickler the first time one tries it: climbing on top of the cars, staggering along the narrow catwalks on their roofs and jumping the spaces between the cars, especially in high-heeled boots. Ordinarily, one waits for stops and inspects from the trackside.

I don't remember how many railroad divisions there are between Benteen and Omaha, but I think we had to change cabooses five or six times, and that it took us three nearly sleepless nights to get there. We considered ourselves lucky that we were not required to accompany the cattle to Chicago.

Once arrived, however, I realized that the other part of what Al had said was also true: our discomforts would be over when we reached Omaha. There the cattle brokers at that time vied with each other for the ranchers' business and nothing Omaha could produce was too good for the poor wrecks who, with their little war sacks, rode into the stockyards behind carloads of fat range beef, ready for the feeders to buy and pass on, corn-fed, to the packers in Chicago.

Members of the brokerage firm to which we had consigned our shipment met us at the yards with plenty of helpers and would not hear of our even sticking around to see the cars unloaded. They would, of course, see that the cattle were well looked after, it being to their advantage to do so. As it was late in the day, they prescribed for us good baths, big steak suppers and plenty of sleep. Then in the morning, when we were well rested, they would take us to the Livestock Exchange to see our steers marketed. In the meantime, our hotel suite with two bedrooms was waiting and paid for. They had a taxicab standing by for us. And, by the way, did we need any cash? They produced great rolls of it, noting that the banks were closed and that if we needed more we would find our credit guaranteed at the hotel.

Our two greeters were both big, strong, healthy-looking men. Each had, himself, a touch of the range clinging to him somehow. As a parting gesture of hospitality when we got into the taxicab, they added that we would find good liquor in the room, with their compliments, and that girls would follow if needed.

It was all as the brokers had said. Our hotel suite had two bedrooms, sitting room and bath. On the dresser top was a package containing two bottles of excellent Scotch, smuggled from Canada. The management called up to see if there was anything special they could get. There wasn't. About half an hour later they called again to see if we had changed our minds. We hadn't. After a week in saddles and cabooses the creature comforts of a hotel felt pretty good and we were enjoying them to the utmost. We had an enormous steak supper and were about to get into bed when the telephone rang. It was some girl friend of our brokers'. She had a pal with her and they would like to ask us something, but not over the telephone. We were too tired to answer questions. Ten minutes later another girl called up and she also wanted to ask us something, but we put her off till the next day.

Before we could get into bed a third girl called. She didn't want to ask us anything. She wanted to show us something. We said that we would look at it next day, but she said she didn't know where it would be next day, so she would have to show it to us now, but there would be absolutely no obligation. We didn't have to take it if we didn't want to, but in case we didn't want to, she thought it only fair that we should know what we were missing. We didn't ask her up. She didn't ask to come up. She simply told us that she was *coming* up.

She was a woman of her word, all right, and no slouch about it. In the time it took us to get our shirts and ties back on again, and rally for defense in our little *salon*, she had arrived at the door. We backed down from our adamant positions to the extent of letting her in and showing her to a chair at the center table, Al and I flanking her on either side. She was not a bad-looking young girl and had a very friendly, open manner about her, so the meeting was cozy. But the conversation, though polite, was somewhat brusque. She began it by asking fearlessly, "Well, I suppose you boys know why I'm here?" I said yes, we were mind readers and had figured that out. "Do you want me to stay?" she inquired next. It was a brutal question, because nobody wishes to tell a girl that she is not wanted and must go. There was an awkward silence while Al and I exchanged glances, each wondering what the other really thought.

"Well?" the girl suggested impatiently, looking at first one of us and then the other expectantly. "If you don't want me, just say so. I have an engagement at eleven o'clock, anyway, but I could break it if you wish."

"We wouldn't ask you to break an engagement for *us*," I stammered. "After all, we're only—"

"Oh, that'd be all right," she cut me short. "There's a whole flock of us. Well, do you want me or not?"

I wondered what kind of engagement it could be.

"It isn't that we don't *want* you," said Al politely. "But, you see, I'm a family man. I have a very wonderful wife, and—"

"I see." She smiled understandingly and turned to me. "Then you're the bachelor?"

"Yes, but I wouldn't want you to give up your engagement for *me*."

"Oh, that's O.K. I can get that kind of work most any time. It's just a stag dinner."

"A stag dinner? What do you do there?"

"I dance . . . nude. I'm the head dancer. I come up out of a big pie, but any of the other girls can do it."

"I should think the stags would be very disappointed if you weren't in their pie. That's really the place for you tonight. Better run along and jump in it," I suggested. Then I poured her a little drink, which she tossed off gratefully.

She rose to go, smoothing out (as I thought) her neat navy-blue tailored suit. But somewhere between the table and the door she whirled, jerked a ripcord and stood as God had made her. "Well, how do you like it?" she asked. "Anybody want to change his mind?" She had a neat, lithe, healthy-looking body and was more graceful than vulgar. I was astounded at the lightning technique of disrobing which she employed and which was most effective in contrast to the standard so-called strippers' methods. Nevertheless, we hustled her off to her pie. On going out she gave us her card, which was a hand-written affair with a telephone number on it, and said, "If you get lonesome, call me up!"

In the morning our brokers joined us bright and early at the hotel. They had already been down to the stockyards and assured us that our steers were doing nicely on plenty of feed and water, in preparation for their going on the market that day. They took us to their offices, where we talked cattle prices until the market opened, then went over to the Livestock Exchange which, I thought, compared favorably with the New York Stock Exchange, except that it was a much nicer location. As I remember, it had three appropriate emblems carved in stone on the façade: a sheep at one end, a hog at the other, and a bull in the middle. I had heard Stock Exchange customers called sheep and it struck me that, with the addition of a bear, the animal foursome might not be too out of character on Wall Street.

From the Livestock Exchange we went out to the pens. It was a beautiful, crisp, sunny autumn day, so we climbed up on the corral fence, watching the proceedings and enjoying the fresh air. Our brokers explained to me what was going on as yard riders, proudly mounted on stock ponies with stock saddles and carrying long slender whips, shuffled different grades of beef around from pen to pen. They worked with an air of careful leisure and were never too busy to pull up for a few pleasant words, seemingly enjoying life and their work. Sometimes they would telephone to the floor of the Exchange, using instruments mounted on corral posts, which they could reach without getting out of the saddle. Their horses seemed to understand all about telephoning, and stood quietly. There was one pony that would even head for the telephone when he heard it ringing. The brokers chatted with other brokers, climbing about on the fences and walking or riding through the pens of cattle. They were very polite about offering you their ponies to ride through the herds and were, I thought, about as cheerful a bunch of businessmen as I had ever seen, each one eager to offer some little act of friendship whether he expected to get a commission out of your cattle or not. They were perhaps not as well dressed as Wall Street businessmen, but they were appropriately dressed, neat and clean with a general tone of Cheyenne pants, warm wool shirts, buckskin jackets and passably polished western boots. Their hats were highly individualized, smaller than our range-type Stetsons, but not making ours feel out of place.

We thus pleasantly whiled away the morning watching sales, being notified of the bid and asked prices for various classes of beef and being advised whether or not to consider a deal. Trading slacked off and finally we went to lunch with a group of stockyards characters such as often include you in their great mass eatings for no special reason other than being friendly. After lunch our steers were sold for a little more than we had expected, so we were very well pleased. Our brokers gave us a minute accounting and, after deducting their commissions, a fat check, which I endorsed with great pride and mailed to our bank. We were taken on a tour of the town, to some of our new-found friends' homes, where we were plied with good liquor, given another large steak dinner and treated to another good night's rest. We reveled in the luxury of sleeping late in the morning, as our train did not leave until around noon. Our friends reappeared to put us on it, wish us good luck and hope that we would consign our beef to them again next year. Our ticket back was as guests of the railroad. On the way home I felt very cocky and rather impatient to explain to Fred and Tom just how well my company was going.

XIX

Fred Lauby

WHEN I got back to the cabin there was somehow or other a noticeable stillness and perfection about it. The place suddenly looked as if it had
been lived in for years. A wisp of blue smoke curled
into the clear autumn sky, like something out of a
Currier and Ives print showing some "wilderness
home" in the old frontier days. Not at all like a
Currier and Ives print were the windows, however:
all sparkling unnaturally bright. It looked almost as
if there had been a woman living in the place.
Could Fred have found romance in the short ten
days that I had been away? He was sitting on the
porch in freshly laundered clothes, with his telescope by his side, reading the *Pathfinder*.

He had some of his special spaghetti simmering
on the stove for supper and, I thought, a rather generous portion of prairie chicken for one who expected to eat alone. He said that there was plenty
for us all, indicating Al and me. But Al was anxious
to get down home for supper. He asked casually if
Tom Bryan would be coming along, and where
Tom was.

"Oh, that crazy sonofabitch!" Fred announced
glibly. "Nobody ever knows where *he* is. I think he's

up Canyon Creek tonight, drinking beer with old Henry Lunk."

Al looked relieved to hear that he was not down at the ranch and Fred hastened to reassure him, "He sure keeps clear of your outfit."

Next morning I strolled about the cabin and our little outbuildings, looking for signs of change since I had left. The signs were all good. For not only were the windows washed and polished, but the floor had recently been scrubbed. In the garage were a still-moist sponge and chamois, bearing mute testimony to Fred's efforts. Al's and my saddles, sent back from Benteen with the roundup outfit, were now on my porch rack, thoroughly cleaned and saddle-soaped. None of this seemed natural.

I tried to piece together the things that Fred had been doing since I had been away on the trip to Omaha. There were signs of carpentry (which, with advancing age, he had taken up along with log work, house painting and gossip). He had been whetting his already very complete knowledge on all scandals about the country. He had been reading voraciously, to increase his useless and enormous store of unrelated facts: such topics as the theory of deep-sea diving or the government-approved way of handling guinea hens. He had kept up a relentless vigil of the terrain through his powerful telescope, clumsily jotting down observations for future reference in an old notebook. And he had all the gory details on some dry farmer's wife who had been caught red-handed and chased by her spouse for four miles down a dry creek bed with a buggy whip. He had collected the latest data on cattle rustlers of the moment, telling me who they were, from whom they rustled, and how many head. He had undoubtedly reached the pinnacle as self-appointed mentor for everyone in the country who had a problem of any kind, which meant just about everybody, including myself.

In fact, Fred was making himself a new place in the community by staying in my cabin. He was developing an official base of operations. Heretofore nobody had paid much attention to him in his own little tumbledown homestead cabin across the river. It was on no route to anywhere and inaccessible except by certain river crossings in certain seasons. Practically nobody ever bucked the odds of trying to visit him, because there was no point involved. Now, however, he had a certain position as part of my little outfit, on the right side of the river. Everything to do with this tiny outfit was new and interesting, and talked about. Tom Bryan alone would give any place at which he stayed a certain amount of *cachet*, even if it were the wrong kind.

Fred Lauby had latched on to this idea, I could see as I wandered about my property marveling at the increase in his personal possessions which had appeared during my absence. There was no doubt about it, he had moved in with me, practically uninvited, but in a perfectly natural sort of way, and

expected to be my official adviser on the pitfalls of
cattle ranching. I couldn't really object to this, as he
was a good cook and had proved a most trustworthy
watchdog for my affairs when I had been away, not
only on this shipping trip but on several trips back
East and to Europe. He looked after, fed and shod
my horses. He kept me posted on the condition of
the cattle. And I was to learn in future years that
nothing of which he ever had charge was lost, stolen
or broken, except one handle on a sugar bowl, for
which he apologized profusely. Considering all this,
and the fact that his own cabin had fallen practically to ruin I felt that he had a lot of natural and not
unreasonable motives for wishing to move into my
nice new one, and I did not mind his practically
hinting that I urge him to do so.

This required very little urging. I realized that,
bit by bit, during my various absences he had been
bringing over his belongings: in the wintertime
across the frozen river on an old, homemade sled
drawn by his docile work horses, in summer by
wagon or, for smaller objects, on horseback. During
my trip to Omaha, he had made a big haul. He now
had *all* his tools at my place, instead of just a few
odd ones for an occasional job. These included not
only his carpenter's tools but other sets: for blacksmithing, plumbing, cobbling and on down to
watchmaking. There was a portable cast iron cobbler's last which turned three ways for different
kinds of shoes; a cobbler's hammer, nails and extra

soles. The collection included everything from heavy tools, such as stone hammers and Stillson wrenches, down to watch-repairing items, such as a jeweler's magnifying eyepiece, a clamp for holding watch springs while inserting them, tiny screwdrivers, watchmaker's oil, a set of quills he had devised for applying it, and extra hairsprings. Fred apparently gave vent to his creative urge by pursuing an odd hobby: collecting old, discarded alarm clocks and making them run again. There were several samples of his handiwork about the cabin in various stages of resuscitation, with their innards partially removed as he studied what made them balky. Some would only run face down, others only on their backs or upside down, but all were gradually convalescing under his treatment. Fred considered all this equipment and paraphernalia necessary and important to our welfare. There remains to this day one tool of his which I still cherish as an interesting item for the reason that I never saw him use it, never asked him what it was for and have never been able to find anyone who could explain it.

Aside from his collection of "necessary" items, he had brought over and stored in my coal shed another trunk—a very old, storybook type with a curved lid and great straps around it—containing various curiosa, some of which I got a glance at during his lifetime, but most of which remained hidden away until he died. Occasionally he would delve into this trunk in search of some other "necessary" item which he could not locate elsewhere. Something really vital, such as, on one occasion, a sailor's palm, when he was sewing up Fashion's nosebag. Sometimes I had a chance to peek over his shoulder. This invariably made him nervous, and he would come forth with such sketchy explanations to my questions as "That? Oh, that's the coat of arms of my mother's family. She was a Van Ness . . . daughter of Cornelius P. Van Ness. He was minister to Spain under President Jackson, I think, and collector of the Port of New York, and something else . . . Oh, yes, his brother was Aaron Burr's second in that duel with Alexander Hamilton." And when I admired a most unusual-looking missal—printed in parallel columns of Spanish and Latin on the finest paper, as a special edition for the Archbishop of Zaragoza, bound in hand-carved mother-of-pearl, velvet and silver—his comment was "That belonged to my mother, a daughter by his second wife, who was a Spanish lady from Madrid."

Toward the end of his life, Fred gave me this missal, saying that he had no known family left to whom he could will it. Later, he also gave me an old album of valentines, written (as they were in those days) by various admirers, to his mother when she was a young girl. Cristina, as her name was, appears from the album to have been very popular. The album is still intact, even to the flowers which have been pressed there for nearly a hundred years. Only one sour note is evident among the mass of tributes to Cristina and the noble emotions she aroused in the palpitating bosoms of her suitors. It is written by some apparently dyspeptic beau on July 21, 1855, which must have been a hot and depressing day indeed, when even thoughts of the fair Cristina could not stir this author from his sense of impending doom as he addressed to her these melancholy lines:

> I saw a Glow Worm on a Grave,
> But its pale light would not scare
> Baser worms which came to crave
> A share of the Banquet there.

The poem goes on for four more stanzas of despair and then closes in a heavy cloud of gloom. I sometimes wonder whatever happened to the poor fellow.

In the trunk were other oddities not so easily explained and, I thought, hardly to be classified as "necessary" equipment. Among these was a collection of feathers and plumes: ostrich, peacock, aigrette, feather boas with a poultry-yard look of Rhode Island Reds about them, and just ordinary feathers. There were several boxes of candy saved from the 1880's; a rather elaborately and beautifully enameled pair of opera glasses made in Paris; about five policeman's clubs of various kinds, and other trivia. Then there was the costume department, which produced an ankle-length automobiling duster of the 1890s, sporting leather-trimmed collar and cuffs, cap and goggles to match, all in a smart, sand-colored whipcord, which must have been very fetching for a Sunday spin in the new Pope Toledo, along some forgotten road of the dim past. Most out of place of all in my coal shed was an undoubtedly genuine court ball dress of the 1830s, beautifully made of the finest silks and so perfectly preserved that, years later, my wife was to wear it with great success at a fancy-dress ball in London. There were also some old-fashioned, square-toed, high button shoes that looked as if they might have been made by the same bootmaker who, apparently, made boots for all the distinguished statesmen whose statues decorate public parks. Finally there was the horror department: a black metal can containing the cremated remains of Fred's brother-in-law, deceased as of April, 1914, according to the label.

All these things and a lot more were jumbled together in this old trunk, regarded by Fred as his treasure trove. They appeared to have come to him from a mysterious sister who visited Tongue River some years before my advent. But the sister hadn't behaved very well and found it wise to leave in a hurry for Texas, from where she never returned or sent any word, leaving the trunk behind. Apparently she had been traveling so fast since 1914 that she never had time to bury her husband's ashes. And Fred, though he didn't travel at all, didn't have time, either. So there they were, in my coal shed, and there they stayed until I discovered them in 1949.

I finally disposed of the ashes to a distant relative for burial, after a long discussion with the railway express agency as to the shipping. They were not allowed to ship "human remains" without a burial permit, and were also keenly interested in the question of how I happened to come into possession of human remains, anyway. With no death certificate, no burial permit and only the explanation that these ashes had been kicking around in my coal shed for twenty-three years while their former guardian was waiting for a chance to bury them, one can hardly blame the express company for being a bit skeptical at first. But as I had shipped lots of cattle by that time, the railroad people knew me and fixed it up with the express company, so that they let the remains go by.

Gradually it dawned on me that Fred's transplanting of his home from across the river to my cabin was a *fait accompli* and that, probably, I should have to accept him as part of my life for some time to come. It turned out to be until the day he died, one bitter winter twenty-three years later. During all of that time he practically never left my property, and even after death events seemed to conspire to keep him there in the cabin. For, being alone, his death went unnoticed for several days, and when the fires flickered out, his body froze just as solid and was just as difficult to handle as that of the old trapper, Lanford, he had told me about. Even the elements lent a hand to keep him clutched there in the cabin, freezing the doors up as water gushed from burst pipes and formed ice on the floor. When the doors were finally forced open, he was found slumped on the edge of the bed, his feet locked in ice on the floor. Then a blizzard came and all but snowed the cabin under, so that it was several days more before an undertaker could reach him. When he was finally ready for burial, another snowfall stalled his hearse and hid the little sagebrush graveyard from all but those who knew it intimately, while intense cold froze the ground so deep that the only way his friends could dig a grave for him was to dynamite it.

But that is getting ahead of the story. At the time of my return from Omaha, he was just settling down to his life-and-death grip on my place. And when I found that I had to go back East again, I felt pretty safe in leaving him there as my watchdog.

My return, next spring, was the first occasion upon which I had been able to slip up to the cabin unnoticed. Neither the gleam of Fred's telescope nor the familiar outline of his massive figure was to be seen on the porch, nor did a few friendly toots on the car horn evoke any sign of life. As I opened the kitchen door, there was a faint odor of chloroform, and I thought of the strange, horrid things people sometimes do when left alone too long. There had been the man who married Buffalo Bill's daughter and lived nearby, on Hanging Woman

Creek, who poured ether into an overshoe, stuck his head into it and expired. But he had long shown an odd behavior pattern.

Fred's body was not sprawled on the kitchen floor. But for odd behavior patterns, when I finally spied him in the big room, he seemed to be running a pretty close second to Buffalo Bill's son-in-law. He was sitting by a window, wearing his jeweler's eyepiece, intently absorbed in some occupation entirely new to me. No alarm clock repair work was this. Between his knees he had my heavy leather batwing chaps, in one leg of which was his cat, upside down, its terrified yowlings rending the air. The cat scratched and struggled mightily, although ineffectually, within the chap leg while Fred, disregarding the flailings of its tail, was inspecting its posterior regions through the magnifying eyepiece. The commotion was such that he had not even heard me enter. I stood aghast in the open kitchen doorway. Suddenly, with a sure, swift stroke of his old-fashioned, British blade razor, he performed his surgical wizardry and applied a few drops of iodine from a small bottle. At this there was a tremendous yelp and the cat emerged from the bottom of the chap leg with the ferocity of a modern guided missile. In a few heroic bounds it negotiated the cabin floor and, still yowling, sailed out the kitchen door between my legs, shedding, as it went, a Bull Durham tobacco sack which, saturated with chloroform, had been affixed to its nose.

"I hated to cut the poor sonofabitch," Fred explained regretfully, "but I made up my mind that I just had to do it or lose him, as he got to roaming around the country so much, and I was afraid the coyotes would get him. They sure love cat meat better than anything I know of."

"Where did you get the chloroform?"

"I sent to town for it. You can get anything like that—even morphine—if you live out on a ranch. Did you know that a ranch boss is even supposed to keep a little morphine on hand for emergencies? All the cattle outfits around here have it, so it was easy for me to get a supply."

I didn't have any, but it sounded logical, and I later learned that it was true. "Do you think you gave that cat enough?"

"Oh, sure," he answered confidently, replacing his razor in its case. "All that hell he was raising don't mean a thing. I've cut lots of cats and they all raise hell. They're more scared than hurt. But he's just as good as new, except for the romantic stuff. And a steer cat always makes a better pet. They stay around more."

By that time the smarting animal had raced about in the sagebrush for a while and, finding nothing else to climb, had perched himself on the chimney top, where he remained for two days, coming down only at night, when we set out food. But he got over the operation quickly and lived to a ripe old age.

Fred then brought me up to date on news of the

outfit. The Whites' hay supply had held out nicely and the cattle had wintered well. "But it's just pure luck," he added skeptically. Tom Bryan had been forgiven his various misdeeds and was back working for Al. "They got sick of fooling with the goddam light plant themselves, not having water and sitting in the dark," he explained. "Tom played his hand just fine. Went on the wagon, sat up here quiet as a mouse and never tried to get in touch with her at all," nodding toward the ranch. "He's been doing a lot of writing to lawyers back East and finally the family put up forty thousand dollars as a starter to jar him loose from his soiled dove. She gets the rest when the final papers are signed." He then confided to me that, although nobody knew it, Tom was fixin' to marry Dorothy Stett, a prediction which later proved true. Al White had bought himself a car, which he couldn't learn to drive, and was the terror of Tongue River when he got out on the county road with it. He had smashed through the corral gate and knocked the dinner bell down three times by backing into its post, until Betty finally had it just left on the ground until he could learn to drive, which didn't look as if it was going to be very soon. He had no driver's license, no insurance and no license plates, but such trivialities were of no consequence to Al, most of whose driving was up side creeks looking at cattle.

"But I haven't told you the *big* news yet," Fred pursued eagerly. "It's about our still—"

"*Our* still?" I interrupted.

"Well, you know . . . that moonshining outfit up in the canyon here." He jerked his thumb over his shoulder in the direction of that boundary line he had promised to survey, but didn't. "The Federal men found it and busted it up."

"*Found* it . . . how?"

"Quite a little excitement around here. First, a flying machine came in the middle of the winter. First one I'd ever seen, and I was suspicious right away. I got a good bead on it with the telescope and watched it flying around in circles all over the country, like it was looking for a place to light, but they must have been on the hunt for stills and looking for smoke, when all of a sudden they flew over the cabin here, real low. There was two of these bastards in it. One of them was driving the outfit and the other had his face poked over the side, looking with field glasses. He looked right at me and I looked right back up at the sonofabitch through the telescope, and I says to myself, "You're a government man, sure as hell."

"Well, nothing happened for a month or so and then along came a hell of a big, powerful-looking car that I knew didn't belong around here anywhere. It turned in the gate here and went down to the ranch, so I put the glass on them and, sure enough, it had a government license plate on the back, and three men got out. They asked Al what was up there in the canyon, and of course he played

dumb. So they started out for it. They knew exactly
where it was. They even knew where the gate was,
leading off the county road, and went right to it.
When I saw them stop at that gate I knew for sure
what they was after, so I saddled up a horse and cut
across the hills, thinking I could still get there first
and warn the boys, as that big car was sliding
around in the mud before it even left the road, and
I figgered it would be a long time getting up to the
canyon."

At this point I had a premonition that, somehow
or other, Fred had implicated himself, and possibly
me, with the government men and that I would hear
more of this when I went to prove up on the title to
my homestead. "Did you ever find out," I asked,
"whether that still was actually on my land?"

"Yes, I surveyed it, like I said I would. It's not on
your claim."

I had a feeling of relief as he continued: "Well,
when I was almost there I saw I couldn't make it.
Their car was stuck about a half a mile down from
the canyon, but they got out and walked and were
almost up to the still. So, I got off my horse and
slipped behind a big rock where there was a good
rest for my telescope and I could see the whole
show just like I was sitting in the front row. These
Federal men had picked the wrong day for a raid,
luckily, as the two moonshiners had gone to town
with a big batch of stuff. They'd hired a little kid
about twelve years old, from some dry farm back up

in the hills, to keep a fire going under the vat till they got back. The kid didn't know what it was all about and he was lying down on a cot under the shed by the boiler, sound asleep, with a six-shooter sticking out from under his pillow. The Federal men eased up to him on tiptoe and grabbed the six-shooter first thing. After that, you could tell they kind of felt sorry for the kid and wanted him to get away. So, they gave him an empty bucket and they must have told him to go down to the spring for some water. Anyway, he started for the spring and they began busting up the outfit with a sledge hammer and an ax, making a big noise. The poor kid got scared and dropped the bucket and ran like hell, back to his dry farm, I suppose. They didn't want him, but I knew they'd keep after the moon-shiners, and probably catch them coming back from town unless somebody got word to them and headed them off. I knew they supplied Sammy Doyle's outfit with booze and he was the man to get hold of, but I didn't dare use the telephone.

"Just then I spotted Ole coming along the road with the mail stage, headed for town, dumping out the waysacks. So, I got back on my horse and whipped up and got down to the road in time to cut Ole off. He said he'd drive as fast as he could and tell Sammy, but that he had to stop at each mail post for the waysacks. But I told him, to hell with the goddam mail and just throw the sacks out as he went by, which he did, and I guess everybody thought it was kind of funny that their sacks weren't in the boxes that day, but no harm came of it, and the moonshiners got away. But it was a close call."

Despite the close call, our moonshiner friends set up shop the very next winter in a neighboring canyon and did a rush business. They were eternally grateful for their timely warning and made special price concessions to Fred's friends in recognition of his having so nobly carried the news "from Ghent to Aix," as it were.

It was a neat piece of detective work, all right, and I asked Fred (with deep respect for his inquiring mind) to what he attributed the discovery of the moonshiners in the first place.

"You know," he said mysteriously, "old Uncle Ebenezer is a teetotaler and doesn't like to see whisky around these ranches. I've got a notion he's at the bottom of this whole business."

XX

Intermission

I HAD returned West fortified by advice from the family lawyers as to how I might better my position in the cattle venture.

The first thing to do was to escape, if possible, from partnership status and its unlimited liability and then to form a corporation. This would at least forestall any chance of my becoming liable for more than my original investment in the cattle, as Tom and Fred feared might happen. It remained to be seen whether I could escape from the partnership, but my hopes were high.

The family attorneys had looked up the name of a lawyer in Billings who was familiar with the Montana laws on livestock procedure, so I went to Billings and retained this man to represent me. But the lawyer admitted frankly that he had very little to work on until I had talked the Whites out of the partnership idea and into favor of a corporation. I thought that he was more or less of a rubber-stamp lawyer with little imagination and overimpressed by this piece of business with the New York flavor to it. The first thing he did was to drag me all over town introducing me to his acquaintances, stopping them on the street and even calling them across the street, or pulling me after them. This, he said, was to reassure me that he knew all the important people in town. But I was not interested in all the important people, I was interested only in protecting myself. Then he asked me for a "retainer." I didn't even know what that was, as I had never had a lawyer of my very own before. I thought a retainer was some kind of servant. Next, he took me into his home, where I was shocked by the way he and his wife spoke to each other. Each addressed the other as "lover." It was sickening. He also introduced me to a girl who, he said, was wonderful, gay and possessed of every attribute a young bachelor could hope for. I found her a stupid, uninteresting dud with a tendency toward tears the very first time I tried to give her a driving lesson in the Cadillac. So, I didn't use my lawyer for much except actually drawing up papers.

I could not detect any outright attack on the part of Uncle Ebenezer, although I knew that he was clever enough to conceal one from me if he wanted to. Al White was a great help in agreeing with everything I said. I drummed up a polite excuse for wanting to dissolve the partnership and form a corporation. Al agreed with my reasoning and for a while it seemed that, even if I could not get the V Bar C brand in my own name, I would at least have some stock to show and my liability limited.

When the idea was put up to Uncle Ebenezer, he didn't like it so much. He rather favored continuing the partnership. I pursued my arguments, however, on several occasions, planning this as an acid test to force his hand. He could not come out in the open with any valid reasoning against a corporation. Yet he did not favor it, and I had some uneasy moments. Finally, I suggested that the valuation of $10 per acre which his company had put on its land to equal my cash investment might be too high. He stoutly maintained that the land was worth every cent of that value, to *them*. After he had gotten quite hot on this topic one day, I suggested that, if he felt so sure about it, he should be willing to take the land back again at the same figure, in a dissolution of the partnership. There was no escape from this logic, and a dissolution was arranged on that basis.

The corporation that followed was a great improvement from the standpoint of my personal safety, and I had an equitable share of stock. But it had one drawback from the standpoint of actually operating the cattle. I had to make occasional trips back East and at such times was always at their mercy. They could call a meeting and, in my absence, make it sound pretty reasonable that certain actions should take place for the benefit of the herd, in the management of which, it could not be denied, they were much more experienced than was I. The herd would still be run the way Uncle Ebenezer wanted it run, whether I liked it or not. I wouldn't have minded this so much had it been just Al and his brother alone, in the spirit of mutual trust which we all felt toward each other. But the coming of Uncle Ebenezer, with his utter control over them, changed all this. The old range spirit seemed to flow out of the picture and to be replaced by the city way of doing things. It was not the openhearted pioneer way of doing business which I had grown to trust, then as I did in later years, whatever its shortcomings might be.

The corporation tagged on for a few months, during which I tried to draw into it other directors sympathetic to my ideas, who could sit in at meetings during my absences back East. But my efforts proved fruitless. Several of my friends politely declined the job, and I couldn't blame them. They also preferred the old-style ways.

I made the Whites a fair proposition to buy me out, and they accepted it. My conditions were: money back plus 6 per cent per annum for the total time of investment. We wound up the deal amicably in 1929.

After that, there came a series of very lean years in the cattle business: bad winters, droughts in summer and two plagues, one of grasshoppers and the other of crickets, similar to those of ancient Egypt. That particular cattle boom was over, and I was considered lucky for having gotten out at the right time. But my erstwhile partners survived the storms and are now riding high again. Needless to say, Uncle Ebenezer did best of all.

Fred Lauby suggested that, if I wished him to, he

The author's cabin in Birney after improvements.

could stay on at my cabin and look after it, as I
never could tell when I might need it again, and
there was no use closing up a cabin and letting the
dry rot settle in. He practically said that it would be
better to let *him* settle in. Then, whenever I wanted
to come West for a visit, I'd always have a place to
stay. He suggested that the world was a funny place,
and who knew but what, someday, I might want to
get back into the cattle business again? When I
asked him what salary he would expect, he looked
down at the alarm clock he was fixing and mumbled, "Hell, boy, don't talk that way. It makes me
feel bad."

Fred never would accept a penny of salary and,
although I let him use my credit everywhere, he
never once abused the privilege. I decided to give
him a home and provide him with food and simple
necessities, in return for all of which he rendered
me a strict accounting, in his sprawling, illiterate
handwriting. His little account book and his scale
soon commanded respect everywhere. And, as
tradesmen quickly learned, God help any of them
who tried to give him short change or short weight!
This situation remained in *status quo* for a dozen or
more years, after which, as Fred had predicted
might happen, I returned West and went into the
cattle business again, although on a much larger
scale and with a different company. The locale,
however, was right next door, so to speak, on the
Crow Indian Reservation, so that I was glad again to

be able to make use of my old headquarters, which I found complete with Fred and all my equipment.

Tom Bryan struggled on with alcohol, his family, his women and his widely vacillating mode of life ranging from palaces to pigpens. He got rid of his soiled dove, eventually came into about seven million dollars, married Dorothy Stett and in a few years was divorced from her. In time he had a third wife, but at that point I lost track of him. He was eventually swallowed up in the vortex of eastern life and, according to last reports, was living in an institution catering to fashionable problem millionaires with his particular problem.

Life rolled on in the Tongue River country, and is still rolling on. The old-timers I knew in my first years there are now mostly gone or forced into retirement made necessary by age and inability to live the strenuous life. Some have moved to nearby towns, like Sheridan, Billings or Miles City. But every once in a while, somehow, they still manage to get in touch with each other.

In place of the old life, a new life has come into being along the Tongue, with much of the same old spirit, although the fairly primitive conditions of the 1920s are now softened for today's ranchers by the advent of modern machinery and conveniences. In 1952 electricity came in through the Rural Electrification Administration, and there is a project to put in regular telephone service. Automobiles are to be seen everywhere, but the old road over which they roll up and down Tongue River has not changed a great deal. Cattle are still run in considerable numbers, but their winter hay is put up by machine on the home ranches. Some of the smaller cattle companies now truck all their steers to the railroad instead of trailing them. Roundup wagons have given way to line camps and there are no more long circles to ride in the chilly dawn.

The small airplane has made its appearance on the range: for spotting lost or scattered livestock, running business errands to town, patrolling the range against rustlers (who still ply a modern version of their trade) and as a godsend in sickness or emergency. Many cowboys are now also pilots. I, too, picked up a bit of flying, but always felt that taking to the air was, as regards ranching proper, a hybrid, inconsistent activity, a sort of cross between driving a car, riding a bicycle and running an elevator in a tall building.

Ole Hansen was one of the first old-timers to go, and he was rather distinctive about it. Not long after his retirement from the mail line, he woke up one morning in the best of health and spirits, but announced to his wife that he thought he ought to die as soon as he had had a good breakfast. They sat down to a hearty meal, after which he said good-bye to his wife and announced again that he thought it was time for him to die. Whereupon he got undressed again, returned to bed, put on his battered old cowpuncher's hat and dozed off to a sleep from which he never awoke. Half an hour later, when his wife went to arouse him from what she considered a senile prank, he had joined the last roundup.

The Whites and their cattle company progressed with the improving times, got financial backing from the various government lending agencies which came into being in the 1930s and, under the iron rule of Uncle Ebenezer, gradually worked out of their difficulties. By 1939, when I had decided to try the cattle business again and began putting out feelers for range, their leases were all stocked up with cattle and they could not take me in on another venture. But again it was Al who came forward with help and suggestions as to locating grass and who drove me in his car (which he still had not learned to control very well) to the Little Big Horn country and introduced me to my future partner, M. H. Tschirgi, owner of the great Antler Ranch, where I was to put in another ten years of happy and profitable operations on the range.

Betty battled on with life through thick and thin, in her gay, indomitable spirit, watching over Al in his declining years, raising her children and getting the next generation started. Through the good old times to the bad old times and on to the good new times again, her spark has never failed, and she survived the shock of Al's death in the same spirit. Always more practical than sentimental, it was she

The living room of the author's cabin as it is today.

who bolstered the ranch morale during his last days and insisted upon riding in the ambulance with him on the night that a cerebral hemorrhage developed. He died in her arms on the way to town. But he will always live in her heart and in the hearts of all the rest of us who knew him. At the head of the long table in the mess house, his empty chair, flanked by the company cattle brands seared all around the under parts of the table, is the only outward indication of her feelings. She will never let anyone sit there. No one could ever fill "Abbit's" place.

The silver-tongued Dan Hawkes continued in his ways of winning friends and influencing cattle movements until he reached a pinnacle never attained by anyone else, before or since. And while one cannot condone this in any way, still one can pause a moment to acknowledge the hand of the master in any undertaking, however unfortunate.

Dan became the only man in history ever to make off with an entire trainload of cattle, comprising some twenty or twenty-five cars, taken from the Cheyenne Indian Reservation. This he did by diverting the shipment from its original destination to a market where there was no government brand inspector, and selling the stock at public auction. It was a magnificent piece of daring; the ultimate in imagination; a feat to be compared only with those earlier deeds of the James boys and even, in a way, surpassing any of them. For the James boys may have held up many a train, but they never *swiped* one!

Not only did he carry out this masterpiece (thereby automatically classifying even the boldest of his followers forever as pikers) but he talked himself out of going to the penitentiary for it. Eventually, however, he did become a guest of the State of Montana, but he quickly captivated the officials and talked his way back to freedom. The occasion of this incident was the unauthorized (and typically carefree) removal of some horses right out of the railroad yards at Sheridan, Wyoming, and the transferring of them across the state line into Montana. But the results of this little slip were talked away before they became too irksome and, thereafter, Dan led a model life. All his successors have been small fry by comparison, the best of them, in 1952, getting up to only a hundred head. Dan had set a world record and retired. It was another milestone in the passing era of the wide-open spaces.

As for the time I had spent on Tongue River, I was satisfied with it. I had not hung up any great records of achievement or amassed any fortune. But financially, I had accomplished what I had set out to do: give a passable account of myself in a strange and intricate business, from a cold start. Even the trustees of the estate, skeptical though they had been at first, finally admitted this. But by far the greatest return I received lay in the valuable experience I stored away and which came in handy during my second round on the range.

Incidentally, I proved up on my homestead and got the title to it, which I still have. This, I think, gives me the dubious distinction of being probably the only Manhattan-born holder of original public domain in Montana. My cabin, now greatly enlarged and improved, still serves me as a home for many months of the year and was an ideal base during the ten years of my second cattle venture, being within ninety miles of the Antler Ranch and near my old friends on Tongue River.

Other rewards came to me during my sojourn on the Tongue, and are still with me. Foremost among these is health, both physical and mental: a sound body where a dubious one existed before; a mind free from all the petty imaginings of crowded eastern thought patterns and a conviction born of firsthand observation that, no matter how discouraging the vista ahead, one can always "make it through somehow." It may take a little faith in something or other. What one uses for faith doesn't matter much. It may be faith in the gods of the churches or just a simple faith in nature, as the Indians express in their various dances. Or, it may be only a feeling that the world will eventually make sense if one will just let it, because someone much smarter than oneself has had it all figured out since the beginning of time.

From 1927 until 1933 I went to work for the

successors to my father's firm in Wall Street. But
after a while hard times came there too, though not
from bitter winters, searing droughts or plagues of
hungry insects. On the whole, this experience was, I
thought, rather futile. Trudging along on the Wall
Street treadmill, with only a very uncertain reward
glowing faintly in the dim, undetermined distance
ahead seemed like a miserable existence whenever I
thought of the sage-scented champagne air, the
clear skies and the big, burning stars of Montana.
There were times, as I struggled with the relentless
mechanical pattern of the Stock Exchange, or had
to call some impoverished widow for more margin,
that I would have exchanged my soul for the feel of
a good horse under me, the sight of a cow hunting
her lost calf, or even the wail of a coyote on a still,
frosty night—with or without Uncle Ebenezer. And
so, eventually, I gravitated back to the free life for
another decade of the only real education I've ever
had, despite an assortment of fancy schools.

My second round on the range also happened to
begin at a most opportune time, which coincidence
earned for me some slight—and totally bogus—reputation as an astute cattleman. However, I believe
that probably there is no such thing as an astute
cattleman. Cattlemen, like other men, though they
sometimes don't care to be considered like other
men, all rise and fall with the conditions governing
their industry. And as in all industries, some of the
wisest and best of them have fallen, never to rise

again, while newcomers often seem to have all the luck. I have seen old-timers in this category of being on the down-side when (it goes without saying) they had forgotten more about the cattle business than I could ever hope to learn. And I have seen other cattlemen, with perhaps less experience than they or, like myself, with practically no experience at all, weather the uncertainties of the range up to the present day. There are in addition, of course, countless cases of ranchers between the extremes of financial success and failure.

Al White lived to see just about every extreme that the cattle business has to offer. And he rode them all like a well-built sailing ship with plenty of ballast, plowing through rough seas and smooth, heedless of the dangers lurking in the waters about him, heading always, as best he could, toward some distant home port. He never lived to see the railroad built, but he did live to see his company back on its feet again and his lands leased to oil prospectors, following the Williston Basin excitement to the north. And through it all he just rolled along, holding his course in the manner of all old-timers who, whether materially successful or not, are of one brotherhood and one heart, a heart big enough to ignore bank accounts or the difference between the sparkling new luxury car and the well-worn little vehicle that is almost old enough to vote. All, having been privileged to taste of our country in its raw state, are branded as of a very special herd. One seldom meets a specimen of this brand who has not hope, a smile on his face and a sense of gratitude in his heart.

Index

INDEX

List of The Lakeside Classics

The Lakeside Classics